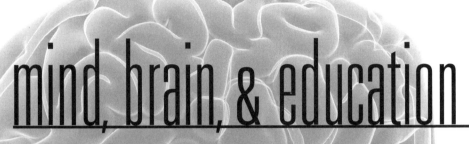

mind, brain, & education

Neuroscience Implications for the Classroom

David A. Sousa (Editor)
Daniel Ansari
Joanna A. Christodoulou
Donna Coch
Stanislas Dehaene
Keith Devlin
Marianna D. Eddy
Matthias Faeth
Kurt W. Fischer
John Gabrieli
Mariale M. Hardiman
Katie Heikkinen
Mary Helen Immordino-Yang
Tricia O'Loughlin
Michael I. Posner
David A. Sousa
Diane L. Williams
Judy Willis

Solution Tree | Press

a division of
Solution Tree

555 North Morton Street
Bloomington, IN 47404
800.733.6786 (toll free) / 812.336.7700
FAX: 812.336.7790

email: info@solution-tree.com
solution-tree.com

Printed in the United States of America

14   13   12   11   10   1   2   3   4   5

FSC
Mixed Sources
Product group from well-managed
forests, controlled sources and
recycled wood or fibre
Cert no. SW-COC-002673
www.fsc.org
© 1996 Forest Stewardship Council

Library of Congress Cataloging-in-Publication Data

Mind, brain, and education : neuroscience implications for the classroom / David A. Sousa ... [et al.].
   p. cm.
 Includes bibliographical references and index.
 ISBN 978-1-935249-63-4
 1. Learning, Psychology of. 2. Cognitive learning. 3. Teaching--Psychological aspects. 4. Brain. I. Sousa, David A.
 LB1060.M5587 2010
 370.15'23--dc22
                 2010016078

Solution Tree
Jeffrey C. Jones, CEO & President

Solution Tree Press
President: Douglas M. Rife
Publisher: Robert D. Clouse
Vice President of Production: Gretchen Knapp
Managing Production Editor: Caroline Wise
Proofreader: Elisabeth Abrams
Text Designer: Amy Shock

Cover Designer: Pamela Rude

Table of Contents

About the Editor

David A. Sousa

David A. Sousa, EdD, is an international consultant in educational neuroscience and author of a dozen books that suggest ways that educators and parents can translate current brain research into strategies for improving learning. A member of the Cognitive Neuroscience Society, he has conducted workshops in hundreds of school districts on brain research, instructional skills, and science education at the preK–12 and university levels. He has made presentations to more than 100,000 educators at national conventions of educational organizations and to regional and local school districts across the U.S., Canada, Europe, Australia, New Zealand, and Asia.

Dr. Sousa has a bachelor's degree in chemistry from Massachusetts State College at Bridgewater, a Master of Arts in Teaching degree in science from Harvard University, and a doctorate from Rutgers University. His teaching experience covers all levels. He has taught senior high school science and served as a K–12 director of science, a supervisor of instruction, and a district superintendent in New Jersey schools. He has been an adjunct professor of education at Seton Hall University and a visiting lecturer at Rutgers University.

Prior to his career in New Jersey, Dr. Sousa taught at the American School of Paris and served for five years as a Foreign Service Officer and science advisor at the USA diplomatic missions in Geneva and Vienna.

Dr. Sousa has edited science books and published dozens of articles in leading journals on staff development, science education, and educational research. His popular books for educators include: *How the Brain Learns,* third edition; *How the Special Needs Brain Learns,* second edition; *How the Gifted Brain Learns; How the Brain Learns to Read; How the Brain Influences Behavior*; and *How the Brain Learns Mathematics,* which was selected by the Independent Publishers Association as one of the best professional development books of 2008. *The Leadership Brain* suggests ways for educators to lead today's schools more effectively. His books have been published in French, Spanish, Chinese, Arabic, and several other languages.

Dr. Sousa is past president of the National Staff Development Council. He has received numerous awards from professional associations, school districts, and educational foundations for his commitment to research, staff development, and science education. He recently received the Distinguished Alumni Award and an honorary doctorate from Massachusetts State College (Bridgewater), and an honorary doctorate from Gratz College in Philadelphia.

Dr. Sousa has been interviewed by Matt Lauer on the NBC *TODAY* show and by National Public Radio about his work with schools using brain research. He makes his home in south Florida.

Introduction

David A. Sousa

You hold in your hands a historical publication. This book is the first to bring together some of the most influential scholars responsible for giving birth to a new body of knowledge: *educational neuroscience.* This newborn's gestation period was not easy. Lasting for several decades, it was difficult and often contentious. Identifying the parents was elusive at best, as more than a few prominent candidates denied kinship. Just naming the offspring was a daunting challenge and more exhausting than herding cats. Nevertheless, the birth occurred recently with the help of the visionaries who have contributed to this book. And teaching will never be the same again.

For centuries, the practice of medicine was an art form, driven by creativity and hope, but with little understanding of how to cure disease. Physicians tried certain treatments and administered specific herbs or potions based largely on their previous experiences or on advice from colleagues. They did not know why some treatments worked on one individual and not another, or why they worked at all. Their practice was essentially trial and error, with an occasional stroke of luck. All that changed when Alexander Fleming discovered penicillin in 1928. Although it took more than a decade for penicillin to be mass produced, it gave physicians their first drug for fighting several serious diseases. Furthermore, by understanding how penicillin disrupted the reproduction of bacteria, physicians could make informed decisions about treatment. Medical practice was not just an art form, but had also crossed the threshold into the realm of a science.

> The birth of educational neuroscience occurred with the help of the visionaries who have contributed to this book. And teaching will never be the same again.

1

Today, a similar story can also apply to teaching. Teachers have taught for centuries without knowing much, if anything, about how the brain works. That was mainly because there was little scientific understanding or credible evidence about the biology of the brain. Teaching, like early medicine, was essentially an art form. Now, thanks to the development of imaging techniques that look at the living brain at work, we have a better understanding of its mechanisms and networks. Sure, the brain remains an enormously complex wonder that still guards many secrets. But we are slowly pulling back the veil and gaining insights that have implications for teaching and learning.

> Until recently, teaching, like early medicine, was essentially an art form.

Since the 1990s, educators all over the world have come to recognize that there is a rapidly increasing knowledge base about the human brain. Through numerous articles, books, videos, and other presentations, they have also become aware that some of this knowledge could inform educational practice. What many educators may not realize, however, is that researchers and practicing educators have worked diligently to establish a legitimate scientific area of study that overlaps psychology, neuroscience, and pedagogy. The result is educational neuroscience (see fig. I.1).

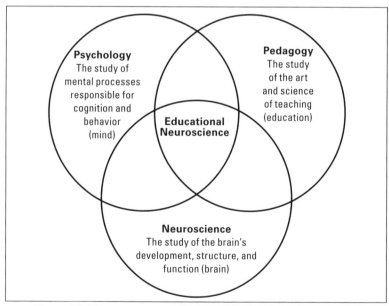

Figure I.1: The emergence of educational neuroscience at the intersection of psychology, neuroscience, and pedagogy.

As exciting as all this seems, understandable skepticism and numerous questions still exist. What specific research applies to pedagogy? Will it benefit students? How do we know the research is being interpreted accurately? Can it be reasonably adapted to our schools and classrooms?

The emergence of a new body of knowledge should be cause for celebration and, in this case, especially among educators. Here in these pages you will discover why we are celebrating. Some of the major pioneers in educational neuroscience explain recent discoveries about the human brain and discuss the influence these discoveries can have on teaching and learning—some now, some in the near future.

The contributors will explore questions such as these:

- How and when did educators get involved with neuroscience?

- How does neuroimaging contribute to our understanding of how the brain learns?

- In what ways is neuroscience research already having an impact on teaching and learning?

- In what ways do emotions affect our ability to learn?

- How does a child acquire spoken language?

- What brain networks are required to learn how to read?

- If we are born with an innate number sense, how can teachers use this to help students learn arithmetic and mathematics more successfully?

- How does the brain represent quantity and numbers?

- What is creativity, and can it be taught?

- In what ways do the arts contribute to brain development?

- What does the future hold for educational neuroscience?

Writing about all the areas researchers are currently investigating that could have an impact on educational neuroscience would fill a volume ten times the size of this one. So it became necessary to focus on those areas that have the greatest potential for affecting educational practice now or in the near future.

We begin with some background on how this new area of study evolved over the past few decades. In chapter 1, I discuss how and why I and a few other educators got so involved following the explosion of brain research in the 1980s and 1990s. Our entry into this new area of study generated considerable controversy, but our tenacity paid off.

The main reason for that explosion was the development of imaging technology that allowed researchers to peek inside the workings of the living brain. Michael Posner was one of the pioneers in using the new imaging devices, and he explains their contribution to neuroscientific research in chapter 2.

Some of the research findings from neuroscience are already being used in educational practice. In chapter 3, Judy Willis, a medical doctor turned classroom teacher, writes about those areas that are already having an impact on instruction and offers numerous suggestions for teachers to consider.

Students do not just develop intellectually in schools, but also socially and emotionally. Despite our understanding that emotions have an impact on learning, some teachers are still unsure how to incorporate emotions into their lessons. Mary Helen Immordino-Yang and Matthias Faeth cite five major contributions in chapter 4 that neuroscience has made to the research on how emotions affect learning, and they suggest three strategies that have proven effective.

Speaking and learning to read are among the early skills that young children learn. In chapter 5, Diane Williams explains what neuroscience research has revealed about the cerebral networks involved in learning spoken language. She debunks popular myths about learning language and discusses some major implications that this research has for teaching and learning.

Because reading is one of the most challenging tasks the young brain will undertake, it has gained a lot of attention from neuroscientists and cognitive psychologists. Consequently, we have devoted two chapters to this topic. In chapter 6, John Gabrieli and his colleagues review the major research findings and current understandings about how a child's brain learns to read, what is different in the brain of a child who struggles to read, and how the neuroscience of reading may come to play an important role in education. Donna Coch in chapter

7 also discusses the complex processes involved as the young brain learns to read, but focuses more on the role of the visual and auditory processing systems as well as the development of the alphabetic principle, semantics, and comprehension.

Another area of great interest to neuroscience researchers is how the brain represents quantity and how it engages neural networks to learn to carry out arithmetic and mathematical computations. Three renowned researchers in this area offer insights for educators. Keith Devlin suggests in chapter 8 that the brain's strength as a pattern-seeker accounts for many of the difficulties people have with basic arithmetic operations. He offers some proposals to educators on instructional approaches in mathematics based on the recent neuroscience research. In chapter 9, Stanislas Dehaene explains how neuroimaging has helped us to understand the three networks our brain uses to evaluate the number of a set of objects and suggests ways this and other discoveries can be used to help students learn arithmetic and mathematics. Not all brains do well with mathematics, however; in chapter 10, Daniel Ansari reviews what is currently known about how the brain computes. He discusses how the brains of individuals with and without mathematical difficulties differ both functionally and structurally. In addition, he suggests ways in which research findings may inform both the thinking and practice of educators.

What is creativity, and can it be taught? How do the arts help students develop competency in other subject areas? These questions are of particular importance because in too many school districts, arts are still thought of as frill subjects and are thus easy targets when budgets get tight. In chapter 11, Mariale Hardiman addresses these important questions and offers suggestions that teachers can use to incorporate the arts in all subjects and at all grade levels.

Because many of the authors refer to specific regions of the brain in their discussion, we have included two diagrams (figs. I.2 and I.3, pages 6–7) that should help readers locate these regions. In addition, we have included a glossary at the end of the book (pages 271–274) that defines the less-familiar scientific terms used by the authors.

With all these promising research findings, where do we go from here? To answer that question, in chapter 12, Kurt Fischer and Katie

Heikkinen suggest that new ways of thinking about teaching will need to emerge if educational neuroscience is to meet its promise in the future.

Exploring these chapters will give the reader a sense of where this new field of educational neuroscience is now, and where it is headed. These authors have been instrumental in supporting this emerging area of study. Their ideas and continuing research are sure to help educators find applications to their practice that will benefit all students.

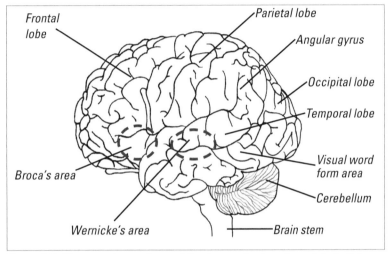

Figure I.2: The exterior regions of the human brain referred to in this book.

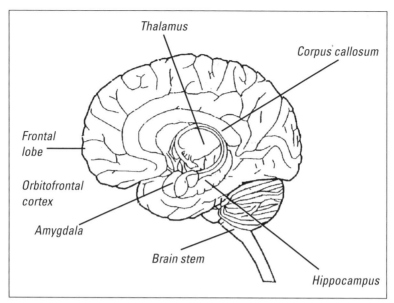

Thalamus

Corpus callosum

Frontal lobe

Orbitofrontal cortex

Amygdala

Brain stem

Hippocampus

Figure I.3: A cross-section of the human brain showing the major regions referred to in this book.

David A. Sousa

David A. Sousa, EdD, is an international consultant in educational neuroscience and author of a dozen books that suggest ways of translating brain research into strategies for improving learning. He has presented to more than 100,000 educators across the U.S., Canada, Europe, Australia, New Zealand, and Asia. In New Jersey, he taught high school chemistry and served in administrative positions, including superintendent of schools. He was an adjunct professor of education at Seton Hall University and a visiting lecturer at Rutgers University.

Dr. Sousa has edited science books and published dozens of articles in leading journals on staff development, science education, and educational research. His books have been published in French, Spanish, Chinese, Arabic, and several other languages. He is past president of the National Staff Development Council. He has received honorary degrees and numerous awards from professional associations, school districts, and educational foundations for his commitment to research, staff development, and science education.

In this chapter, Dr. Sousa reviews the history of how some educators became deeply interested in the emerging research on the brain and began to look for applications in schools and classrooms. Despite criticism from some researchers that any such applications were premature, a cadre of determined educators sought to collaborate with neuroscientists—a dialogue that continues to grow to this day.

Chapter 1

How Science Met Pedagogy

David A. Sousa

No one can say exactly when the area of study now known as educational neuroscience was born. Rather, the domain emerged slowly after at least four decades of research on the brain and amid heated battles between well-intentioned parties who held drastically different views about the application of neuroscientific discoveries to educational practice. To understand why these conflicting views developed, it is helpful to review how advances in brain research and imaging technology forever changed cognitive psychology and neuroscience.

Scientific Developments

Psychologists, of course, have been studying the brain for over a century. Behavioral psychologists made inferences about brain function by watching how people responded to certain stimuli (remember Pavlov and his dogs?). Cognitive psychologists drew conclusions about brain growth and development by watching how and when children acquired certain skills. Neurologists had to infer brain function by looking at case studies in which a patient's behavior changed as a result of some sort of brain trauma, such as stroke, lesion, or hemorrhage. But those studying the brain at that time had to face one inescapable fact: the only way they could actually look at a human brain was in an autopsy. In an autopsy, one can learn about the location and size of various brain structures, but nothing about their true function. Even neurologists had to wait until an autopsy was performed to confirm which area of the brain had sustained damage. Conventional X-rays were no help because they revealed only hard tissue, such as bones and teeth, and they damaged healthy brain cells.

In the early 1970s, a new technology was developed independently by Godfrey Hounsfield at the EMI Laboratories in London and Allan Cormack at Tufts University in Massachusetts. Called computerized axial tomography, or CAT or CT scan, this instrument manipulated low-power X-rays to detect variations in soft body tissues. Here, at last, was a device that revealed structures in the living human brain. Hounsfield and Cormack shared the 1979 Nobel Prize in Medicine for their discovery. A few years later, another technology for looking at body tissue, called magnetic resonance imaging, or MRI, was developed by Paul Lauterbur at Stony Brook University in New York and enhanced by Peter Mansfield at the University of Nottingham in the United Kingdom. The Nobel Prize in Medicine was awarded to Lauterbur and Mansfield in 2003 for their discoveries that led to MRI.

CAT and MRI scans were remarkable tools for medical diagnosis of brain trauma. But these devices showed brain *structure*. Neuroscientists needed a technology that could look at brain *function*. The first of these was positron emission tomography, or PET scans, developed in the late 1970s as a result of the work of Michel Ter-Pogossian, Michael Phelps, and others at the Washington University School of Medicine in St. Louis. PET scans revealed which parts of the brain were more or less active at any given moment. However, they were not practical for looking at the brains of otherwise normal individuals because they required the injection of a radioactive substance. A noninvasive technology, called functional magnetic resonance imaging, or fMRI, was developed in the early 1990s by Seiji Ogawa about the same time that U.S. President George H. W. Bush declared the 1990s the "Decade of the Brain." A massive infusion of federal research dollars and advances in imaging technology resulted in an explosion in the number of studies in the neurosciences.

From that time forward, findings from brain research regularly flooded the professional journals and popular media. Almost weekly a major news story appeared regarding research on the brain. It was only a matter of time before educators began to explore whether any of this research would have an effect on what they did in schools and classrooms. Little did they realize what a hornet's nest they would stir up.

Educators began to explore whether this research would have an effect on what they did in schools and classrooms. Little did they realize what a hornet's nest they would stir up.

Educators Wade Into the Fray

Every educator and consultant who spread the word about the findings of brain research has a story to tell. My own story revolves around my love for science and my passion for teaching. Seeing these two important areas beginning to merge was an exhilarating experience that set the stage for major changes in my life and career. Because I was fortunate to be there at the beginning, describing my experiences also reveals much about how the domain of educational neuroscience evolved and the barriers that had to be overcome.

Professional Development in the 1980s

In the early 1980s, I was working in a fine New Jersey school district as the K–12 supervisor of science. A new superintendent arrived and asked me to remake the district's staff development program into a cutting-edge experience with a long-term focus on positively affecting teacher growth and student achievement. I had other new duties as well, but upgrading the professional development program was my main task.

I started going to national education conferences to get a sense of which cutting-edge issues could form the framework of an effective and long-range professional development program. The learning styles movement was already underway. It was an offshoot of research by Roger Sperry in the 1960s (and later by Michael Gazzaniga), who worked with so-called split-brain patients. These were patients with severe epilepsy whose treatment involved severing the nerve fibers connecting the two cerebral hemispheres. As the patients recovered, Sperry observed that each hemisphere of these split brains had distinctly different functions that were not readily interchangeable (Sperry, 1966). Sperry won the 1981 Nobel Prize in Medicine for this work.

In the late 1970s and 1980s, the notion that various regions of the brain performed different functions formed the basis for explaining why students seem to have different learning styles. Educational researchers Rita and Ken Dunn of St. John's University developed a model that identified about twenty components of learning styles (Dunn & Dunn, 1978). Other models, such as Bernice McCarthy's 4MAT and Susan Kovalik's integrated thematic instruction, also claimed to be tied to brain research. Although these models had little research support from cognitive psychology, they were very attractive to educators because teachers' own experiences suggested that students learn in various ways.

One of the most popular speakers at that time was Madeline Hunter. She had served as a psychologist at Children's Hospital and Juvenile Hall in Los Angeles. She wanted to work full-time with typical children, however, and soon became a professor at the University of California, Los Angeles and principal of the UCLA lab school. At national conferences she often remarked on how surprised she was that teachers were working hard in the classroom but were not using instructional strategies based on recent research in behavioral and cognitive psychology.

As a former chemistry teacher and science educator, I found Hunter's message exciting because she was advocating the linking of my two loves—science and teaching. In 1985, I had an opportunity to talk with her privately for a few minutes after her keynote speech at an education conference. She suggested that I research the findings from cognitive psychology and neuroscience and share this with the district's teachers as part of our professional development program. She was convinced that once teachers understood the research, they could find ways to translate it into educational practice. Furthermore, she believed that we would continue to unlock the mysteries of the human brain and how it processes and learns. Now we can enable teachers to use that knowledge to accelerate the learning process. Her favorite expression was that "teaching is no longer a 'laying on of hands.'" Instead, she said, it was becoming a profession that combines science with art to create a better, more productive classroom in which all children learn (Hunter, 1982).

Hunter had her critics, but her work greatly influenced the nature of professional development programs for teachers all over the world. Today, numerous state and federal programs require that professional development in school districts be based on scientific research. Of course, Hunter's belief that science would discover more about how the brain works was dramatically bolstered by the development of the brain-imaging technologies that I discussed earlier.

> In the early 1980s, Madeline Hunter predicted that teaching would become a profession that combines science with art.

Increased Awareness About the Brain

Hunter was not the only important voice urging educators to look at the connections between science and pedagogy. Researchers Michael Posner and Michael Gazzaniga were working as early as the 1970s toward integrating neuroscience and psychology. In 1983, Leslie Hart published *Human Brain and Human Learning*. In this seminal work, Hart argued that teaching without an awareness of how the brain learns is like designing a glove with no sense of what a hand looks like. If classrooms are to be places of learning, Hart continued, then the brain—the organ of learning—must be understood and accommodated (Hart, 1983).

The same year, Howard Gardner (1983) of Harvard University published *Frames of Mind: The Theory of Multiple Intelligences.* He suggested that humans possess at least seven different intelligences (now up to nine) in varying degrees. Robert Sternberg (1985) at Yale proposed a triarchic theory of intelligence that distinguished three types of intelligence. Although not directly connected to neuroscience, Gardner's and Sternberg's theories shook some fundamental beliefs about intelligence. They suggested that people can be smart in many different ways and thus upset the long-held notion of intelligence as a singular construct. Furthermore, they caused educators (and parents) to refocus their attention on the workings of the brain and to ask whether this new information should be getting to classroom teachers.

Along with other educators, I began recognizing during the late 1980s that some of the findings from brain research could have definite implications for educational practice, which would require updating teachers about these new discoveries—no small task. Whenever I asked teachers and administrators to tell me what they knew about how the brain actually learned, I almost always heard references to Ivan Pavlov, Jean Piaget, and John Dewey, and some ideas about time on task and repetition. If I asked them to tell me two or three new things they had recently learned about the brain, there was usually an awkward silence. We had our work cut out for us.

In 1994, after serving for several years as superintendent of schools in New Jersey, I felt it was time to move onto the national scene and join the growing cadre of respected educators who were spreading the word about the potential benefits to education of research in the neurosciences. This cadre included, among others, Geoffrey and Renate Caine, Eric Jensen, Robert Sylwester, and Patricia Wolfe.

One of the more perplexing issues facing our cadre was selecting a short title to describe what we were advocating. Our mission was to encourage teachers to use instructional strategies in their classrooms that were consistent with research in brain-related sciences. "Brain-based education" was one of the earlier labels. It seemed attractive at first, but then I thought, "Isn't all learning brain based? What's the alternative?" Others preferred "brain-compatible" and "brain-friendly." I finally settled on "translating brain research into classroom practice." And off I went to spread the word.

What Was Brain Research Revealing?

Much of what was being revealed in the 1990s about the brain had little to do with teaching and learning. Most of the studies focused on understanding brain trauma, disease, and developmental problems. But within this expanding sea of information, one discovered little islands where the research findings could have an impact on pedagogy. Many more discoveries have been made since then, but the following are some of the major ones of that time:

- **Movement enhances learning and memory.** The typical classroom setting in which students "sit and get" was challenged by research findings showing that the brain is more active when learners are moving around. Movement brings additional fuel-carrying blood to the brain. It also allows the brain to access more long-term memory areas (an ancient survival strategy), thereby helping students make greater connections between new and prior learning (Scholey, Moss, Neave, & Wesnes, 1999). Furthermore, exercise was shown to be strongly correlated with increases in brain mass and cell production, as well as in improved cognitive processing and mood regulation. These findings should encourage teachers to get students up and moving in their classrooms. It also should discourage administrators from eliminating recess and physical education classes, a common practice in the current era of high-stakes testing.

- **Emotions have a great impact on learning.** Teachers of the elementary grades are accustomed to dealing with their students' displays of emotion. In contrast, teachers at the secondary level are trained to deliver content—and lots of it! They have little time to deal with their students' emotional development and often assume that students should simply "act like adults." Daniel Goleman's book *Emotional Intelligence* described the influence and power of emotions and how important it is for individuals to learn at an early age the connections between their feelings and their actions (Goleman, 1995). The immense popularity of Goleman's book prompted educators to look at the impact of emotions in the classroom, especially in secondary schools. Teachers need to understand the biology of emotions, especially stress, and to recognize that students cannot focus on the curriculum unless they feel physically safe (for example, from weapons or violence) and emotionally secure (they perceive that teachers respect them and care about their success).

- **The varying pace of brain development explains the behavior of children and adolescents.** Teachers and parents are well aware of the unpredictable, often risky behavior of preteens and adolescents. Emotional outbursts and physical aggression are common ways for these youngsters to deal with situations. We often blame these behaviors on changing hormones. A landmark longitudinal study of brain growth using imaging technology revealed that the emotional areas of the brain are fully developed by about age ten to twelve, but the regions responsible for rational thought and emotional control mature closer to age twenty-two to twenty-four (Giedd et al., 1999). This finding does not excuse child and adolescent misbehavior, but it explains it and suggests that there are more appropriate, effective interventions than saying, "You should have known better."

- **The school's social and cultural climates affect learning.** Schools tend to be so focused on academics and testing that they often are unaware of the powerful effect that social and cultural forces have on students. Humans are social beings, and students are constantly interacting with their peers and teachers. To what degree do students feel welcomed and respected by their peers and teachers? How much will they succumb to peer pressure? What risks are they willing to take to feel socially accepted? Imaging studies have revealed brain regions that appraise the meaning of an event and decide what emotional response to use in a social context (Heatherton et al., 2006; Zahn et al., 2007). These and other findings have spawned a new field of study called social cognitive neuroscience. This area of inquiry combines social psychology with cognitive neuroscience and aims to describe behavior using data from brain imaging and similar technology. School culture is characterized in part by openness of communication, level of expectations, amount of recognition and appreciation for effort, involvement in decision making, and degree of caring. All of these affect an individual's self-esteem. Educators need to pay much more attention to strengthening the positive aspects of the school's social and cultural climates. Regrettably, we have seen the kinds of violent acts that students can commit when they feel disaffected from their school.

- **The brain can grow new neurons.** For a long time scientists were convinced that neurons were the only body cells that did not regenerate. The number of neurons an individual had was always declining. But in the late 1990s, researchers found that the brain does indeed grow new neurons, at least in a part of the brain called the hippocampus, an area responsible for encoding long-term memories (Kempermann & Gage, 1999). Later research indicated that this regrowth, called neurogenesis, was highly correlated with mood, memory, and learning. Moreover, it could be enhanced by good nutrition and regular exercise as well as by maintaining low levels of stress (Kempermann, Wiskott, & Gage, 2004). By knowing this, teachers can help students understand how their brain grows and can explain the kinds of behaviors that lead to consistent neural growth and brain health.

- **The brain can rewire itself.** Previous notions about neural networks held that they changed very slowly and even slower as we passed middle age. Early in the 2000s, new research evidence showed that the brain could rewire itself (a process called neuroplasticity) as a result of environmental input, and at a faster pace than originally thought. This finding led researchers to examine the brain scans of young struggling readers (many diagnosed with dyslexia) and eventually to devise computer programs and protocols that actually rewired these students' cerebral networks to perform more like those of good readers (Shaywitz, 2003; Simos et al., 2002). What an amazing discovery and application to pedagogy (Sousa, 2005)! Furthermore, the good news for adults is that neuroplasticity continues throughout our lifetime.

- **Short-term memory is not so temporary.** Ask teachers anywhere in the world how long they want their students to remember what they taught them, and the answer is always the same: "Forever!" Yet they all know this is just not reality. Why do students forget so much of what they are taught, especially in high school? As a result of extensive research on memory systems, two findings in particular helped shed light on this question (Squire & Kandel, 1999). First, short-term memory seems to consist of two components: a brain area that initially processes incoming information for just a few seconds, referred to now as immediate memory, and another area where information is consciously processed for extended periods, called working memory. Conventional wisdom used to be that working memory held items from a few minutes up to a day or so before it faded from the system. But it seems that a student actually can carry items for up to several weeks in working memory and then discard them when they serve no further purpose—in other words, after the student takes the test. That explains why students often fail to recall topics that the teacher taught a few months earlier.

Second, in the typical classroom, sense and meaning appeared to be among the major criteria that the brain uses in deciding what to encode to long-term memory. Teachers work hard at having their presentations make sense, but they do not always do enough to make the learning meaningful or relevant. These two findings suggest the need to focus on strategies that enhance retention of learning and on curricula that students perceive as relevant to their lives (Sousa, 2006).

- **Sleep is important for memory.** Parents always tell their children how important it is to get enough sleep. This advice usually is based on the need to give the body, including the brain, sufficient rest so that one can wake up refreshed and tackle the activities of the new day. Researchers found that the brain is incredibly active during sleep, carrying out processes that help the brain to learn, make connections, remember, and clear out clutter (Schacter, 1996). A brain that is sleep deprived has trouble capturing all sorts of memories. Studies showed that sleep-deprived students were more likely to get poorer grades than students who slept longer and also more likely to get depressed (Wolfson & Carskadon, 1998). Many secondary students (and their teachers) come to school sleep deprived because their average sleep time is only five to six hours. By knowing about sleep research, teachers can emphasize to students the importance of getting adequate sleep; most teenagers need about nine hours. With sufficient sleep, students have a better chance of remembering all the good information and skills they learn in school that day.

For centuries, effective teachers discovered through experience what strategies to use and how to implement them. But they did not know why the strategies worked, or did not work, on different occasions. That is what the findings from these studies in cognitive neuroscience were providing—the *why*. When teachers know the why, they can be much more masterful in applying instructional strategies.

We Begin to Spread the Word

Neuroscientists in the 1990s were working hard at finding new evidence of how the brain works, but they were not thinking much about applications to pedagogy. One neuroscientist said to me, "My job is to discover the inner workings of the brain. I haven't a clue as to whether my findings have any applications to teaching. You're the educator, so that's your job." And that is exactly what I and other educators who were intently following the brain research did. We looked for potential applications to pedagogy, wrote about them, and traveled internationally to tell other educators about them.

Neuroscientists in the 1990s were working hard at finding new evidence of how the brain works, but they were not thinking much about applications to pedagogy.

During the 1990s, just about every regional and national education conference had one or more workshop sessions on brain research. I presented a number of these workshops and found most educators to be very interested in the information. Meanwhile, individual school districts in the United States, Canada, and other countries were exposing their professional staff to the implications of brain research on pedagogy. Articles on the subject began appearing in professional journals. Ron Brandt, editor of *Educational Leadership,* the widely read journal of the Association for Supervision and Curriculum Development (ASCD), saw the emerging research as a significant development and encouraged contributions on this subject. Books by educators linking brain science to pedagogy flooded the market. All of this activity attracted the attention of psychologists, and it did not take them long to make their views known.

The Critics Pounce

Some psychologists admitted that there were potential applications of neuroscience to pedagogy but advised caution. Still others insisted that teachers did not think scientifically and thus were not qualified to judge the applications of neuroscientific research. They criticized educators for not reflecting on their daily practice and not documenting their own successful (and unsuccessful) instructional strategies. The psychologists' argument was that although educators could potentially make significant contributions to understanding of the brain, most failed to apply the scientific method and did not know how to do reliable research in their own classrooms. Consequently, much of the information gathered in education was anecdotal, poorly documented at best, and of little value to the profession. Cognitive psychologists felt that they should be the ones assessing which research findings have applications to pedagogy and that they alone should be the bridge between neuroscientists and educators.

One of the most vocal critics was John Bruer. In the late 1990s, he wrote several articles criticizing the linking of brain research to education. He said educators should resist trying to understand brain research, implying that they weren't smart enough. Instead, he suggested, they should look to cognitive psychology for research guidance and applications. In one article he jibed that if brain-based education were true, then "the pyramids were built by aliens—to house Elvis" (Bruer, 1999, p. 656). Furthermore, he insisted that it would take twenty-five years before there would be any practical applications of brain research to the classroom. Fortunately, Bruer's prediction was way off. By 2006, he took a more moderate stand, saying that focusing solely on neuroscience gives insufficient attention to cognitive psychology (Bruer, 2006). Nevertheless, many of his criticisms have been overtaken by the impressive amount of brain research continuing to emerge. Ironically, two of the researchers that Bruer often cites in his articles, Michael Posner and Stanislaus Dehaene, support a strong relationship between neuroscience and education and are contributors to this book.

Any field of serious study, especially an emerging one such as educational neuroscience, should be monitored by qualified skeptics. Healthy skepticism has often advanced scientific thought. However, some of the skeptics intentionally selected marginal issues to criticize the myths that they claimed educators and consultants were perpetuating. Gender differences, left-right hemisphere specialization, and sensitive developmental periods were topics that psychologists chose most frequently as examples, calling them "neuromyths." They argued that nothing from the research in these areas would have any practical application to pedagogy.

Anyone taking that stand even ten years ago was not keeping up with the research. Neuroscientists did not dispute that there are definite differences in the structure and function of male and female brains. Nor did anyone dispute that areas of the cerebral hemispheres have specialized functions in most people. And there already was ample evidence that there are sensitive as well as critical periods during the development of the young brain when neural networks are growing and consolidating. The question was the degree to which these factors affected learning in children.

In the critics' defense, it is true that some less-informed consultants were stretching the applications of these research findings beyond what was appropriate. Statements such as "Girls aren't that good at math" or "He's too left-brained to be creative" did not serve our cause and lent further ammunition to the critics. Add to this the unfortunate "Mozart effect" misunderstandings (Rauscher, Shaw, & Ky, 1993) and the "water bottle on every desk" mantra, and it was no surprise that even those of us who were trying to define legitimate research applications were under fire. Nonetheless, some neuroscientists, cognitive psychologists, and educators were slowly recognizing that there was a common ground within their three respective fields where they could meet and seriously discuss the present and future effects that discoveries in neuroscience might have on pedagogy.

> Despite the critics, some neuroscientists, cognitive psychologists, and educators were slowly recognizing that there was a common ground within their three respective fields.

The Dust Settles

With the advent of the 21st century, the tide turned and the battles subsided, especially when prestigious universities established programs and institutes around the link between neuroscience and education. Some of the schools sponsoring these programs included Cornell University, Dartmouth College, Harvard University, University of Southern California, University of Texas at Arlington, and University of Washington. Various professional associations also had become involved. They include the American Educational Research Association Special Interest Group on the Brain and Learning, the Dana Foundation, the International Mind, Brain, and Education Society, the Organisation for Economic Co-operation and Development, and the Society for Neuroscience. One major contribution to these efforts came from the U.S. National Research Council, which published a book called *How People Learn* (Bransford, Brown, & Cocking, 2003).

Interest in the applications of neuroscience to pedagogy also was rapidly developing in other countries. Institutes and study groups were forming in Australia, Canada, Japan, France, India, Italy, Mexico, the Netherlands, and the United Kingdom, among others. Several international conferences, such as Learning Brain Europe, are now held regularly around the world, centered on areas of brain research that have an impact on teaching and learning.

One recent study that helped shed light on possible areas of agreement was prompted by the work of Tracey Tokuhama-Espinosa, a doctoral candidate whose thesis focused on the development of standards in the new field that she referred to as "neuroeducation," or "mind, brain, and education science." Her work involved a review and meta-analysis of more than 2,200 related documents, plus asking a panel of twenty recognized leaders in neuroscience, psychology, and education for their views on what should be the standards for this new field, now also referred to as educational neuroscience (Tokuhama-Espinosa, 2008).

The result was a compilation of several dozen beliefs about the brain and learning that were filtered through the panel, which classified them as to whether they were well established, probably so, intelligent speculation, or popular misconceptions (those "neuromyths" mentioned earlier). Not surprisingly, the panel members' ratings varied, but there was enough consistency between the panel's ratings and the findings from the author's extensive meta-analysis of the literature that she was able to extract twenty-two "principles" that describe how the brain learns (Tokuhama-Espinosa, 2008).

This study and other published articles make clear that there is not yet broad agreement on the standards that define educational neuroscience. Perhaps those who continue to focus on the somewhat contrived and now stale neuromyths will shift their efforts instead to the research findings that have real potential for enhancing educational practice.

We have come a long way since 2000, and the future looks promising. More teachers are now paying attention to this area. Teachers are, after all, the ultimate "brain changers." They are in a profession of changing the human brain every day. So as neuroscientists continue to discover the inner workings of the brain, as cognitive psychologists continue to look for explanations of learning behavior, and as educators continue to apply research to improve their teaching, not only will this new field gain independence, but, most important, also greatly improve the quality and effectiveness of educational experiences for our children.

> Teachers are, after all, the ultimate "brain changers." They are in a profession of changing the human brain every day.

References

Bransford, J. D., Brown, A. L., & Cocking, R. R. (Eds.). (2003). *How people learn: Brain, mind, experience and school.* Washington, DC: National Academies Press.

Bruer, J. T. (1999, May). In search of . . . brain-based education. *Phi Delta Kappan, 80,* 645–657.

Bruer, J. T. (2006, Summer). Points of view: On the implications of neuroscience research for science teaching and learning: Are there any? *CBE-Life Sciences Education, 5,* 104–110.

Dunn, R., & Dunn, K. (1978). *Teaching students through their individual learning styles: A practical approach.* Reston, VA: Reston Publishing Company.

Gardner, H. (1983). *Frames of mind: The theory of multiple intelligences.* New York: Basic Books.

Giedd, J. N., Blumenthal, J., Jeffries, N. O., Castellanos, F. X., Liu, H., Zijdenbos, A., et al. (1999, September). Brain development during childhood and adolescence: A longitudinal MRI study. *Nature Neuroscience, 2,* 861–863.

Goleman, D. (1995). *Emotional intelligence: Why it can matter more than IQ.* New York: Bantam.

Hart, L. (1983). *Human brain and human learning.* New York: Longman.

Heatherton, T. F., Wyland, C. L., Macrae, C. N., Demos, K. E., Denny, B. T., & Kelley, W. M. (2006). Medial prefrontal activity differentiates self from close others. *Social Cognitive and Affective Neuroscience, 1,* 18–25.

Hunter, M. (1982). *Mastery teaching.* Thousand Oaks, CA: Corwin Press.

Kempermann, G., & Gage, F. (1999, May). New nerve cells for the adult brain. *Scientific American, 280,* 48–53.

Kempermann, G., Wiskott, L., & Gage, F. (2004, April). Functional significance of adult neurogenesis. *Current Opinion in Neurobiology,* 186–191.

Rauscher, F. H., Shaw, G. L., & Ky, K. N. (1993). Music and spatial task performance. *Nature, 365,* 611.

Schacter, D. (1996). *Searching for memory: The brain, mind, and the past.* New York: Basic Books.

Scholey, A. B., Moss, M. C., Neave, N., & Wesnes, K. (1999, November). Cognitive performance, hyperoxia, and heart rate following oxygen administration in healthy young adults. *Physiological Behavior, 67,* 783–789.

Shaywitz, S. E. (2003). *Overcoming dyslexia: A new and complete science-based program for reading problems at any level.* New York: Knopf.

Simos, P. G., Fletcher, J. M., Bergman, E. , Breier, J. I., Foorman, B. R., Castillo, E. M., et al. (2002, April). Dyslexia-specific brain activation profile becomes normal following successful remedial training. *Neurology, 58,* 1203–1213.

Sousa, D. A. (2005). *How the brain learns to read.* Thousand Oaks, CA: Corwin Press.

Sousa, D. A. (2006). *How the brain learns* (3rd ed.). Thousand Oaks, CA: Corwin Press.

Sperry, R. (1966). Brain bisection and consciousness. In J. Eccles (Ed.), *How the self controls its brain.* New York: Springer-Verlag.

Squire, L. R., & Kandel, E. R. (1999). *Memory: From mind to molecules.* New York: W. H. Freeman.

Sternberg, R. J. (1985). *Beyond IQ: A triarchic theory of human intelligence.* New York: Cambridge University Press.

Tokuhama-Espinosa, T. N. (2008). *The scientifically substantiated art of teaching: A study in the development of standards in the new academic field of neuroeducation (mind, brain, and education science).* Unpublished doctoral dissertation, Capella University.

Wolfson, A., & Carskadon, M. (1998). Sleep schedules and daytime functioning in adolescents. *Child Development, 69,* 875–887.

Zahn, R., Moll, J., Krueger, F., Huey, E. D., Garrido, G., & Grafman, J. (2007, April). Social concepts are represented in the superior anterior temporal cortex. *Proceedings of the National Academy of Sciences, 104,* 6430–6435.

Michael I. Posner

Michael I. Posner, PhD, is Professor Emeritus at the University of Oregon and Adjunct Professor of Psychology in Psychiatry at the Weill Medical College of Cornell University, where he served as founding director of the Sackler Institute. With Marcus Raichle, he developed studies of imaging the human brain during cognitive tasks. He has also worked on the anatomy, circuitry, development, and genetics of three attentional networks underlying maintaining alertness, orienting to sensory events, and voluntary control of thoughts and ideas. His methods for measuring these networks have been applied to a wide range of neurological, psychiatric, and developmental disorders, and to normal development and school performance.

His current research, a longitudinal study of preschool children, is designed to understand the interaction of specific experience and genes in shaping attention and self regulation. His work has been recognized by his election to the National Academy of Sciences, by the 2009 National Medal of Science, by seven honorary degrees, and by the Distinguished Science Award of the American Psychological Association, the Karl Spencer Lashley Award by the American Philosophical Society, and the Mattei Dogan Award from the International Union of Psychological Science, among others.

In this chapter, Dr. Posner explains how advances in neuroimaging technology led to deeper understandings about how the brain works. He also suggests how these understandings may apply to educational practice.

Chapter 2

Neuroimaging Tools and the Evolution of Educational Neuroscience

Michael I. Posner

The key element in the evolution of educational neuroscience was the development of cognitive neuroimaging in the late 1980s. In this chapter, I review the historical record of developments in brain imaging methods such as measurement of changes in blood flow and of electrical and magnetic activity (in both healthy patients and in patients with brain damage). Together, these methods have illuminated the acquisition of literacy, numeracy, expertise, and other aspects of education.

Hemodynamic Imaging

Efforts to image the human brain are ancient, but the modern era began with computerized tomography, or CT scans, which use mathematical algorithms to combine X-rays in such a way as to produce a picture of the brain's structure. However, the images most needed were those showing the brain's *function* during performance of everyday tasks. Efforts to map the function of the brain began by measuring

> The images most needed were those showing the brain's *function* during performance of everyday tasks.

blood flow. Using radionucleides that emit photons when in contact with matter, researchers counted the frequency of emissions to map changes in blood flow at various locations in the brain. The major methods used to develop these maps were single photon emission computed tomography (SPECT) and positron emission tomography (PET) (for an extensive history of this field, see Savoy, 2001).

Using PET Imaging

In the late 1980s, it became possible to examine changes in the intact brain while people carried out tasks involving thinking. One method used was called positron emission tomography. PET took advantage of the fact that when brain cells are active, they change their own local blood supply. Using PET, it is possible to show which portions of the brain are active. The PET mapping method was first employed to show how, during tasks such as reading or listening to music, much of the brain, but not the whole brain, exhibited increased blood flow (Lassen, Ingvar, & Skinhoj, 1978). In an important early study, researchers compared specific tasks such as navigating from place to place while reading and listening; the results showed clear regional distribution of brain activity—activity that differed depending on the task (Roland & Friberg, 1985). Prior to the development of functional brain imaging, cognitive psychologists had already broken down tasks such as reading, attention, and visual imagery into component operations or subroutines sufficient to program a computer to perform the tasks (Kosslyn, 1980; Posner & Raichle, 1994). Relating these subroutines to specific brain areas was an important step toward making brain maps useful in psychology and education.

An initial step in connecting subroutines to specific brain areas used PET to examine brain activity while participants listened to and read individual words (Petersen et al., 1988). Participants performed a set of hierarchical tasks (shown in table 2.1) that required looking at a fixed point, reading a word out loud, or generating a use for a word. By "subtracting" the imaging results for each subtask, researchers could roughly isolate the mental operations for each step as participants moved up the hierarchy of increasingly complex tasks.

Table 2.1: Hierarchy of Tasks Designed to Understand the Processing of Single Words and Based on a Theory of Internal Codes in Word Processing (Adapted from Petersen et al., 1988)

Control State	Stimulated State	Areas Activated After Subtraction
Fixation point only	Passive words	Passive word processing
Passive words	Repeat words	Articulatory coding Motor programming and output
Repeat words	Generate uses	Semantic association Selection for action

For example, in the simplest situation, researchers compared the brain activity when participants looked at a screen that showed only a fixation point (this was the control state, shown in the first column of table 2.1) with their brain activity when a single visual or auditory noun was presented at intervals of about a second (the stimulation state, the second column). Subtracting the fixation-only condition from the words provided a measure of where seeing or hearing words activated the brain (the third column, in this case, passive word processing). The visual words strongly activated the visual system and the auditory words the auditory system, thus confirming what would be expected. At the next level, brain activity for the presentation of visual words was subtracted from the activity shown when participants read the same words aloud; thus researchers were able to identify those parts of the brain needed to translate the visual letters into a name and articulate the output. When participants read words aloud, the PET showed major activity in motor areas. At the highest level in table 2.1, participants were asked to generate a use of the presented word: for example, to think of and say a word such as *pound* when presented with the word *hammer*. When they had to produce a use of each noun presented, a brain network was activated that included the left anterior frontal gyrus, the anterior cingulate, parts of the cerebellum, and a posterior temporal-parietal area.

In other words, the highly automated task of reading a word activated one set of areas in the brain, but when subjects had to make a new association with the word, then a different set of areas was activated. During the naming of new associations, it might be concluded, the anterior cingulate was involved in attending to the task, the left frontal area held the input word "in mind," while the posterior area provided the associated meaning. If the same list of words was repeated and participants made the same association, then the strength of the activations decreased. After a few repetitions, producing the association resulted in the same brain activity as simply reading the word aloud (Raichle et al., 1994). Apparently, a few minutes of learning had automated the associations, and they were made more reliably and faster than when they were novel. The brain pathway functioned as though the association was as directly connected to the image of the word as to the process of reading the word. These findings supported the notion that mental operations occur in separate brain areas and showed how quickly these activations could be changed by practice.

Using Functional Magnetic Resonance Imaging (fMRI)

A major development in 1990 was the use of magnetic resonance (MR) to measure localized changes in blood oxygen. PET had required the use of radioactivity to detect blood flow, while MR used no radioactivity—only a high magnetic field—and thus could noninvasively map brain activity (Ogawa et al., 1990). This technology (fMRI) not only was able to reveal much more localized activity than PET, but also had two other features that were very important for cognitive and educational work. First, since fMRI did not use any radioactivity, it could be used with children and to map differences in one individual's brain activity by scanning repetitively. Second, because an individual could be scanned repeatedly without harm, fMRI allowed researchers to combine trials of different types (for example, naming words and generating their uses) within the same series of trials so that participants could not develop a special strategy for each task. Later, the experimenter could average all the word-naming trials separately from the use-generating trials and make the subtraction needed to reveal the networks of brain areas used to generate a simple association.

A major 1990 development was the fMRI that used no radioactivity, was noninvasive, and could be used with children.

Much subsequent work has confirmed and elaborated the meaning of brain-area activations, particularly with respect to reading.

For example, in a skilled reader, two important posterior brain areas operate automatically: the left fusiform gyrus and the left temporal parietal lobe (see fig. 2.1). The first of these two areas appears to be involved in chunking visual letters into a unit. Often called the *visual word form area* (McCandliss, Cohen, & Dehaene, 2003), it appears to be of special importance in languages that are irregular in pronunciation. English is a particularly irregular language. For example, the "-ave" in *wave* and *have* are pronounced quite differently. While there has been dispute about this area of the brain (Price & Devlin, 2003), most studies have found that it responds to any group of letters that can be pronounced (for example, *iske* is not a word but can be pronounced using the rules of English and would activate the word form area). The second area, the left temporal parietal lobe, is closer to the auditory system and appears to represent the sound of the word. These two areas operate automatically in skilled readers but did not seem to work well in children having difficulty in learning to read (Shaywitz, 2003).

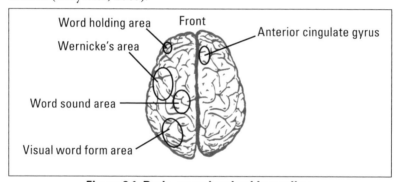

Figure 2.1: Brain areas involved in reading.

These two posterior areas operate in coordination with areas involved in (1) giving effort or attention to the printed word and (2) understanding sentences and longer passages. The anterior cingulate gyrus is a major structure in the executive attention system and is important for regulating other brain networks, including those involved in reading. It operates in conjunction with a left lateral frontal area to hold words in mind while lexical meanings are retrieved from Wernicke's area and from the other highly distributed areas that deal with meaning. Understanding the connotation of a word may also involve information stored in sensory and motor areas.

Use of fMRI has allowed the study of many brain networks not only related to cognitive processes, such as reading, listening, imaging, and so forth, but also to emotional, social, and personality-related processes. A partial list of these networks is shown in table 2.2.

Table 2.2: Some Neural Networks Studied by Neuroimaging

Arithmetic
Autobiographical memory
Faces
Fear
Music
Object perception
Reading and listening
Reward
Self-reference
Spatial navigation
Working memory

Connectivity

As the studies of reading and brain activity show, several neural areas must be orchestrated to carry out any task. One approach to investigating this connectivity uses fMRI to study the timeline of activity and the correlations between active areas of the brain. Figure 2.2 illustrates the connectivity of the anterior cingulate during tasks that involve attention, such as reading and listening. This area of the brain has large-scale connectivity to many other brain areas and is ideally situated to exercise executive control over other brain networks (Posner, 2008).

The executive attention network resolves conflict among competing responses. For example, if you are asked to name the color of ink (such as blue) in which the word *red* is written, there is a conflict between the usual reading response and the instructed response to name the ink color. The executive attention network allows us to inhibit the word name while responding to the ink color. The anterior cingulate is part of this executive network. According to Bush, Luu, and Posner (2000), an analysis of a number of conflict tasks shows that the more dorsal, or rear, part of the anterior cingulate is involved in the regulation of cognitive tasks, while the more ventral, or front,

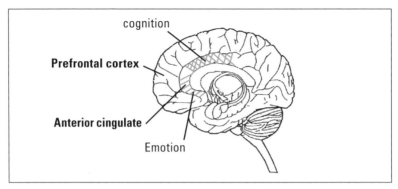

cognition

Prefrontal cortex

Anterior cingulate

Emotion

Figure 2.2: The anterior cingulate portion of the prefrontal cortex, shaded in the regions that process emotion and cognition.

part of the cingulate is involved in regulation of emotion. The dorsal part of the anterior cingulate has strong connections to frontal and parietal areas that are also involved in cognitive processes; during task performance, it establishes contact with these brain areas involved in processing information. In one study, for example, participants selected either visual or auditory information in separate blocks of trials. During the selection of visual information, the dorsal cingulate showed correlation with visual brain areas; during the selection of auditory information, it switched, showing correlation to auditory areas (Crottaz-Herbette & Mennon, 2006). In other studies involving emotional stimuli, the more ventral parts of the cingulate became active and became connected to limbic areas related to the emotion being processed (Etkin et al., 2006).

Another approach to measuring connectivity uses noninvasive diffusion tensor imaging (DTI) to reveal the white matter fiber tracts that connect neural areas. This form of imaging measures the diffusion of water molecules in particular directions due to the presence of myelinated fibers (Conturo et al., 1999). Thus it provides a way to examine the physical connections in the brain and trace fiber pathways during different stages of human development.

As noted earlier, because fMRI is noninvasive, it is possible to use multiple scans of the same individual to examine changes that occur with learning and development (Kelly & Garavan, 2005). This obviously is an important tool for educational applications. It is common for learning on a task to decrease the number and extent of cerebral activation. The rate of these changes may vary from milliseconds to years, depending on what is being learned (see table 2.3 for time courses to acquire different kinds of learning). The connectivity of the involved networks also can be enhanced by practice (McNamara et al., 2007). Studies of changes in connectivity as an individual develops show that the local connections dominant in children are supplemented with the longer connections more prominent in adults (Fair et al., 2009). This process is often accompanied by a reduction in the number and extent of activations, as when practicing a given task.

Table 2.3: Time Required to Show Brain Changes Based on Different Causes

Time Course	Cause	Example
Milliseconds	Attention	Conjunctions
Seconds to minutes	Practice	Generation of task
Minutes to days	Learning	New associations
Weeks to months	Rule learning	Orthography
Months to years	Development	Attention system

Electromagnetic Imaging

Because fMRI depends upon changes in blood flow, it develops relatively slowly, and small differences over time may be hard to detect. However, the use of electrical activity recorded from the scalp in the form of the electroencephalogram (EEG) is an old method that can yield high temporal accuracy. Before the development of neuroimaging, it was not possible to tell from an EEG recorded at the scalp where the signal originated in the brain. However, by combining electrical or magnetic recording from outside the head with fMRI, it is possible to get high temporal *and* spatial resolution.

Event-Related Potentials

When a stimulus such as a word is presented many times, the electrical or magnetic activity can be averaged to eliminate the background, not time locked to the stimulus, and form an *event-related potential*. The event-related potential represents the effect of the stimulus on the brain millisecond by millisecond following the stimulus. It is a picture of the brain activity induced by the signal.

For example, Dehaene (1996) used electrical recording from scalp electrodes to map out the time course of mental activity involved in determining whether a number shown visually was above or below five. He used a computer to display a sequence of numbers, which participants had to classify as above or below 5 by pressing a key, then averaged the brain electrical activity following the presentation of each number. During the first hundred milliseconds after the presentation of the input number, the visual system showed activity. When the input was an Arabic numeral (6), both hemispheres were active; when it was a spelled digit (*six*), however, activity was in the visual word form system of the left hemisphere that we described earlier. In the next hundred milliseconds, brain activity varied depending on how close to or far from 5 the number was. This effect of the distance from 5 was shown in the parietal brain areas known to be involved in representing the mental number line. Before the participant pressed the key to indicate above or below 5, electrodes above the motor areas were active. After pressing the key, if the person was in error (for example, had mistakenly indicated that the digit 6 was below 5), activity showed in the frontal midline near the anterior cingulate. Although being able to recognize the quantity of a number is a very elementary aspect of numeracy, training in the appreciation of the value of a number has been shown to be an important contributor to success in learning elementary school arithmetic (Griffin, Case, & Siegler, 1995).

Oscillations

The complex electrical signals coming from scalp electrodes can be separated by analysis into sine and cosine waves. There is a great deal of interest in these oscillations, both in how they show changes of brain state and integration of brain activity in different brain systems. During sleep, for example, deep slow waves predominate; in the awake resting state, created by closing the eyes, alpha frequency (about 10 Hz) dominates, particularly over electrodes at the back of the scalp. When someone realizes he or she has made an error, activity occurs in the theta electrical band (3 Hz) (Berger, Tzur, & Posner, 2006). It has been hypothesized that high-frequency gamma activity (40 Hz) is important in order to tie together distant brain regions that are analyzing a single object (Womelsdorf et al., 2007).

Infants and Young Children

Electrical recordings are sufficiently noninvasive to use with young children, which makes them valuable for understanding what happens in the brain during infancy. For example, infants come into the world already able to discriminate among the units of language (phonemes) in all languages. That is, if an infant hears one phoneme sounded over and over again (for example, *ba*), its novelty effects are reduced. However, a recovery of the novelty effect occurs when the infant discriminates a different phoneme (for example, *da*) from the *ba* that has just been repeated. Thus, the infant exhibits an auditory system that can discriminate between phonemes not only in his native language, but in all of the world's languages. In the period between six and ten months of age, there is considerable shaping of this phonemic structure (Kuhl, 2000). Those sounds to which the infant is exposed tend to solidify and form a unit, while the ability to discriminate unfamiliar sound units begins to disappear. Studies have shown that infants raised in English-speaking homes can maintain their ability to discriminate phonemes in Mandarin Chinese, for instance, if exposed to a speaker of those sounds during this period (Kuhl, Tsao, & Liu, 2003). In addition, phonemes in English (their native language) are also facilitated (Kuhl et al., 2006).

Unfortunately, the studies also revealed that learning did not occur when the language exposure was to a video rather than an actual person. Current research is attempting to determine the most important aspects of these social interactions between an infant and a tutor that facilitate language acquisition in the hope that they could be incorporated into an electronic media presentation. The tutor in these studies used elaborate methods to maintain the interest of the infant, and we simply do not know if these methods can be duplicated by a nonsocial, computer-based system. However, these findings and others like them show that the auditory system of infants is trained by the speech patterns of their community.

Experiments with infants have also shown that the effectiveness of this training can be measured by variations in the electrical signals that follow a change from a frequent to an infrequent phoneme (Guttorm et al., 2005; Molfese, 2000). As noted earlier, the brain shows its discrimination between the two phonemes by responding differently when the novel phoneme occurs. This electrical difference can be used to measure the efficiency of the brain in making the discrimination. Consequently,

> Brain activity may be measured to help determine the efficiency of a child's language acquisition.

we can examine the effectiveness of caregivers in establishing the phonemic structure of their native language and other languages that they desire to teach. From these recordings, it is also possible to predict later difficulties in spoken language and reading (Guttorm et al., 2005; Molfese, 2000). It is still unknown exactly how accurate these predictions can be. Currently, brain stem electrical activity recorded from the scalp allows early detection of deafness in infants. Similarly, use of electrical recording should make it possible to check for the development of a strong phonemic structure even during infancy.

Lesions

Not all parts of an active brain network are needed to carry out a task. In the past, the effects of brain lesions have been studied as a primary way to identify brain areas that, when lost, will prevent a person from performing certain tasks. A good example of the use of lesion data in conjunction with imaging occurred in a study of a patient who had suffered a stroke. He was unable to read words when they were presented to the left of where he was looking (called *fixation*), but he could read them fluently when the words were presented to the right of fixation (Cohen et al., 2004). Imaging revealed an interruption of the neural fibers that conducted information from the right hemisphere occipital lobe (where visual signals are first processed) to the visual word form area (see fig. 2.1, page 31). Typically, the left visual field has direct access to the right hemisphere but must cross over the corpus callosum to access the left hemisphere. In this patient, when words were presented to the left of fixation (that is, presented directly to the right hemisphere of the brain), the patient could only sound them out letter by letter. He demonstrated that he had retained all of his reading skills, however, when words were presented to the right visual field (that is, presented directly to the left hemisphere—the visual word form area). This study illustrates the importance of the visual word form systems for fluent reading.

It is now possible to apply brief magnetic pulses (transcortical magnetic stimulation, or TMS) to the scalp overlying the brain area of interest to disrupt parts of a network at particular times in order to observe the effects on task performance. One striking finding of this technology showed that readers of Braille use the brain's visual system. When TMS was applied to the visual cortex, Braille readers had a specific problem in reading words, suggesting that the visual system was being used to handle spatial aspects of the tactile input from the Braille characters (Pascale-Leone & Hamilton, 2001).

Data from lesion studies may reveal causes of learning difficulties such as dyslexia and dyscalculia.

Lesion data and imaging techniques can be used to confirm and extend theories on learning and brain development. While educators are not usually dealing with patients with specific brain lesions resulting from stroke, findings from these patients can often illuminate specific learning difficulties, such as dyslexia (problems with reading) or dyscalculia (problems with arithmetic).

Genes: Individual Differences in Network Efficiency

Educators are interested in individual differences among students, and this interest has usually involved the study of intelligence(s). Neuroimaging has provided a new perspective on the nature of individual differences. Although most of the networks studied by neuroimaging (see table 2.2, page 32) are common to all people, their efficiency varies, which may be partly due to genetic variations. But the expression of these genetic variations is also influenced by experience. Genes code for different proteins that influence the efficiency with which modulators, such as dopamine, are produced and/or bind to their receptors. These modulators are in turn related to individual differences in the efficiency of one's brain networks.

Humans have much in common in the anatomy of their high-level networks, and this must have a basis within the human genome. The same genes that are related to individual differences are also likely to be important in the development of the networks that are common to all humans. Learning can build on pre-existing brain networks to achieve new functions. For example, primitive appreciation of number is present in infancy. However, when used together with language networks, this primitive sense of numeracy can form a basis for numerical calculation (Dehaene & Cohen, 2007).

In the study of attention, individual differences have been linked to differences in genetic variation. Recall that the executive attention network is involved in the resolution of conflict between other brain systems. The association of the executive attention network with the neuromodulator dopamine is a way of searching for candidate genes that might relate to the efficiency of the network. For example, several studies employing conflict-related tasks found that alternative forms (alleles) of the catechol-o-methyl transferase (COMT) gene were related to the ability to resolve conflict. A number of other dopamine genes have also proven to be related to this form of attention. In addition, research has suggested that genes related to serotonin transmission also influence executive attention (see Posner, Rothbart, & Sheese, 2007, for a review). In studies using brain imaging, it was also possible to show that some of these genetic differences influenced the degree to which the anterior cingulate was activated during the performance of a task. In the future, it may be possible to relate genes to specific points within neural networks, allowing a much more detailed understanding of the origins of brain networks.

While genes are important for common neural networks and individual differences in efficiency, specific experiences also play an important role. Several genes, for instance, including the DRD4 gene and the COMT gene, have been shown to interact with aspects relating to the quality of parenting. For example, one study (Sheese, Voelker, Rothbart, & Posner, 2007) found that in the presence of one version of the DRD4 gene, parents are influential in reducing the impulsivity of their two-year-olds. In children without that version of the gene, however, the quality of parenting did not influence impulsivity. This provides evidence that aspects of the culture in which children are raised can influence the way in which genes shape neural networks—ultimately influencing child behavior (Posner, 2008).

> Several genes have been shown to interact with aspects related to the quality of parenting.

If brain networks are affected by parenting and other cultural influences, it should be possible to develop specific training methods to influence underlying brain networks. For example, one study tested the effect of training during the period of major development of executive attention, which takes place between four to seven years of age. Training methods were adopted from primate studies and taught the children to manage conflict. Trained children showed an improvement in conflict resolution skills as well as changes in the underlying brain network—changes that generalized to an IQ test using materials quite different from those involved in the training. Similar studies have shown improvement of attention in classrooms that carry out training in executive function through working-memory training tasks as well as through meditation (see Rothbart et al., 2009, for a review of this work).

Given the wide range of individual differences in the efficiency of attention, it is expected that attention training could be especially beneficial for those children with poorer initial efficiency. These could be children with pathologies that involve attentional networks, children with genetic backgrounds associated with poorer attentional performance, or children raised in various degrees of deprivation.

Summary

Neuroimaging has provided a means of understanding how the human brain operates during tasks similar to those performed in school, such as reading and arithmetic. Networks of brain areas are connected to carry out most tasks of daily life. With practice, the connectivity between brain areas is strengthened, and tasks can be carried out more efficiently. Interrupting networks by temporary or permanent lesions can lead to loss of particular functions. The results of imaging studies have also provided important links between the general networks that are present in all people and the differences in the efficiency of these networks that lead to individuality. Much of the neuroimaging work so far deals with studies common to early education. However, the field is expanding to deal with differences between the expert and the novice brain (Anderson, 2007; Posner, in press). These studies should further expand the usefulness of imaging in secondary and higher education.

References

Anderson, J. R. (2007). *How can the human mind occur in the physical universe?* New York: Oxford University Press.

Berger, A., Tzur, G., & Posner, M. I. (2006). Infant brains detect arithmetic errors. *Proceedings of the National Academy of Sciences, 103,* 12649–12653.

Bush, G., Luu, P., & Posner, M. I. (2000). Cognitive and emotional influences in the anterior cingulate cortex. *Trends in Cognitive Science, 4/6,* 215–222.

Cohen, L., Henry, C., Dehaene, S., Martinaud, O., Lehericy, S., Lemer, C., & Ferrieux, S. (2004). The pathophysiology of letter-by-letter reading. *Neuropsychologia, 42*(13), 1768–1780.

Conturo, T. E., Lori, N. F., Cull, T. S., Akbudak, E., Snyder, A. Z., Shimony, J. S., McKinstry, R. C., Burton, H., & Raichle, M. E. (1999). Tracking neuronal fiber pathways in the living human brain. *Proceedings of the National Academy of Sciences, 96,* 10422–10427.

Crottaz-Herbette, S., & Mennon, V. (2006). Where and when the anterior cingulate cortex modulates attentional response: Combined fMRI and ERP evidence. *Journal of Cognitive Neuroscience, 18,* 766–780.

Dehaene, S. (1996). The organization of brain activations in number comparison: Event-related potentials and the additive-factors method. *Journal of Cognitive Neuroscience, 8,* 47–68.

Dehaene, S., & Cohen, L. (2007). Cultural variation in neural networks. *Neuron, 56,* 384–398.

Etkin, A., Egner, T., Peraza, D. M., Kandel, E. R., & Hirsch, J. (2006). Resolving emotional conflict: A role for the rostral anterior cingulate cortex in modulating activity in the amygdala. *Neuron, 51,* 871–882.

Fair, D., Cohen, A. L., Power, J. D., Dosenbach, N. U .F., Church, J. A., Meizin, F. M., et al. (2009). Functional brain networks develop from a local to distributed organization. *Public Library of Science, 5*(5), 1–13.

Griffin, S. A., Case, R., & Siegler, R. S. (1995). Rightstart: Providing the central conceptual prerequisites for first formal learning of arithmetic to students at risk for school failure. In K. McGilly (Ed.), *Classroom lessons: Integrating cognitive theory* (pp. 25–50). Cambridge, MA: MIT Press.

Guttorm, T. K., Leppanen, P. H. T., Poikkeus, A. M., Eklund, K. M., Lyytinen, P., & Lyytinen, H. (2005). Brain event-related potentials (ERPs) measured at birth predict later language development in children with and without familial risk for dyslexia. *Cortex, 41*(3), 291–303.

Kelly, A. M. C., & Garavan, H. (2005). Human functional neuroimaging of brain changes associated with practice. *Neuroimage, 15,* 1089–1102.

Kosslyn, S. (1980). *Image and mind.* Cambridge, United Kingdom: Cambridge University Press.

Kuhl, P. K. (2000). A new view of language acquisition. *Proceedings of the National Academy of Sciences, 100,* 11855–11857.

Kuhl, P. K., Stevens, E., Hayashi, A., Deguchi, T., Kiritani, S., & Iverson, P. (2006). Infants show a facilitation effect for native language phonetic perception between 6 and 12 months. *Developmental Science, 9*(2), F13–F21.

Kuhl, P. K., Tsao, F. M., & Liu, H. M. (2003). Foreign-language experience in infancy: Effects of short-term exposure and social interaction on phonetic learning. *Proceedings of the National Academy of Sciences, 100,* 9096–9101.

Lassen, N. A., Ingvar, D. H., & Skinhoj, E. (1978). Brain function and blood flow. *Scientific American, 238,* 62–71.

McCandliss, B. D., Cohen, L., & Dehaene, S. (2003). The visual word form area: Expertise for reading in the fusiform gyrus. *Trends in Cognitive Sciences, 7*(7), 293–299.

McNamara, A., Tegenthoff, M., Hubert, D., Buchel, C., Binkofski, F., & Ragert, P. (2007). Increased functional connectivity is crucial for learning novel muscle synergies. *NeuroImage, 35,* 1211–1218.

Molfese, D. L. (2000). Predicting dyslexia at eight years of age using neonatal brain responses. *Brain and Language, 72,* 238–245.

Ogawa, S., Lee, L. M., Kay, A. R., & Tank, D. W. (1990). Brain magnetic resonance imaging with contrast dependent blood oxygenation. *Proceedings of the National Academy of Sciences, 87,* 9868–9872.

Petersen, S. E., Fox, P. T., Posner, M. I., Mintun, M., & Raichle, M. E. (1988, February). Positron emission tomographic studies of the cortical anatomy of single word processing. *Nature, 331,* 585–589.

Pascale-Leone, A., & Hamilton, R. (2001). The metamodal organization of the brain: Vision—From neurons to cognition. *Progress in Brain Research, 134,* 427–445.

Posner, M. I. (in press). The expert brain. In J. J. Staszewski (Ed.), *Expertise and skill acquisition: The impact of William G. Chase.* New York: Psychology Press.

Posner, M. I. (2008). *Evolution and development of self-regulation.* 77th Arthur Lecture on Human Brain Evolution, New York: American Museum of Natural History.

Posner, M. I., & Raichle, M. E. (1994). *Images of mind.* New York: W. H. Freeman.

Posner, M. I., Rothbart, M. K., & Sheese, B. E. (2007). Attention genes. *Developmental Science, 10,* 24–29.

Price, C. J., & Devlin, J. T. (2003). The myth of the visual word form area. *NeuroImage, 19,* 473–481.

Raichle, M. E., Fiez, J. A., Videen, T. O., McCleod, A. M. K., Pardo, J. V., Fox, P. T., et al. (1994). Practice-related changes in the human brain: Functional anatomy during non-motor learning. *Cerebral Cortex, 4,* 8–26.

Roland, P. E., & Friberg, L. (1985). Localization of cortical areas activation by thinking. *Journal of Neurophysiology, 53,* 1219–1243.

Rothbart, M. K., Posner, M. I., Rueda, M. R., Sheese, B. E., & Tang, Y.-Y. (2009). Enhancing self-regulation in school and clinic. In D. Cicchetti & M. R. Gunnar (Eds.), *Minnesota Symposium on Child Psychology: Meeting the challenge of translational research in child psychology* (vol. 35, pp. 115–158). Hoboken, NJ: John Wiley.

Savoy, R. L. (2001). History and future directions of human brain mapping and functional neuroimaging. *Acta Psychologica, 107,* 9–42.

Shaywitz, S. (2003). *Overcoming dyslexia.* New York: Knopf.

Sheese, B. E.,Voelker, P. M., Rothbart, M. K., & Posner, M. I. (2007). Parenting quality interacts with genetic variation in dopamine receptor DRD4 to influence temperament in early childhood. *Development and Psychopathology, 19,* 1039–1046.

Womelsdorf, T., Schoffelen, J. M., Oostenveld, R., Singer, W., Desimone, R., Engel, A. K., et al. (2007). Modulation of neuronal interactions through neuronal synchronization. *Science, 316,* 1609–1612.

Judy Willis

Judy Willis, MD, MEd, attended UCLA School of Medicine, where she was awarded her medical degree and where she completed a neurology residency. She practiced neurology for fifteen years before obtaining her teaching credential. She then taught in elementary and middle schools for ten years and currently is an associate lecturer at University of California, Santa Barbara.

An authority in brain research regarding learning and the brain, Dr. Willis presents at educational conferences and professional development workshops nationally and internationally about classroom strategies derived from this research. She has written six books and numerous articles for professional journals, and was honored as a 2007 Finalist for the Distinguished Achievement Award for her educational writing by the Association of Educational Publishers.

Dr. Willis is a research consultant and member of the board of directors for the Hawn Foundation, an international foundation developed and directed by Goldie Hawn to implement educational programs in schools to teach students about their brains so they can lead smarter and happier lives. When not teaching, writing, consulting, or making presentations, Dr. Willis is a home winemaker and writes a weekly wine column.

In this chapter, Dr. Willis discusses how important it is for educators to understand the recent research in neuroscience that can have an impact on teaching and learning. Based on this research, she suggests a number of strategies that educators can consider in designing their instructional approaches that are likely to lead to improved student understanding and achievement.

Chapter 3

The Current Impact of Neuroscience on Teaching and Learning

Judy Willis

The convergence of laboratory science and cognitive research has entered our classrooms. Interpretations of this research and its implications for increasing the effectiveness of instruction are welcomed by many educators who seek ways to breathe life into increasingly compacted curricula that must be "covered" for standardized tests. Other teachers, who have been forced to use curricula claiming to be brain based that in fact are neither effective nor adequately supported by valid scientific research, are rightfully hesitant and cynical about using laboratory research as evidence on which to base classroom strategies.

In this chapter, I offer information about the brain processes involved in learning and memory to give educators foundational knowledge with which to evaluate the validity of "brain-based" claims. In addition, understanding how one's most successful lessons and strategies correlate with neuroscience research promotes the expansion and modification of these successful interventions for use in more situations and for the varying needs and strengths of individual students.

My background as an adult and child neurologist is the lens through which I evaluate the quality and potential applications of the new science of learning. However, it is my own schooling (I returned to school in 1999 to earn a teaching credential and Master of Education degree) and my past ten years of classroom teaching that allow me to incorporate the theoretical wisdom and observations of great educators, past and present, with laboratory analysis of neuroimaging, neurochemistry, and electrical monitoring of regions of the brain in response to different environmental influences and sensory input. Pairing theoretical interpretations of observations about teaching and learning with the interpretations of the current laboratory research offers what I call "neuro-*logical*" strategies applicable to today's classrooms.

A Brief Warning

It is striking how the accumulated scientific research since the early 1990s supports theories of learning from educational and psychological visionaries, such as William James, Lev Vygotsky, Jean Piaget, John Dewey, Stephen Krashen, Howard Gardner, and others. As I share stories of scientific support for these educational visionaries' theories, I hope also to illuminate the pathways through the brain that we see through neuroimaging.

However, the neuroscience implications of brain and learning research for education are still largely suggestive rather than empirical in establishing a solid link between how the brain learns and how it metabolizes oxygen or glucose. Teaching strategies derived from well-controlled neuroimaging research are at best compatible with the research to date about how the brain seems to deal with emotions, environmental influences, and sensory input.

Although what we see in brain scans cannot predict exactly what a strategy or intervention will mean for individual students, the information can guide the planning of instruction. I use the term *neuro-logical* in referring to strategies suggested by research and consistent with my neuroscience background knowledge that I correlate with research implications and have applied successfully in my own classrooms.

Learning Life Support

Research can suggest the most suitable emotional, cognitive, and social environments for learning. It is up to professional educators with knowledge about the brain to use the findings from scientific research to guide the strategies, curriculum, and interventions they select for specific goals and individual students. Knowing the workings of the brain makes the strategies we already know more adaptable and applicable.

When educators learn about how the brain appears to process, recognize, remember, and transfer information at the level of neural circuits, synapses, and neurotransmitters, and then share that knowledge with students, the empowerment for both enriches motivation, resilience, memory, and the joys of learning. The purest truth, I suggest, is the least open to statistical analysis and comes not from my twenty years as a physician and neuroscientist, but from my past ten years as a classroom teacher. There is no more critical life support than passionate, informed teachers who resuscitate their students' joyful learning.

This chapter describes the evolution of several current neuroscience-to-classroom topics in which interpretations of the new sciences of learning correlate strongly with past theories that were based on observations of students without the benefit of looking into their brains. A look backward and forward at the lab-to-classroom implications of attention, emotion, and neuroplasticity theories and research suggests practical implications for instruction, curriculum, and assessment for today's learners—tomorrow's 21st century citizens.

The Neuroscience of Joyful Learning Emotions

Remember the adage, "No smiles until after winter holidays"? Do you recall the time when proper learning behavior was represented by students sitting quietly, doing exactly what they were told without question or discussion, and reporting back memorized facts on tests? Where did those notions come from? Certainly not from the education luminaries of the past. A few thousand years ago, Plato advised against force-feeding facts to students without providing opportunities for them to relate learning to interest or evaluating their readiness:

> Calculation and geometry and all the other elements of instruction . . . should be presented to the mind in childhood; not, however, under any notion of *forcing* our system of education.

Because a freeman ought not to be a slave in the acquisition
of knowledge of any kind. Bodily exercise, when compulsory,
does no harm to the body; but knowledge which is acquired
under compulsion obtains no hold on the mind. (Plato, trans.
2009, p. 226; italics added)

Jump ahead several thousand years, and we discover Lev Vygotsky's zone of proximal development (ZPD) theory. He suggested that students learn best when guided by adults or more capable peers through the distance between their level of independent problem solving and their level or zone of potential development (Vygotsky, 1978). Similarly, Stephen Krashen (1981) supported the need for individualizing and differentiating instruction in the ZPD, which he called "comprehensible input." Krashen also described the negative effect of stress on learning: "Language acquisition does not require . . . tedious drill. The best methods supply comprehensible input (a bit beyond the acquirer's current level) in low anxiety situations, containing messages that students really want to hear" (Krashen, 1982, p. 25).

Incremental, Achievable Challenge

The compelling nature of computer games is an excellent example of the success of differentiating instruction to the students' ZPD or level of comprehensible input. Studies of what makes computer games so captivating show that variable challenge, based on the player's ability, is the key element (Reigeluth & Schwartz, 1989).

The most popular computer games take players through increasingly challenging levels. As skill improves, the next challenge motivates practice and persistence because the player feels the challenge is achievable. Similar incremental, achievable challenges in the classroom, at the appropriate level for students' abilities, are motivating and build mastery by lowering the barrier, not the bar.

Incremental, achievable challenges in the classroom, at the appropriate level for students' abilities, are motivating and build mastery by lowering the barrier, not the bar.

In computer games, the degree of challenge for each level is such that players are neither bored nor overwhelmed and frustrated. Practice allows players to improve and thus experience the neurochemical response of pleasure. Players succeed at the short-term goals provided by multiple levels of incremental challenge, while moving toward the long-term goal of completing the game. This is the power of achievable challenge: opportunities for students to see their effort-related improvement along the way to an ultimate goal, instead of having only the feedback of a final test or other end-point assessment. The computer game does not give prizes, money, or even pats on the back, yet it remains compelling. This may be attributed to the powerful brain response to intrinsic reward, described in the next section as the dopamine-reward effect.

Before the research on the dopamine-reward system, it was Krashen's theory of an affective (emotion-responsive) filter that started my search for how the brain's physical structures or neurochemicals are influenced by emotions. Research now supports recommendations to avoid high-stress instructional practices such as use of fear of punishment and to incorporate appropriate environmental, social, emotional, and cognitive considerations into instruction. We recognize that the brain has filters that influence what information enters our neural networks, as we see the effects of stress and other emotions on these filters.

Neuroimaging studies (Pawlak, Magarinos, Melchor, McEwen, & Strickland, 2003) show how stress and pleasure influence the way the brain filters sensory input and the effects of such emotions on the amygdala (Krashen's affective filter), a gateway that sends input either to the thinking brain (the prefrontal cortex) or to the lower, involuntary reactive brain. When stress directs sensory input to the lower brain, that input is not available for higher cognitive processing. To reduce the stress of frustration and increase information processing and memory at the higher cognitive level, we can encourage students by recognizing effort as well as achievement and providing opportunities for them to work at their achievable challenge level.

Intake Filters

The brain's first sensory intake filter, the reticular activating system (RAS), is a primitive network of cells in the lower brain stem through which all sensory input must pass if it is to be received by the higher brain. Out of the millions of bits of sensory information available to the brain every second, only several thousand are selected to pass through the RAS—and that selection is an involuntary, automatic response rather than a conscious decision. Much as in other mammals, in humans, the RAS is most receptive to the sensory input that is most critical to survival of the animal and species. Priority goes to changes in the individual's environment that are appraised as threatening. When a threat is perceived, the RAS automatically selects related sensory information and directs it to the lower, reactive brain, where the involuntary response is fight, flight, or freeze (Raz & Buhle, 2006). The RAS is an editor that grants attention and admission to a small fraction of all the sensory information available at any moment. This survival-directed filter is critical for animals in the wild, and it has not changed significantly as humans evolved.

Implications for the Classroom

The implications for the classroom are significant. Reducing students' perception of threat of punishment or embarrassment in front of classmates for not doing homework, concern about whether they will be chosen last for a kickball team, or anxiety that they will make an error in front of classmates because they are not fluent in English is not a "touchy-feely" option. During stress or fear, the RAS filter gives intake preference to input considered relevant to the perceived threat, at the expense of the sensory input regarding the lesson (Shim, 2005). Unless the perception of threat is reduced, the brain persists in doing its primary job—protecting the individual from harm. During fear, sadness, or anger, neural activity is evident in the lower brain, and the reflective, cognitive brain (prefrontal cortex) does not receive the sensory input of important items, such as the content of the day's lesson.

Neuroimaging has also given us information about which sensory input gets through the RAS when no threat exists. The RAS is particularly receptive to novelty and change associated with pleasure and to sensory input about things that arouse curiosity. Novelty—such as a changed room arrangement, a new wall or display color, discrepant events, posters advertising upcoming units, costumes, music playing when students enter the room, and other curiosity-evoking events—alerts the RAS to pay attention because something has changed and warrants further evaluation (Wang et al., 2005).

Students are often criticized for not paying attention when they may simply not have their RAS attuned to what their teachers think is important. Knowing how the RAS works means we can promote learning communities in which students feel safe and can count on adults to consistently enforce the rules that protect their bodies, property, and feelings from classmates or others who threaten them.

Students are often criticized for not paying attention when they may simply not have their RAS attuned to what their teachers think is important.

Priming the RAS

Our increasing understanding about what gains access through the RAS once a threat (stress) is removed also offers clues to strategies that promote attentive focus on lessons (Raz & Buhle, 2006). The following are a few examples of how you can build novelty into learning new information:

- Modulate your voice when presenting information.

- Mark key points on a chart or board in color.

- Vary the font size in printed material.

- Change seating arrangements periodically.

- Add photos to bulletin boards.

- Advertise an upcoming unit with curiosity-provoking posters, and add clues or puzzle pieces each day. Then ask students to predict what lesson might be coming. This can get the RAS primed to select the sensory input of that lesson when it is revealed.

- Play a song as students enter the room to promote curiosity and focus, especially if they know that there will be a link between some words in the song and something in the lesson.

- Behave in a novel manner, such as walking backwards at the start of a lesson about negative numbers. Curiosity primes students' RAS to follow along when you then unroll a number line on the floor to begin that unit about negative numbers.

Other RAS alerting strategies include engaging curiosity by asking students to make predictions. For example, you can get the RAS to focus on a lesson about estimating by overfilling a water glass. When students react, you respond, "I didn't estimate how much it would hold." Even a suspenseful pause before saying something particularly important builds anticipation as students become alert to the novelty of silence and the RAS is prompted by curiosity about what you will say or do next.

Similarly, there may be several minutes of curious excitement when students enter the classroom and find, say, a radish on each desk. A radish? The students' RAS will be curious, and so their attention will promote intake of sensory input cues to the puzzle of this novel object on their desk. They will be engaged and motivated to discover why the radishes are there. Younger students, learning the names and characteristics of shapes, now have the opportunity to develop a concept of roundness and evaluate the qualities that make some radishes rounder than others.

The radish lesson for older students might address a curriculum standard, such as analysis of similarities and differences. Their RAS will respond to the color, novelty, and peer interaction of evaluating the radishes they usually disdain in their salads. In the meantime, students develop skills of observation, comparison, contrast, and even prediction as to why the radish that seemed so familiar at first reveals surprises when examined with a magnifying glass. Stress levels remain low when students can choose their individual learning strengths to individually record their observations using sketches, verbal descriptions, or graphic organizers (such as Venn diagrams). They then feel they have something to contribute when groups form to share observations about what the radishes in their group have in common and how they differ.

As a survival mechanism, the RAS admits sensory input associated with pleasure. Animals have adapted to their environments and seek to repeat behaviors that are pleasurable and survival related, such as eating tasty food or following the scent of a potential mate. Engaged and focused brains are alert to sensory input that accompanies the pleasurable sensations. These associations increase the likelihood of the animal finding a similar source of pleasure in the future. As students enjoy the investigation with the radishes, the required lesson content can flow through the RAS gateway to reach the higher, cognitive brain.

A novel experience also has a greater chance of becoming a long-term memory because students are likely to actually answer their parents' often-ignored queries about what they learned in school that day. Students will summarize the day's learning as grateful parents give the positive feedback of attentive listening. The effect of the radish as a novel object—something parents probably never expected to hear described by their child—now alerts the parents' RAS, and the stage is set for a family discussion of the lesson.

Where Heart Meets Mind

Neuroimaging reveals that the amygdala and associated neural networks function very much like Krashen's affective filter, reducing successful learning when students are stressed. Until recently it was thought that the amygdala responded primarily to danger, fear, or anger. But neuroimaging studies show that it also responds to positive emotional influences. In experiments using fMRI (Pawlak et al., 2003), subjects were shown photographs of people with happy or grumpy expressions. After viewing the faces, the subjects were shown a list of words and instructed that the words would then appear mixed into a longer series of words. If they recognized a word from the initial list, they were to respond with a clicker. The results revealed better recall by subjects who viewed the happy faces, and their scans during recall had higher activity in the prefrontal cortex (PFC).

Neural networks converge in the PFC to regulate cognitive and executive functions, such as judgment, organization, prioritization, risk assessment, critical analysis, concept development, and creative problem solving. Unlike the RAS, which is proportionately the same size in humans as in other mammals, the PFC is proportionally larger in humans than in other mammals. For learning to occur and be constructed into conceptual long-term knowledge, sensory input needs to pass through the RAS and be processed by the PFC.

> For learning to occur, sensory input needs to pass through the RAS and be processed by the prefrontal cortex.

The subjects in these studies who viewed the grumpy faces showed increased metabolic activity in the amygdala, but significantly lower activity in the PFC than was exhibited by the control group when recalling the words they were instructed to remember. The studies suggest that when we are in a negative emotional state, the amygdala directs input to the lower, reactive (fight/flight/freeze) brain. When the subjects viewed pleasant faces, the metabolic activity was lower in the amygdala and higher in the reflective PFC, suggesting the nonthreatening condition favors conduction of information through the amygdala networks to the PFC (Pawlak et al., 2003).

The Influence of Dopamine

Dopamine is one of dozens of neurochemicals and hormones that not only influence learning, but also can be activated by certain environmental influences and teaching strategies. Dopamine is one of many neurotransmitters that carry information across gaps (synapses) between the branches (axons and dendrites) of connecting neurons. Certain experiences have been associated with the increased release of dopamine, which in turn produces pleasurable feelings. Engaging students in learning activities that correlate with increased dopamine release will likely get them to respond not only with pleasure, but also with increased focus, memory, and motivation (Storm & Tecott, 2005).

What Goes Up Must Come Down—Even in the Brain

Just as dopamine levels rise in association with pleasure, a drop in dopamine can be associated with negative emotions. A dopamine storage structure located near the prefrontal cortex, called the *nucleus accumbens* (NAcc), releases more dopamine when one's prediction (one's choice, decision, or answer) is correct and less dopamine when the brain becomes aware of a mistake. As a result of the lowering of dopamine, pleasure drops after making an incorrect prediction. When an answer is correct, the increased release of dopamine creates positive feelings (Salamone & Correa, 2002). This set of effects makes dopamine a learning-friendly neurotransmitter, promoting motivation, memory, and focus along with pleasurable feelings. It allows us to put a positive value on actions or thoughts that resulted in the increased dopamine release, and the neural networks used to make the correct predictions are reinforced. Just as valuable is the modification of the network that was used to make an incorrect prediction; the brain wants to avoid the drop in pleasure the next time. However, there needs to be timely corrective feedback for this memory storage correction to take place (Galvan et al., 2006).

This dopamine-reward system explains the compelling aspects of achievable challenge in computer games. When players make progress toward the achievement of their goals and feel the pleasure of the dopamine reward for their correct decisions (that is, their actions, choices, or answers), they remain intrinsically motivated to persevere through the next challenges of the game (Gee, 2007). Similarly, when students experience the dopamine pleasure of a correct prediction in class, they are intrinsically motivated to persevere through the challenges and apply effort to reach the next level of learning (O'Doherty, 2004).

The increased dopamine release in response to the satisfaction of a correct response reinforces the memory of the information used to answer the question, make a correct prediction, or solve the problem. The brain favors and repeats actions that release more dopamine, so the involved neural memory circuit becomes stronger and is favored when making similar future choices. However, if the response is wrong, then a drop in dopamine release results in some degree of unpleasantness. The brain responds negatively to mistake recognition by altering the memory circuit to avoid repeating the mistake and experiencing another drop in the dopamine pleasure (Thorsten et al., 2008).

> When students experience the dopamine pleasure of a correct prediction in class, they are motivated to persevere through the challenges of the next level of learning.

The value of the brain's dopamine disappointment response is associated with brain changes through neuroplasticity. Neuroplasticity is the ability of neural networks to extend, prune, reorganize, correct, or strengthen themselves based on acquiring new information, obtaining corrective feedback, and recognizing associations between new and prior knowledge. Changes in the neural circuits develop so that the brain is more likely to produce a correct response the next time and avoid the pleasure-drop consequences of making a mistake (van Duijvenvoorde et al., 2008).

Reducing the Fear of Mistakes

We know that understanding increases with corrective feedback after the brain makes incorrect predictions. However, making predictions means taking the risk of participating and being wrong, and most students' greatest fear is making a mistake in front of their peers. In order to construct and strengthen memory patterns (networks) of accurate responses and revise neural networks that hold incomplete or inaccurate information, students need to participate by predicting correct or incorrect responses. The goal is to keep all students engaged and participating because *only the person who thinks, learns.*

Students who risk making mistakes benefit from the dopamine pleasure fluctuations. The dopamine response to correct or incorrect predictions increases the brain's receptivity to learning the correct response. When immediate corrective feedback follows the students' incorrect predictions, the brain seeks to alter the incorrect information in the neural network that resulted in the wrong prediction so as to avoid the mistake in the future.

The Value of Frequent Assessment

Frequent formative assessment and corrective feedback are powerful tools to promote long-term memory and develop the executive functions of reasoning and analysis. Frequent assessment provides teachers information about students' minute-to-minute understanding during instruction. Your awareness of students' understanding from the ongoing feedback allows you to respond and adjust instruction accordingly so students do not become frustrated by confusion and drop into the fight/flight/freeze mode, in which cognitive processing and learning lesson content cannot take place.

For the process of assessment and expedient feedback to work, students must participate. The interventions I suggest are twofold: first, keep students' amygdala pathway open to the PFC and reduce their fear of participation. When students are in this low-anxiety state, they remain engaged, participate, and learn from feedback provided in a nonthreatening manner. Second, obtain frequent assessment of individual students' understanding throughout the class period without calling on specific students. For example, ask whole-class questions with single-word or multiple-choice (by letter) answers, and then have students respond by writing on individual whiteboards. Students need only hold up their whiteboards long enough for you to see their responses and nod to signify you have seen them.

About every ten minutes, do a walkabout and respond to the whiteboard assessments. This will allow you to prompt students whose responses demonstrate understanding to move on to preplanned higher-challenge activities while you work with those who need further explanation or practice. The students at mastery level are no longer stressed by the frustration of repeated explanation, drill, and grill on information they already know. Instead, these students can discuss a challenge question with a partner, create a graphic organizer comparing the new material to prior knowledge, or predict how what they learned can be transferred to other uses related to their interests. When the whiteboard assessment/feedback process becomes a regular part of the class, the amygdala-stressing frustration of confusion or boredom is reduced because students know within a few minutes that they will have help in acquiring the understanding needed to proceed or opportunities to move on to an enrichment activity in their higher achievable challenge range.

Positivity

Strategies to promote input to the prefrontal cortex overlap with those associated with increased dopamine levels. Examples of these amygdala-friendly and dopamine-releasing interventions include:

- Allowing students to move around in class periodically in learning activities. Examples are using pantomime while they guess which vocabulary word is being enacted or doing a ball toss to review high points of a lesson.

- Reading to students or shared reading by student pairs

- Creating opportunities for students to experience intrinsic satisfaction from incremental progress, not just feedback after final product (test, project, or report) assessment

- Using humor, not sarcasm

- Structuring positive peer interactions

- Using well-planned collaborative group work
- Providing some opportunities for student choice of practice or assessment options

Mind Controls Matter Through Neuroplasticity

Scientists are certainly on to something regarding neuroplasticity, and I enjoy reading current claims about this concept that has been in use for over a hundred years. Neuroplasticity changes neural networks by adding or pruning synapses and dendrites and producing layers of insulating myelin around axons. The construction of stronger, more efficient networks (faster retrievals, greater transfer) in long-term memory is stimulated by repeated activation of the circuit, such that *practice makes permanent* (Rivera, Reiss, Eckert, & Menon, 2005; Sousa, 2006).

> The construction of stronger, more efficient networks in long-term memory is stimulated by repeated activation of the circuit, such that *practice makes permanent.*

This neuroplasticity information, shared with students by teaching them a "Brain Owner's Manual," has significantly increased my students' motivation to study and review. When you share with students that their brain networks and memories are strengthened with the neural activation of review and practice, just as their muscles strengthen with repeated exercise, they begin to believe you when you tell them, "This can be the last time you'll ever have to learn what a least common denominator is."

A great study to share is the example of the neuroplasticity in the visual cortex. When we develop memory from visual information, the memory is ultimately stored in the cortex of the occipital lobes, located at the back of the brain. When we gain information by touching something, that sensation is recognized, and the memory ultimately stored in the parietal lobes at the top of the brain.

However, when subjects were blindfolded for a week and received intense tactile-sensory Braille practice, their occipital visual cortex, which before the experiment did not respond to tactile stimuli, demonstrated new neural-circuit plasticity and fMRI activity. Their visual cortex became similar to those found in people blind from birth (Merabet et al., 2008).

Pattern Development for More Successful Prediction

The extension and modification of neural network connections follows the patterning theories described by Piaget (Ginsberg & Opper, 1988). When students' knowledge increases through pattern recognition and by matching new information to memories, the neural networks become more extensive. Further modification, correction, and strengthening of the networks continue because of the dopamine feedback in response to accuracy of predictions (discussed earlier). Whenever students participate in a mental or physical activity that activates a specific pathway of neurons, the pattern that binds the connections is strengthened. When new information is added to the pattern, the network is extended, and future predictions (answers or choices) are more accurate (Dragansk & Gaser, 2004).

Patterning and Memory

To survive successfully, we need to collect information from the environment. Our brains perceive and generate patterns and use these patterned networks to predict the correct response to new stimuli. *Patterning* refers to the meaningful organization and categorization of information. Sensory data that pass through the brain's filters need to be successfully encoded into patterns that can be connected to existing neuronal pathways. The brain evaluates new stimuli for clues that help connect incoming information with stored patterns, categories of data, or past experiences, thereby extending existing patterns with the new input.

Strategies for Enhancing Pattern-Based Memory

When sensory input reaches the hippocampus—a structure located next to the amygdala—it is available for consolidation into memory. For consolidation to occur, prior knowledge from stored memory must be activated and transferred to the hippocampus to bind with the new information (Davachi & Wagner, 2002; Eldridge, Engel, Zeineh, Bookheimer, & Knowlton, 2005).

Using strategies that help students relate new information with memories they have already acquired enables students to detect the patterns and make connections. Such strategies include:

- Making analogies and recognizing similarities and differences

- Brainstorming about what they already know and what they want to learn about a new unit

- Administering pre-unit assessments, self-corrected for corrective feedback, and not counted for grading purposes

- Having class discussions, particularly using current events of high interest so that students can relate the new unit to prior knowledge

- Using ball-toss activities, in which students say what they think they know or make predictions about an upcoming topic or a book they will read

- Making cross-curricular connections, such as examining what students learned about the topic from the perspective of another class or subject

- Using activities that build pattern recognition skills. This is especially beneficial for younger students. For example, ask students to guess the pattern you are using as you call on students with a similar characteristic (such as asking students wearing blue shirts to stand up one at a time until students predict what they have in common). You can give examples and nonexamples of a concept and ask students to make predictions about the category or concept that the items share.

- Using graphic organizers, because they are nonlinguistic visual, pictorial, or diagrammatic ways to organize information so that the student's brain discovers patterns and relationships

- Using multisensory learning, which extends patterns because stimulation promotes the growth of more connections between dendrites and more myelination. Each of the senses has a separate storage area in the brain. In multisensory learning, more areas of the brain are stimulated (Wagner et al., 1998). Activities that use multiple senses mean duplicated storage of information and thus more successful recall (Rivera et al., 2005).

When new information is recognized as related to prior knowledge, learning extends beyond the domain in which it occurred. It is available through transfer to create new predictions and solutions to problems in other areas beyond the classroom or test.

Yes, You Can Change Your Intelligence

Children, as well as many adults, mistakenly think that intelligence is determined at or before birth by their genes and that effort will not significantly change their potential for academic success. Especially for students who believe they are "not smart," the realization that they can literally change their brains through study and review strategies is empowering. This is also true of my neurology patients who lose function as a result of brain disease or trauma. Through practice, beginning with visualizing of moving the paralyzed limb or imagining themselves speaking, neuroplasticity constructs new neural networks as undamaged parts of their brains take over the job of the damaged regions (Draganski, Gaser, Busch, & Schuierer, 2004).

Intelligence can be considered as a measure of students' ability to make accurate connections between new input and existing patterns of stored information. As children grow and learn, they expand their experiential databases. The more experiences they have, the more likely their brains will find a fit when comparing new experiences with previous ones. These connections allow them to acquire and apply the new knowledge to solve problems. In this way, more successful, extensive patterning leads to more accurate predictions (answers). Through practice, experience, and mental manipulation, the brain builds intelligence (more accurate predictions) by extending, correcting, and strengthening neural networks.

A great positivity-building tool comes from students' learning about their brain's ability to change through this neuroplasticity process. When students understand that their brains can develop stronger, more efficient, accessible, and durable neural networks through their actions, they have the positivity, resilience, and motivation to do their part to develop the skills, knowledge, and intelligence to achieve their goals. Teachers can help their students recognize how effort and practice change their brains, resulting in improved memory, information retrieval, and knowledge

> Through practice, experience, and mental manipulation, we develop intelligence by extending, correcting, and strengthening neural networks.

transfer so that learning in one setting can readily be applied to new situations. I explain to my students: "Your own mental efforts in all types of higher thinking, practicing and reviewing, as well as making conscious choices to delay immediate gratification, working to achieve goals, and evaluating the strategies you used when you were most successful actually build your brain into a more efficient and successful tool that you control."

I have been teaching my upper elementary and middle school students about the brain filters that determine what information reaches their higher, thinking brains (PFC) and how they can consciously influence those filters. They learn about changes in their brains that take place through neuroplasticity. I show them brain scans, and we draw diagrams and make clay models of connections between neurons that grow when they learn new information. I call their lesson summaries "Dend-Writes," and we discuss how more dendrites grow when information is reviewed. I even send home electron microscope photos of growing dendrites and synapses and assign students to explain the neuroanatomy to family members and report their families' responses, because teaching new learning to someone else is strong memory cement.

I use sports, dance, and musical instrument analogies. I ask them to recall how their basketball shots or their guitar or ballet performances improved when they practiced more. Then we discuss that their brains respond the same way when they practice their multiplication facts or reread confusing parts of a book because, through neuroplasticity, practice makes permanent. Their results are wonderful. One ten-year-old boy said, "I didn't know that I could grow my brain. Now I know about growing dendrites when I study and get a good night's sleep. Now when I think about playing video games or reviewing my notes, I tell myself that I have the power to grow brain cells if I review. I'd still rather play the games, but I do the review because I want my brain to grow smarter. It works and feels great."

The Future

The most rewarding jobs of this century will be those that cannot be done by computers. The students best prepared for these opportunities need conceptual thinking skills to solve problems that have not yet been recognized. For 21st century success, students will need a skill set far beyond the current subject matter evaluated on standardized tests. The qualifications for success in the world that today's students will enter will demand the abilities to think critically, communicate clearly, use continually changing technology, be culturally aware and adaptive, and possess the judgment and open-mindedness to make complex decisions based on accurate analysis of information. The keys to success for today's students will come through the collaboration of the laboratory scientist and the classroom teacher.

The Science

Neuroscience is showing us more of the brain's potential to modify intelligence through neuroplasticity. With increasing developments in the genetic-environmental connection, fMRI scanning, and collaboration among neuroscientists, cognitive scientists, and all professionals in the mind, brain, and education fields, we will continue to add to our understanding of how different people learn and the role of environment and experience. We will have more predictive information earlier to enable individualizing learning for each student. With a better understanding of the brain's information-processing functions, neurotransmitters, and which networks do what, we will know more about the strategies best suited for different types of instruction.

Technology will surely play an increasing role in the classrooms of tomorrow. Already more online classes and computerized instruction (especially for foundational knowledge at all grade levels) are in use than ever before, and the possibilities for the future seem almost infinite. Models are developing to use neuroimaging, EEG, and cognitive evaluations to predict the best instructional modes for individual students.

Collaboration

An equally exciting trend is the development of learning communities within schools or districts, in which classroom teachers, resource specialists, and administrators use books and videos and share information from professional development workshops to evaluate strategies appropriate for students' needs. Educators who teach and observe classrooms discuss their successful use of these strategies, and teachers collaborate and reflect on neuro-*logical* strategies they try in their classrooms that appear to result in identifiable patterns of learning benefits.

In the learning communities I observe when I travel, I see dedicated professionals who chose to become educators because of their dedication to making a difference for all students. Teachers are drawn to their career choices for admirable reasons. Creativity, imagination, perseverance, and motivation endure in the educators I meet, even in these times of teacher blame and over-packed curriculum.

I observe as educators coach one another in research-based strategies and share the knowledge they acquire about the science of learning, and how they have or want to apply new research implications to further enhance students' positive and successful learning experiences. I see these groups then go beyond the boundaries of their schools and contribute to the growing global teacher-researcher community.

Increasingly it is evident that the most valuable assets for improving education won't be developed through neuroimaging in a laboratory, but rather by improving the effectiveness of educators. Given access to tools—time, ongoing professional development to acquire foundational knowledge about the science of learning, and professional learning communities to evaluate and share potential classroom applications of laboratory research about mind, brain, and education—educators will be the leaders in raising the level of preparation, optimism, and outcomes of the students who pass through their classrooms.

The interface of science and learning can continue to guide educators in the development of the strategies, interventions, and assessments to prepare today's students for the world of tomorrow. The more educators know about the research-supported basis for a strategy or procedure, the more they feel invested in it and the more comfortable they are using and modifying the strategy. This empowers and encourages teachers to extend lessons beyond rote memory into conceptual understanding and transferable knowledge. These educators help students become lifelong learners because they embrace the neuroscience of joyful learning.

Collaboration will propel the education advancements of this century. The one-way street of scientists telling teachers what to do, without having spent time observing in classrooms, has been modernized to a bridge between classroom and laboratory. The future developments with the most extensive and useful classroom applications will likely arise from input that educators provide to scientists. Through this collaboration, the seeds planted in a single classroom by a creative, resourceful teacher may be analyzed, replicated, expanded, and disseminated to benefit students worldwide. After all, isn't sharing what we teachers do so well?

References

Davachi, L., & Wagner, A. (2002). Hippocampal contributions to episodic encoding: Insights from relational and item-based learning. *Journal of Neurophysiology, 88*(2), 982–990.

Dragansk, D., & Gaser, C. (2004). Neuroplasticity: Changes in grey matter induced by training. *Nature, 427,* 311–312.

Draganski, B., Gaser, C., Busch, V., & Schuierer, G. (2004). Neuroplasticity: Changes in grey matter induced by training. *Nature, 427*(22), 311–312.

Eldridge, L. L., Engel, S. A., Zeineh, M. M., Bookheimer, S. Y., & Knowlton, B. J. (2005, March). A dissociation of encoding and retrieval processes in the human hippocampus. *Journal of Neuroscience, 25*(13), 3280–3286.

Galvan, A., Hare, T. A., Parra, C. E., Penn, J., Voss, H., Glover, G., et al. (2006, June). Earlier development of the accumbens relative to orbitofrontal cortex might underlie risk-taking behavior in adolescents. *Journal of Neuroscience, 26*(25), 6885–6892.

Gee, J. P. (2007). *What video games have to teach us about learning and literacy* (2nd ed.). New York: Palgrave Macmillan.

Ginsburg, H. P., & Opper, S. (1988). *Piaget's theory of intellectual development* (3rd ed). Englewood Cliffs, NJ: Prentice Hall.

Krashen, S. (1981). *Principles and practice in second language acquisition.* English language teaching series. London: Prentice Hall International (UK) Ltd.

Krashen, S. (1982). *Theory versus practice in language training.* In R. W. Blair (Ed.), *Innovative approaches to language teaching* (pp. 25–27). Rowley, MA: Newbury.

Merabet, L. B., Hamilton, R., Schlaug, G., Swisher, J. D., Kiriakopoulos, E. T., Pitskel, N. B., Kauffman, T., & Pascual-Leone, A. (2008). Rapid and reversible recruitment of early visual cortex for touch. *PLoS One, 3*(8), 1–12.

O'Doherty, J. P. (2004, December). Reward representations and reward-related learning in the human brain: Insights from neuroimaging. *Current Opinion in Neurobiology, 14,* 769–776.

Pawlak, R., Magarinos, A. M., Melchor, J., McEwen, B., & Strickland, S. (2003, January). Tissue plasminogen activator in the amygdala is critical for stress-induced anxiety-like behavior. *Nature Neuroscience, 6,* 168–174.

Plato. (2009). *The republic* (B. Jowett, Trans.). Thousand Oaks, CA: BN Publishing.

Raz, A., & Buhle, J. (2006). Typologies of attentional networks. *Nature Reviews Neuroscience, 7,* 367–379.

Reigeluth, C. M., & Schwartz, E. (1989). An instructional theory for the design of computer-based simulations. *Journal of Computer-Based Instruction, 16*(1), 1–10.

Rivera, S. M., Reiss, A. L., Eckert, M. A., & Menon, V. (2005, November). Developmental changes in mental arithmetic: Evidence for increased functional specialization in the left inferior parietal cortex. *Cerebral Cortex, 15*(11), 1779–1790.

Salamone, J. D., & Correa, M. (2002, December). Motivational views of reinforcement: Implications for understanding the behavioral functions of nucleus accumbens dopamine. *Behavioral Brain Research, 137,* 3–25.

Shim, J. (2005). Automatic knowledge configuration by reticular activating system. In L. Wang, K. Chen, & Y. S. Ong (Eds.), *Advances in natural computations* (pp. 1170–1178). New York: Springer.

Sousa, D. A. (2006). *How the brain learns* (3rd ed.). Thousand Oaks, CA: Corwin Press.

Storm, E. E., & Tecott, L. H. (2005, August). Social circuits: Peptidergic regulation of mammalian social behavior. *Neuron, 47,* 483–486.

Thorsten, T., Hariri, A., Schlagenhauf, F., Wrase, J., Sterzer, P., Buchholz, H., et al. (2008). Dopamine in amygdala gates limbic processing of aversive stimuli in humans. *Nature Neuroscience, 11*(12), 1381–1382.

van Duijvenvoorde, A. C. K., Zanolie, K., Rombouts, S. A., Raijmakers, M. E. J., & Crone, E. A. (2008, September). Evaluating the negative or valuing the positive? Neural mechanisms supporting feedback-based learning across development. *Journal of Neuroscience, 28*(38), 9495–9503.

Vygotsky, L. (1978). *Mind and society: The development of psychological processes.* Cambridge, MA: Harvard University Press.

Wagner, A. D., Schacter, D. L., Rotte, M., Koutstaal, W., Maril, A., Dale, A. M., et al. (1998, August). Building memories: Remembering and forgetting of verbal experiences as predicted by brain activity. *Science, 281,* 1188–1191.

Wang, J., Rao, H., Wetmore, G. S., Furlan, P. M., Korczykowski, M., Dinges, D. F., et al. (2005, December). Perfusion functional MRI reveals cerebral blood flow pattern under psychological stress. *Proceedings of the National Academy of Sciences, 102*(49), 17804–17809.

Mary Helen Immordino-Yang

Mary Helen Immordino-Yang, EdD, is a cognitive neuroscientist and educational psychologist who studies the brain bases of emotion, social interaction, and culture and their implications for development and schools. A former junior high school science teacher, she earned her doctorate at the Harvard Graduate School of Education. She is the associate North American editor for the journal *Mind, Brain, and Education*, the recipient of the Proceedings of the National Academy of Sciences Cozzarelli Prize, and the inaugural recipient of the International Mind, Brain, and Education Society's Award for Transforming Education through Neuroscience. She is currently Assistant Professor of Education at the Rossier School of Education and Assistant Professor of Psychology at the Brain and Creativity Institute, University of Southern California.

Matthias Faeth

Matthias Faeth is a doctoral student at the Harvard Graduate School of Education. His interest is the interaction of emotions and learning from an educational, psychological, and neuroscientific perspective. He is currently living in Montreal where he is also pursuing his research at the Centre de Recherche en Neuropsychologie et Cognition (CERNEC) at the Université de Montréal.

In this chapter, the authors present a neuroscientific view of how emotions affect learning new information and suggest a set of socially embedded educational practices that teachers can use to improve the emotional and cognitive aspects of classroom learning.

Chapter 4

The Role of Emotion and Skilled Intuition in Learning

Mary Helen Immordino-Yang and Matthias Faeth

Advances in neuroscience have been increasingly used to inform educational theory and practice. However, while the most successful strides forward have been made in the areas of academic disciplinary skills such as reading and mathematical processing, a great deal of new evidence from social and affective neuroscience is prime for application to education (Immordino-Yang & Damasio, 2007; Immordino-Yang & Fischer, in press). In particular, social and affective neuroscience are revealing more clearly than ever before the interdependence of cognition and emotion in the brain, the importance of emotion in guiding successful learning, and the critical role of teachers in managing the social environment of the classroom so that optimal emotional and cognitive learning can take place (van Geert & Steenbeek, 2008).

The message from social and affective neuroscience is clear: no longer can we think of learning as separate from or disrupted by emotion, and no longer can we focus solely at the level of the individual student in analyzing effective strategies for classroom instruction. Students and teachers socially interact and learn from one another in ways that cannot be done justice by examining only the "cold" cognitive aspects of academic skills. Like other forms of learning and interacting, building academic knowledge involves integrating emotion and cognition in social context. Academic skills are hot!

Beyond Neuromyths

In this chapter, we aim to help educators move beyond the oversimplified and often misleading "neuromyths" that abound in education (Goswami, 2004, 2006) by replacing them with a set of strategies for fostering the sound development of academic emotions (Pekrun, Goetz, Titz, & Perry, 2002). These strategies are guided by the use of emotionally relevant and socially contextualized educational practices (Brackett, Rivers, Shiffman, Lerner, & Salovey, 2006). These strategies are not taken directly from the details of neuroscience findings, as drawing such a direct connection would be inappropriate and premature. Instead, we interpret these findings to present a neuroscientific view of the functionality of emotions in learning new information. We then build from this discussion a set of socially embedded educational practices that teachers can use to improve the emotional and cognitive aspects of classroom learning.

Before we proceed, we would like to insert a strong cautionary note. While the emerging field of mind, brain, and education is making strong strides toward informing educational practice with neuroscientific findings, it is important to maintain a cautious stance (Fischer et al., 2007). Too often in education, out of the sincere desire to understand and help students, educators have grabbed onto various "brain-based" teaching strategies that are based either in misunderstandings or misapplications of neuroscientific information to education. The education literature and popular media are rife with examples, from the categorizing of elementary school students as specific kinds of learners (such as kinesthetic or auditory) to the notion that young babies should listen to Mozart to develop better spatial cognition than they might otherwise develop. At best, these neuromyths have wasted educational resources; at worst, they may even have been harmful or dangerous to children.

We take a different approach. Rather than presenting details about brain systems and findings that are not directly relevant to the question of how best to educate children, we instead aim to interpret findings from a body of neuroscience research that has made use of a very productive paradigm for studying the emotional and body-related signals underlying learning. This paradigm, known as the Iowa Gambling Task, was designed by Antoine Bechara and others some years ago (Bechara, Damasio, Tranel, & Damasio, 2005), and it has taught neuroscientists a great deal about the formative role of emotions in cognition and learning. In this chapter, we aim to distill what neuroscientists have learned into a series of neuroscience-based recommendations about emotion and learning in social context that can inform teachers' practice. These recommendations are likely to be reliable and usable because they reflect not one experiment or brain area, but rather a consensus on the principles of brain functioning that has accumulated over several years of neuroscientific experimentation and debate.

To do this, we first describe the Iowa Gambling Task and the important insights it has revealed into the role of nonconscious emotional "intuition" in successful, efficient learning. We present a typical participant's performance in this paradigm to illustrate the

> The Iowa Gambling Task has taught neuroscientists a great deal about the formative role of emotions in cognition and learning.

reliable patterns that have been revealed through the many emotion and learning experiments that have made use of this paradigm, and we interpret this typical pattern in light of various researchers' findings with normal and brain-damaged patients. We then go on to describe how interference with emotional processing during learning—either from the intrusion of other emotions irrelevant to the task at hand or, in extreme cases, because of damage to relevant brain regions—can interfere with the building of sound emotional intuitions that guide skilled, rational behavior.

In the second half of the chapter, we explicitly address strategies that teachers can use to help students manage and skillfully recruit their emotions in the service of meaningful learning, building from what neuroscience experiments have taught us.

Thus the overall aim of the first part of the chapter is to describe five contributions from neuroscience research that have taught neuroscientists about the relationship between emotion and cognition in learning and that we feel have important implications for teaching in social settings such as schools. The overall aim of the second half of the chapter is to distill the implications of these contributions into a series of three strategies that can be used to improve teaching and learning in schools. Taken together, we hope this chapter will guide teachers in beginning to incorporate meaningful emotional experiences into their students' learning.

The Brain and Learning: Why Does Emotion Matter?

Consider the following intriguing scenario from the Iowa Gambling Task (IGT): a participant in a study is seated at a table with a card game before her. Her task is to choose cards from four decks. With each card she draws, she has the chance to win some amount of money. Unbeknownst to her, some decks contain cards with larger wins than other decks, but these decks also result in occasional enormous losses that make these decks a bad choice in the long run. How does a typical person learn to play this game and deduce the rules for calculating and weighing the relative long-term outcomes of the different decks?

1. Emotion Guides Cognitive Learning

In examining our IGT player's performance, we will see that the process of learning how to play this game involves both emotional and cognitive processing. It begins with the development of (generally) nonconscious emotional intuitions that eventually become conscious rules, which she can describe in words or formulas. The development and feeling of these intuitions is critical to construct successful, usable knowledge. As she begins the game, she at first randomly selects cards from one deck or another, noting wins and losses as they come. But soon, before she is consciously aware that the decks are biased, she begins to show an anticipatory emotional response in the moment before choosing a card from a high-risk deck (her palms begin to sweat in microscopic amounts, measured as *galvanic skin response*, or GSR). Nonconsciously, she is accumulating emotional information about the relative riskiness of some decks. As she proceeds, this emotional information steers her toward the "safe" decks and away from those with high gains but the possibility of large losses. After playing for awhile longer, she accumulates enough information about the decks that she is able to describe the rule about which decks to play and which to avoid, and we would say that she has "learned."

The Iowa Gambling Task and other experiments have taught neuroscientists about the importance of emotion in the learning process, an importance that probably applies not only here, but also to math learning, social learning, and to learning in various other arenas in which a person must accumulate information from his or her experiences and use that information to act advantageously in future situations (Bechara & Damasio, 1997). Emotion guides the learning of our participant much like a rudder guides a ship (Immordino-Yang & Damasio, 2007). Though it and its influence may not be visible, it provides a force that stabilizes the direction of a learner's decisions and behaviors over time. It helps the learner recognize and call up relevant knowledge—for example, knowledge about which deck to pick from or which math formula to apply (see fig. 4.1, page 74). In the diagram, the solid ellipse represents emotion; the dashed ellipse represents cognition. The extensive overlap between the two ellipses represents the domain of "emotional thought." Skilled intuitions are often an important step in the development of emotional thought and are built through repeated revisiting of real or simulated bodily sensations in the light of the "cognitive" aspects of knowledge.

2. Emotional Contributions to Learning Can Be Conscious or Nonconscious

In the example of the Iowa Gambling Task, the anticipatory emotional response guiding the participant's choice is not present from the very beginning. It must be slowly learned from experience playing the game. Although she understands that she is engaging in a game of chance with uncertain outcomes, our participant at first has no information—intuitive or factual—that might help her to distinguish between the decks. As she draws, she will at first surely be attracted to the large-gain/large-loss decks as long as she is experiencing the delivery of higher rewards. At this stage, she will already be developing a nonconscious emotional reaction to these decks, one of excitement and attraction.

It is only after her first encounter with an enormous loss that her reaction will change, rapidly shifting from excitement to disappointment. Was the loss an isolated event? Or should she learn from it and adjust her future choices accordingly? From then on, she will not draw from the decks in the same way as before. She will likely continue to draw from the high-risk deck occasionally, feeling tempted by the higher rewards, but she will do so while at the same time fearing to be

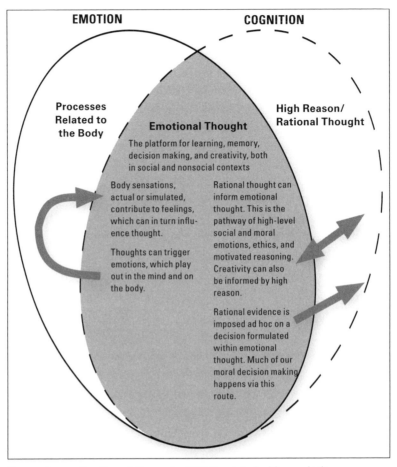

Source: Immordino-Yang & Damasio, 2007. Reprinted with permission.

Figure 4.1: How emotion and cognition come together to produce the thought processes that educators care about, among them learning and memory.

punished again for taking the risk. As we can see, her emotional rudder is steering her behavior and teaching her about the decks, making her reluctant to reach for the risky decks, helping her to overcome the temptation of higher rewards, and giving her the energy and impetus to think twice. And as the neuroscience experiments show, all of this can be happening underneath her level of conscious awareness. She may still report that she does not know yet how to play the game or what to expect from the different decks. Only her sweating palms give away the hidden force of her unconscious emotional learning at this early point in the learning process.

3. Emotional Learning Shapes Future Behavior

Having an emotional rudder is helpful when playing the Iowa Gambling Task, but it is just as helpful in many other situations—both in school and elsewhere. Consider the third-grade student who incorrectly solves a math problem and receives a red X on his paper or, alternatively, correctly solves the problem and gets a good grade. Consider the community college student whose essay draft misses the mark, or who raises his hand in class and gets an encouraging nod from the instructor.

Just as we observed in the IGT player, learners' emotional reactions to the outcomes of their behavioral choices become implicitly attached to the cognitive knowledge about the domain—in the previous examples, either school culture or math or essay writing. These academic activities are no longer neutral to the learner; they become "risky" and uncomfortable, or else exciting and challenging, depending in part on the learner's emotional interpretation of the outcome. In each of these examples, the learner's emotional reaction to the outcome of his efforts consciously or nonconsciously shapes his future behavior, either inciting him to behave in the same way the next time or to be wary of situations that are similar.

4. Emotion Is Most Effective at Facilitating the Development of Knowledge When It Is Relevant to the Task at Hand

In the context of schools, emotion is often considered ancillary or secondary to learning, rather than an integral part of the knowledge being learned. We expect children, for example, to "get their feelings out of the way" so that they can focus on their studies. In this view, emotions are seen as a disruptive force, antagonistic to good cognition and in need of regulation and suppression in the interest of mature judgment—be it with respect to social dilemmas such as how to treat your friends, moral dilemmas such as dealing with an instance of cheating (Haidt, 2001), or cognitive dilemmas such as deciding which

Efficient learners build useful and relevant intuitions that guide their thinking and decision making.

equation to apply to a problem in math class (Immordino-Yang & Fischer, in press).

However, as the IGT task demonstrates, neuroscience is revealing that rather than working to eliminate or "move beyond" emotion, the most efficient and effective learning incorporates emotion into the cognitive knowledge being built. In effect, efficient learners build useful and relevant intuitions that guide their thinking and decision making (Damasio, 1994/2005; Immordino-Yang & Damasio, 2007). These intuitions integrate their emotional reactions with their cognitive processing and incorporate what has been learned from experience. Intuitions are not randomly generated nonconscious whims. Rather, because they are shaped and organized by experience with a task or domain, they are specific and relevant to the particular contexts in which they are learned.

But how can we distinguish between relevant and irrelevant emotions, and how does this distinction affect academic learning? To understand how the development of the emotional rudder can go wrong, let's return to the previous example. How effectively would the gambler learn the game if she were so anxious that she could not "feel" the subtle emotional changes telling her about the valence of the decks? Alternatively, what if she were so excited about, say, an upcoming football game that she could not concentrate on the task at hand? In both cases, she would clearly have an emotional reaction, but with respect to the task, her reaction would be static. She would be anxious or excited independent of which deck she drew from and independent of the outcome obtained. In both of these examples, she would quite possibly not learn to effectively distinguish the different decks based on her emotional intuition, because all decks would be experienced with undifferentiated emotionality. Her learning of the game would fail. Taken together, these examples show that effective learning does not involve removing emotion; rather, it involves skillfully cultivating an emotional state that is relevant and informative to the task at hand.

5. Without Emotion, Learning Is Impaired

Consider now an alternate scenario: A different person is gambling in the task and trying to win the money. However, this person is a neurological patient with damage to an area of the brain that lies just above the eyes (the ventromedial prefrontal cortex) and mediates between the feeling of the body during emotion and the learning of cognitive strategies. How would this person's performance differ from the person in the previous example? This patient has perfectly intact cognitive abilities; she solves logic problems and does fine on standardized IQ tests. Will she be able to learn how to play the game successfully, though, given that her choice of cognitive strategy cannot be subtly informed by her nonconscious emotional reactions to risky decks? Maybe getting emotion out of the way will allow for a more direct assessment of the game's rules?

Sadly, this is not the case. The patient would start out just like the typical player, randomly selecting cards from one deck or another. However, instead of developing the anticipatory emotional response that would tell her about the differential riskiness of the decks, her emotional reaction to choosing the cards would not inform her future choices. While normal participants gradually shift to picking from the "safe" decks, the ventromedial prefrontal cortex patient would remain attracted to the large-gain/large-loss decks, picking from them at least as often as from the "safe" decks. Although she would notice that some decks produce high losses and feel disappointed when these losses occurred, she would not use this information to guide her future playing strategy.

Most normal participants are able to identify a conscious rule about which decks to play and which to avoid by the time they have picked a total of eighty cards. Even the normal participants who fail to state the rule fully and correctly have developed an advantageous pattern of choosing from the decks by then. But among the group of ventromedial prefrontal cortex patients, things look very different. They continue to choose disadvantageously *even if* they succeed in identifying a conscious rule about which decks to play and which to avoid. Put another way, they never successfully learn to play the game. Their conscious knowledge, emotional reactions, and cognitive strategies are not integrated or aligned. The result is that these patients are unable to learn from their experiences and unable to use what they may consciously appear to know. (Notably, this deficit extends into decisions these patients make in their daily lives. They are unable to manage their lives as effectively as they did prior to sustaining the brain injury and must be constantly supervised.)

For the interaction of emotion and cognition, all of this means that factual knowledge alone is useless without a guiding emotional intuition. Some ventromedial prefrontal patients know very well which decks are good or bad, but this information has no relevance for them when it comes to making decisions. Students in the classroom struggle with much the same problem. If they feel no connection to the knowledge they learn in school, then the academic content will seem emotionally meaningless to them. Even if they manage to regurgitate factual information, it will not influence their decisions and behavior. Sure, unlike the ventromedial prefrontal patients, they have the capacity to develop emotional reactions to the material they learn. But if the curriculum does not support the development of emotional reactions—if it does not accommodate the reactions when they occur and allow them to influence decisions and behavior in the classroom—then the effective integration of emotion and cognition in learning will be compromised. For effective cognition to manifest itself in the classroom and beyond, emotions need to be a part of the learning experience all along.

> If students feel no connection to the knowledge they learn in school, then the academic content will seem emotionally meaningless to them.

Bringing Emotions Back Into Classroom Learning: Three Strategies for Teachers

In this section, we provide three guiding strategies to help teachers accommodate and support the development of emotional learning.

Foster Emotional Connection to the Material

The first and possibly most important strategy that teachers can use to foster meaningful learning through emotion is to design educational experiences that encourage relevant emotional connection to the material being learned. Such fostering of emotional connection can start with the selection of the topic to be explored. Sometimes teachers have some leeway in deciding which topics to present and how to engage their students in them. Why not, in a serious and responsible manner, involve students in the selection process? For example, if the topic is learning about ancient Rome, why not allow students a choice among writing and performing a play about key events, writing a research report, or designing a model senate that mimics that of the early Romans? When students are involved in designing the lesson, they better understand the goal of the lesson and become more emotionally invested in and attached to the learning outcomes. This participatory approach has the power to instill in students a sense of ownership that can go a long way toward making later learning meaningful and the emotions they experience relevant.

In addition, teachers can relate material to the lives and interests of their students. Relating can mean showing how new learning can affect students' everyday experiences, or it can mean students themselves identifying and probing connections. As much as possible, teachers should encourage students to follow their interests and passions and help them to see the relevance and usefulness of the academic material to these choices. How, for example, did Caesar feel and think about war? That question, applied to students or today's national leaders, is as relevant now as it would have been in Caesar's time. When students are encouraged to engage and identify with academic material in a meaningful way, the emotional intuitions they develop also will be relevant to decisions they face in their everyday lives.

Another effective tool for emotional engagement is teaching students to solve open-ended problems. Such problems allow students to wrestle with the definition of the task, recruiting their intuitive knowledge regarding relevance, familiarity, creativity, and interest in the process (Ablin, 2008). Portfolios, projects, and group work, although usually more closely guided, also can be effective in enabling the emotional aspects of thought. In general, teachers should strive to design activities that create space for emotional reactions to appear and space to make mistakes and learn from them. For some teachers, so doing likely will mean breaking away from a highly prescriptive approach that aims to move students along the fastest and most direct path toward mastery of specific content, because this fast, direct path often is emotionally impoverished.

It is in the detours and missteps as well as in rediscovering the path that students experience rich emotionality, accumulate valuable emotional memories, and develop a powerful, versatile emotional rudder. In a time of heavily used standardized testing and curricula packed to the brim, this idea might sound unorthodox. But from an affective neuroscientific perspective, the direct and seemingly most efficient path turns out to be inefficient, leading too often to abundant factual knowledge that is poorly integrated (and therefore ineffective) in students' real lives.

Encourage Students to Develop Smart Academic Intuitions

Once a topic is chosen, teachers should encourage students to use their own intuitions when engaging in learning and problem-solving activities in the classroom. From a neuroscientific perspective, intuition can be understood as the incorporation of the nonconscious emotional signals into knowledge acquisition. Recall the Iowa Gambling Task, in which typical participants playing the game began to show signs of emotional unease before choosing from risky decks. Eventually this emotional reaction was incorporated into the participants' conscious understanding of the rules of play. That is, even before a participant can consciously describe the rules, she has nonconscious intuitions about how things will turn out when she chooses from one or the other card decks. The development of these experience-based intuitions increasingly guides the participant's decisions and eventually facilitates the formation of conscious, cognitive rules for the game—in educational language, she has "learned"!

Just as the Iowa Gambling Task participant needs both positive and negative experiences to learn the relevance of the different decks and the implications for various choices, so too must students have opportunities to develop intuitions about how and when to use academic material. They will learn to ask relevant questions, such as "Is the use of this mathematical procedure warranted in this instance?" and "Am I getting closer to the correct solution?" Students' private (or collective) reflections on such questions are critical to the development of useful, generalizable, memorable knowledge. And, at their base, answering these questions requires integrating emotional and cognitive knowledge to produce skilled intuitions—the kind that will transfer to other academic and real-life situations.

Neuroscience suggests that learning may be more effective if teachers judiciously build into their curricula opportunities for students to develop skilled intuition.

It is understandable that teachers feel pressured to help their students learn a large amount of information as quickly as possible, and at least initially students may be slow to attain mastery. However, neuroscience suggests that in the long run, learning may be more effective if teachers judiciously build into their curricula opportunities for students to develop skilled intuition. Without the development of sound intuitions, students likely will not remember the material over the long term. And even if they do remember it in an abstract sense, they will have difficulty applying it to novel situations.

Actively Manage the Social and Emotional Climate of the Classroom

The development of students' intuitions also depends on the social aspects of the classroom climate. While allowing for the development of skilled intuition is important, simply providing students with space to make mistakes will not be enough. Students will allow themselves to experience failure only if they can do so within an atmosphere of trust and respect. Thus classroom climate and social relationships between the teacher and students have crucial contributions to make.

Faced with the challenge of bringing positive emotions back into the classroom, teachers may feel tempted to take the easy route and stir up students' emotions in artificial and non-task-related ways, such as by telling jokes, showing cartoons, doling out prizes, or turning a blind eye when students act out. Indeed, a carefully timed dose of humor or an incentive certainly can help students invest in the classroom culture as an enjoyable place to belong. Such activities also can go a long way in helping students feel safe expressing themselves, learning from their mistakes, and building social cohesion—all necessary ingredients of engaged learning.

At the same time, emotions that are irrelevant to tasks at hand may actually interfere with students' ability to feel the subtle emotional signals that steer the development and application of new conceptual knowledge. As we saw in the Iowa Gambling Task, overanxious, overexcited, or distracted participants may have trouble learning the game. For emotion to be useful, it has to be an integral part of knowing when and how to use the skill being developed. Especially in young learners or students whose engagement or connection to academic learning is tenuous, the emotional signals that undergird skilled intuition could easily be drowned out.

Effective teachers are faced with a balancing act. On the one hand, task-irrelevant emotions can serve an important initial role in establishing a safe and enjoyable social climate in the classroom. On the other hand, too much irrelevant emotion can undermine the development of students' ability to feel appropriately emotional about their academic learning. For teachers to manage the social-emotional climate of their classroom effectively, they must strike a balance between these two kinds of emotion by actively managing the emotions of their students, helping learners to attend to, trust, and thrive on the subtle emotional signals they build as they accumulate meaningful academic experiences. As learners become more emotionally skilled, task-irrelevant emotional activities can fade, leaving actively engaging emotional learning experiences in their place.

> As learners become more emotionally skilled, task-irrelevant emotional activities can fade, leaving actively engaging emotional learning experiences in their place.

A Neuroscientific Perspective on Emotions, Intuitions, and Learning

A rich body of recent neuroscience research has demonstrated the interrelatedness of emotions and cognition and the importance of emotion in rational thought (Greene, Sommerville, Nystrom, Darley, & Cohen, 2001; Haidt, 2001; Immordino-Yang, 2008). Yet much of contemporary educational practice considers emotion as ancillary or even as interfering with learning. As we have shown in this chapter, the role of emotion in learning is critical. Students' accumulation of subtle emotional signals guides meaningful learning, helping them to build a set of academic intuitions about how, when, and why to use their new knowledge.

Rather than trying to remove emotions from the learning context, teachers can use this neuroscientific perspective to orchestrate an emotional climate in the classroom that is conducive to students feeling these subtle emotional signals. As students learn to notice and refine these signals, learning will become more relevant and meaningful to them and ultimately more generalizable and useful in their everyday lives.

References

Ablin, J. L. (2008). Learning as problem design versus problem solving: Making the connection between cognitive neuroscience research and educational practice. *Mind, Brain, and Education, 2*(2), 52–54.

Bechara, A., & Damasio, H. (1997). Deciding advantageously before knowing the advantageous strategy. *Science, 275*(5304), 1293–1295.

Bechara, A., Damasio, H., Tranel, D., & Damasio, A. R. (2005). The Iowa Gambling Task and the somatic marker hypothesis: Some questions and answers. *Trends in Cognitive Sciences, 9*(4), 159–162.

Brackett, M. A., Rivers, S. E., Shiffman, S., Lerner, N., & Salovey, P. (2006). Relating emotional abilities to social functioning: A comparison of self-report and performance measures of emotional intelligence. *Journal of Personality and Social Psychology, 91*(4), 780–795.

Damasio, A. R. (1994/2005). *Descartes' error: Emotion, reason and the human brain.* London: Penguin Books.

Fischer, K. W., Daniel, D. B., Immordino-Yang, M. H., Stern, E., Battro, A., & Koizumi, H. (2007). Why mind, brain, and education? Why now? *Mind, Brain, and Education, 1*(1), 1–2.

Goswami, U. (2004). Neuroscience and education. *British Journal of Educational Psychology, 74*, 1–14.

Goswami, U. (2006). Neuroscience and education: From research to practice? *Nature Reviews Neuroscience, 7*(5), 406–411.

Greene, J. D., Sommerville, R. B., Nystrom, L. E., Darley, J. M., & Cohen, J. D. (2001). An fMRI investigation of emotional engagement in moral judgment. *Science, 293*(5537), 2105–2108.

Haidt, J. (2001). The emotional dog and its rational tail: A social intuitionist approach to moral judgment. *Psychological Review, 108*(4), 814–834.

Immordino-Yang, M. H. (2008). The smoke around mirror neurons: Goals as sociocultural and emotional organizers of perception and action in learning. *Mind, Brain, and Education, 2*(2), 67–73.

Immordino-Yang, M. H., & Damasio, A. R. (2007). We feel, therefore we learn: The relevance of affective and social neuroscience to education. *Mind, Brain, and Education, 1*(1), 3–10.

Immordino-Yang, M. H., & Fischer, K. W. (in press). Neuroscience bases of learning. In V. G. Aukrust (Ed.), *International Encyclopedia of Education, 3rd Edition, Section on Learning and Cognition.* Oxford, England: Elsevier.

Pekrun, R., Goetz, T., Titz, W., & Perry, R. P. (2002). Academic emotions in students' self-regulated learning and achievement: A program of qualitative and quantitative research. *Educational Psychologist, 37*(2), 91–105.

van Geert, P., & Steenbeek, H. (2008). Brains and the dynamics of "wants" and "cans" in learning. *Mind, Brain, and Education, 2*(2), 62–66.

Diane L. Williams

Diane L. Williams, PhD, is an assistant professor in the Department of Speech-Language Pathology at Duquesne University in Pittsburgh. She is also Co-Director of the Center for Excellence in Autism Research at the University of Pittsburgh. Dr. Williams is the recipient of a Research Career Development Award from the National Institute on Deafness and Other Communication Disorders, through which she received training in conducting structural and functional magnetic resonance imaging studies of cognitive and linguistic processing. She continues this work, studying the neurofunctional bases of social cognition, language processing, and learning in autism, in collaboration with colleagues at Carnegie Mellon University.

Dr. Williams has extensive clinical experience working with young children and adults with developmental disorders. She has served as a consultant to early intervention programs, special education agencies, and school districts in the design and implementation of programming for children with problems with the development and use of language. She is the author of numerous scientific articles and book chapters on the neuropsychology and neurophysiology of cognition and language. Her book *Developmental Language Disorders: Learning, Language, and the Brain* is written for clinicians and special educators and presents a summary of current research on the neurological basis of developmental disorders and the application of this research to the learning process.

In this chapter, Dr. Williams explains what neuroscience research has revealed about the cerebral networks involved in learning spoken language. The findings of this research are at odds with many popular myths about learning language. Dr. Williams discusses major implications that this research has for teaching and learning.

Chapter 5

The Speaking Brain

Diane L. Williams

Spoken language is a unique human capability that is not only the major way that we communicate with each other, but also a major means by which we make judgments about each other. For example, we can generally tell where someone is from by the dialectal pattern of his or her speech. As teachers, we rely on what children say to make judgments about what they know. When we do so, we are making assumptions about how the child's brain is functioning by her ability to answer our questions, to describe what she did, or to explain new concepts using spoken language. In addition to this more general assumption about the connection between spoken language and brain functioning, several more specific assumptions about the brain bases of spoken language have taken hold in the popular imagination. In this chapter, we'll discuss what these common assumptions are and whether modern neuroscience research supports or undermines them.

Early Assumptions About the Brain and Language

Knowledge about the neurological basis of spoken language was initially acquired through the study of individuals who had suffered injuries to the brain, and through the use of procedures such as the Wada test, in which a substance was injected into the carotid artery to disrupt language processing (Wada & Rasmussen, 1960). The reasoning used in these studies was negative—if someone had a lesion or injury in a particular brain region, the thinking went, what that person could no longer do must be a function of that region. A number of assumptions about the brain basis of spoken language were developed based on these studies and on behavioral research that used measures believed to reflect brain function.

One of the major assumptions was that language is a lateralized function, or a function that is stronger on one side of the brain than the other, with one of the hemispheres of the cortex being the dominant or primary hemisphere for language. This is a conclusion that is typically traced back to a paper by Dr. Paul Broca published in 1865 based on his lesion studies (Josse & Tzourio-Mazoyer, 2004). For most people, the left hemisphere is dominant for language (Pujol, Deus, Losilla, & Capdevila, 1999). That is why a child who is facile at language-based learning is frequently referred to as being "left-brained." A second closely related assumption was that the right hemisphere did not process language per se but did process or interpret aspects of language such as prosody and nonverbal communication (Ross & Mesulam, 1979). A third assumption was that different aspects of language processing were localized across separate brain regions for spoken words, speech sounds, and sentences (Fodor, 1983).

Another set of early assumptions about the development of spoken language in children was not based on direct observations of brain function, but rather on observations of behaviors that were the result of brain function. Explanations of what was happening in the brain were then crafted to fit with the behavioral evidence. Some of the main assumptions about children's brain function had to do with the developmental progression of the brain. For example, behavioral measures indicate a plateau in the development of sentence length in early childhood. Therefore, it was assumed that the brain areas in the temporal and frontal lobes that are responsible for semantics (word processing) and syntax (grammatical processing) were fully developed in young children (Krashen, 1973). Further development in these skills was considered to be related not to development in brain areas, but rather to experience and practice with language. At school age,

> Early assumptions about the development of spoken language in children were not based on observations of brain function, but rather on observations of behaviors.

typically developing children were assumed to have a fully developed spoken language system that could serve as the basis for learning to read and to write (Brown & Fraser, 1964).

Another behavior-to-brain assumption was based on the observation that most girls were better at language-based learning than boys (Maccoby, 1966). The brain basis of this difference was not specified but instead was attributed to a more general difference in the rate of maturation between boys and girls that has long been considered to underlie differences in academic performance between the sexes (Clark, 1959).

Learning two languages or bilingualism has given rise to particular behavior-to-brain assumptions. It has long been assumed that if children were exposed to two spoken languages, their brains would become confused and would fail to develop an adequate model for either language (see discussion in Petitto, 2009). This decades-old assumption actually pre-dated scientific research in this area. However, it was perpetuated by behavioral research that indicated that bilingual toddlers mixed their two languages and were slower to develop language compared to monolingual speakers (Redlinger & Park, 1980; Vihman, 1985). The interference or confusion between the two languages was thought to occur because the dedication of an area in the brain to the processing of the first language resulted in reduced neural resources for processing the second language (Petitto et al., 2001). That is, when children were simultaneously exposed to two languages, they were thought to have inadequate brain resources to learn either of the languages well. Therefore it was argued that children should wait until they were older to learn a second language. This is one of the reasons why many children in the United States are not exposed to a second language until high school (Petitto, 2009).

Finally, yet another behavior-to-brain assumption was that after early adolescence, language learning primarily involves the acquisition of new vocabulary (McNeill, 1970). Behavioral studies indicated that the development of an adult grammar, or the use of sentences with clauses to modify the meaning, was completed by about age eight, which was considered a marker of the upper limit of grammatical development (Muma, 1978). The behavioral observation of a plateauing in language development at adolescence was attributed to a loss of brain plasticity that was assumed to be associated with the onset of puberty (Lenneberg, 1967).

As modern neuroimaging techniques have come into use, some of these early assumptions about the brain and spoken language have been supported, others have undergone refinements, and still others have given way to newer understandings of brain function and development related to the acquisition and use of spoken language. In this chapter, I will review major recent findings about the brain basis of spoken language and discuss the implications of this knowledge for teaching and learning.

Left Hemisphere Dominance for Speech and Language

Speech and language processing have long been considered to occur predominantly in one hemisphere of the brain, with the left hemisphere being dominant for language in most people. People who are good at speaking and reading may be referred to as "left-brained"; if they are strong artistically, they may be referred to as "right-brained." This assumption about the dominance of the left hemisphere for language processing has been supported by modern structural and functional imaging studies. Neuroimaging studies indicate that the dominance of the left hemisphere for language processing is true not only for the vast majority of people who are right-handed, but also for three-quarters of the people who are left-handed. In a functional imaging study of fifty right-handed and fifty left-handed healthy adult volunteers, 96 percent of the right-handers and 76 percent of the left-handers processed language in the left hemisphere (Pujol et al., 1999). Speech and language are the most lateralized functions in the human brain. For most people, language is lateralized to the left hemisphere.

For most people, language is lateralized to the left hemisphere.

The left hemispheric dominance for language appears to be a measurable trait of brain function early in life. Therefore, it is assumed to be genetically determined rather than a result of environmental factors. At least one fMRI study with young children has demonstrated that the processing of spoken language occurs primarily in the left hemisphere even at ages at which experience with language is limited (Dehaene-Lambertz, Dehaene, & Hertz-Pannier, 2002). In that study, when infants from birth to three months old were exposed to human speech, the brain activation occurred predominantly in left hemisphere language areas. This finding supports the notion that use of these brain areas for language processing is innate. Left lateralization of language has also been reported in other functional imaging studies of children as young as five years of age (Balsamo et al., 2002; Wood et al., 2004).

In addition to confirming the left lateralization of language processing, modern neuroimaging research has further refined our understanding of this feature of brain function. An fMRI study of 170 healthy individuals, ages five to seventy, performing a verb-generation task provided initial evidence about the developmental time course of the functional lateralization of language to the dominant hemisphere (Szaflarski, Holland, Schmithorst, & Byars, 2006). According to the results of this study, the lateralization of language does not appear to be a constant feature across the age span. Rather, it appears to increase in individuals between ages five and twenty with a plateau between ages twenty and twenty-five. A decline in lateralization occurs between ages twenty-five and seventy. Therefore, the development of the brain basis of spoken language appears to be an ongoing process, at least until early adulthood.

> The development of the brain basis of spoken language appears to be an ongoing process, at least until early adulthood.

The Right Hemisphere and Language

Although the left hemisphere has a dominant role in the speaking brain, this does not mean that the right hemisphere is not involved in language processing. However, the specific nature of that role has been a matter of debate (Beeman & Chiarello, 1998). Prior to modern neuroimaging, assumptions about right hemispheric language functions were based on studies of individuals with right hemisphere brain damage. Whatever these persons could no longer do was assumed to be a function of the right hemisphere. Using this logic, the right hemisphere has long been considered to be important for understanding and producing prosody—that is, the intonational and emotional aspects of spoken language (Ross, Thompson, & Yenkosky, 1997).

Prosody is how we change the meaning of spoken words even when the words are the same. For example, the question, "Where is your homework?" can be asked with a neutral tone, meaning the teacher is simply collecting the assignment, or it can be asked with an irritated or impatient tone with emphasis on the word *where*, meaning the teacher is becoming concerned over constantly missing assignments. Whereas these prosodic elements contribute essential information to verbal communication, they are not considered to be language in the same sense as phonological, semantic, and syntactic elements of language. Other language-related functions thought to be located in the right hemisphere are interpreting humor and metaphors, making inferences, and understanding sarcasm or irony (Beeman, 1993; Bihrle, Brownell, Powelson, & Gardner, 1986; Bottini et al., 1994; Brownell, Potter, Bihrle, & Gardner, 1986; Brownell, Simpson, Bihrle, Potter, & Gardner, 1990; Shammi & Stuss, 1999; Tompkins, 1990). Language tasks that require processing larger units of language, such as comprehending discourse (Benowitz, Moya, & Levine, 1990) and identifying the central theme of a story (Hough, 1990), are thought to result in the recruitment of right hemisphere processing as the left hemisphere processing resources are taxed. It has also been proposed that the right hemisphere is required for more demanding semantic tasks, such as processing distantly related words (Beeman, 1998), deriving connotative word meanings (Brownell, Potter, Michelow, & Gardner, 1984), and resolving lexical ambiguity (Burgess & Simpson, 1988; Tompkins, Baumgaertner, Lehman, & Foassett, 1997).

Assumptions about the function of the right hemisphere language areas have been supported by recent functional imaging investigations. Right hemisphere activation has been observed during the generation of inferences (Mason & Just, 2004; St. George, Kutas, Martinez, & Sereno, 1999; Virtue, Haberman, Clancy, Parrish, & Beeman, 2006), interpretation of metaphors (Bottini et al., 1994; Mason & Just, 2004), generation of the theme from untitled stories (St. George et al., 1999), and during comprehension of narratives (Schmithorst, Holland, & Plante, 2006).

In general, proposed contributions of the right hemisphere to language function fall into two general categories. According to the first view, all of the parameters of language (such as semantics and syntax) have complementary right and left hemispheric functions that perform parallel processes. These complementary processing streams interact to produce full comprehension of language (Beeman & Chiarello, 1998). A second view considers the right hemisphere to be part of the more general cognitive resources available for demanding processing tasks. According to this latter view, the right hemisphere is involved in language processing when a task becomes so demanding that the left hemisphere cannot accomplish it alone and additional processing resources are needed (Monetta & Joanette, 2003; Murray, 2000).

Neuroimaging research has provided brain activation results that can be interpreted as supporting both views. In addition, functional imaging studies have refined our understanding of the specialized functions of the right hemisphere regions. A common denominator among these functions is that they involve interpretation of language based on world knowledge or context. They also typically involve an understanding of the thoughts or intentions of the speaker, a cognitive skill referred to as "theory of mind" (Premack & Woodruff, 1978). Theory of mind is the understanding that other people have thoughts and the ability to infer what those thoughts might be. Theory of mind processing is important for making inferences, understanding figurative language such as irony, and comprehending discourse. Functional imaging studies suggest that processing associated with a theory of mind is accomplished by a right hemisphere network that includes right middle temporal, right superior temporal sulcus, and medial frontal gyrus (Mason & Just, 2006).

The nature of the contributions of the right hemisphere to language processing is still being determined. However, based on current behavioral and neurofunctional studies, both the left and the right hemispheres appear to make important contributions to the interpretation of spoken language. While language is predominantly a left-brain function, both hemispheres are necessary for a fully functioning, flexible spoken language system.

> While language is predominantly a left-brain function, both hemispheres are necessary for a fully functioning, flexible spoken language system.

Is Language Function Localized?

Based on studies from the late 19th century with brain-damaged patients, the two primary left hemispheric areas for speech and language processing were determined to be Wernicke's area (the posterior part of the left superior temporal gyrus; Brodmann Area 22) and Broca's area (the left inferior frontal gyrus; Brodmann's 44/45). According to traditional models of speech and language processing, Wernicke's area is used for auditory comprehension or understanding of spoken language, and Broca's area is used for formulating sentences and providing the motor plan for articulation, or the production of speech. Wernicke's and Broca's areas are connected by a fiber bundle, or tract, called the arcuate fasciculus (see figure 5.1). The direct connection between the two brain areas means that understanding and production of spoken language can be highly synchronized, making the rapid back and forth of conversational speech possible.

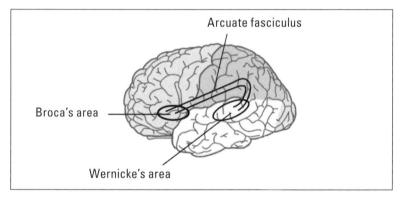

Figure 5.1: A view of the left hemisphere showing the arcuate fasciculus, a fiber bundle that connects Wernicke's area to Broca's area.

According to the late 18th/early 19th century models of brain localization such as that of Franz Joseph Gall (Zola-Morgan, 1995), language functions were localized in structures that were connected anatomically to form a complete language system. Language was generally considered to be modular, with specific parameters of language controlled by specific areas of the brain. The identification of Wernicke's and Broca's areas as brain regions with distinct and separate language functions fit with these early localization models.

Modern neuroimaging and neurophysiological studies have confirmed these traditional functions for Wernicke's and Broca's areas and have expanded our understanding of what these two brain areas do. According to numerous neuroimaging studies, activation occurs in Wernicke's area during language comprehension, particularly semantic processing, or the processing of word meaning (reviewed in Cabeza & Nyberg, 2000). But semantic processing does not appear to be limited strictly to Wernicke's area. Adjacent areas of the temporal gyrus also appear to be involved in semantic processing. For example, listening to spoken words has been reported to elicit activation in the anterior and posterior regions of the left superior temporal gyrus (Giraud & Price, 2001). In addition, the left middle temporal gyrus (Brodmann area 21) has been found to be active during semantic retrieval when viewing both words and pictures (Martin, Haxby, Lalonde, Wiggs, & Ungerleider, 1995; Martin, Wiggs, Ungerleider, & Haxby, 1996; Vandenberghe, Price, Wise, Josephs, & Frackowiak, 1996). The left temporal lobe appears to be a key region for both comprehension of spoken language and retrieval of word knowledge. A working left temporal lobe is important for activities such as learning new vocabulary words and interpreting the meaning of printed words.

As expected, activity in Broca's area is observed during syntactic processing (Caplan, Alpert, & Waters, 1998; Friederici, Rüschemeyer, Hahne, & Fiebach, 2003; Hagoort, 2003; Just, Carpenter, Keller, Eddy, & Thulborn, 1996; Moro et al., 2001). In addition, Broca's area appears to be involved in some semantic and working memory processes (Chein, Ravizza, & Fiez, 2003; Fiez, 1997; Gabrieli, Poldrack, & Desmond, 1998; Price, 2000). Activation in this area has been reported during reading and semantic generation tasks (reviewed in Cabeza & Nyberg, 2000; reviewed in Fiez & Petersen, 1998). In general, Broca's area is thought to be recruited with increased demands during language tasks when coordination of processing is required, rather than being restricted to the processing of syntax (Brauer & Friederici, 2007). Paralleling the functions of other frontal lobe areas, Broca's area appears not to simply process sentences or develop articulation plans, but also to provide coordination and integration of neural information from other language-processing areas of the brain. Hence when young children are just learning to read, a really difficult language task, they may say the words aloud because of the increased activation in Broca's area, which then triggers articulation or the speech motor system.

Language as a Network Function

Neuroimaging and neurofunctional measures have confirmed the basic functions of Wernicke's and Broca's areas. At the same time, they have expanded our understanding of how language is processed in the brain. It appears that these larger brain regions may actually be comprised of smaller processing areas with narrower but related functions (Bookheimer, 2002). Additionally, each specialized functional area does not accomplish language processing by itself. Rather, these functions are highly interactive, both within a region of the cortex and across cortical areas. Instead of arising from distinct processing modules with localized language functions, current models consider language processing to be a distributed network function that can involve very diverse and distant cortical areas. Therefore, inferior frontal and temporal areas function as part of a larger corti-cal network to accomplish various types of language processing. For some aspects of language, the network primarily involves regions in the dominant hemisphere; for other aspects, the network is bilateral (Vannest, Karunanayaka, Schmithorst, Szaflarski, & Holland, 2009).

More complex language tasks involve more elaborated networks. For example, discourse processing is thought to involve five different networks that make unique but integrated contributions to accomplish the processing task (Mason & Just, 2006). These processing networks include one for understanding semantics (right middle and superior temporal), one for monitoring coherence (bilateral dorsolateral prefron-tal), one for integrating text (left inferior frontal-left anterior temporal), one for interpreting the perspective of the agent or actor (bilateral medial frontal/posterior right temporal/parietal), and one for imaging spatial information (left dominant, bilateral intraparietal sulcus). So, when a child is listening to the teacher explain a historical event, he or she is not simply using left hemisphere language areas. The child is using a large network that includes brain areas on both the left and right sides of the brain. The more challenging the task (for example, because it includes abstract language or requires lots of inferencing or "filling in the blanks"), the more areas of the brain are needed.

Depending on the type of task being performed, the language network interacts with other cognitive processing networks, such as the working-memory network and the episodic-memory network. These networks can contribute to or interfere with the processing of language. For example, the working-memory network typically includes the prefrontal cortex and the parietal lobes, depending on the stimulus and task demands (Owen, McMillan, Laird, & Bullmore, 2005). It is incorporated into any language task in which language must be held on line while another process is performed. For example, during a spelling test, the child must hold the dictated sentence "on line" as he or she converts the spoken words into orthographic symbols and prepares the motor plan to produce the written letters. The episodic-memory network is comprised of the medial temporal lobe, prefrontal regions, and the parietal lobe (Wagner, Shannon, Kahn, & Buckner, 2005). It is used to recall an experience before that knowledge is translated into spoken language. For example, when asked to give an oral lab report, the student must retrieve the tasks that were performed from episodic memory and then translate the remembered experience into language before delivering the report. Therefore, the language network is only one part of much larger cortical processing networks that are used to perform the myriad of tasks children are asked to do throughout the school day. The efficiency of the functioning of the language network is affected by the allocation of brain resources to other competing functions or tasks.

Implications for Children Processing Language

Speech and language are part of the general well of cognitive resources, not separate from them. Therefore, if cognitive resources are being spent on another process or processes, there are fewer resources to be used for understanding and production of spoken language. Similarly, if cognitive resources are being spent on understanding or producing spoken language, there are fewer resources for other cognitive activities. Some children cannot listen to orally presented information and take notes at the same time—not because they are being noncompliant, but because they

> Some children cannot listen to orally presented information and take notes at the same time because they have only enough cognitive resources to do one or the other.

have only enough cognitive resources to do one or the other. Listening and interpreting what they hear may be using their entire language network resources, leaving no resources to convert what they are hearing into the written language system.

Similarly, if resources are being devoted to emotional processing, this processing may interfere with the processing of language. Therefore, the child may be unable to comprehend what he or she is hearing or to formulate what he or she wants to say. Reducing the cognitive load in one area of the network frees up resources that other network processes can use.

Speech and Language Development

Prior to the advances made possible by neuroscience, models of language were primarily cognitive and perceptual. They emphasized what develops when, not the location or nature of the neural processing of spoken language. Models of speech and language development were based on behavioral studies of young children; in fact, there were no methods for the measurement of neurological development in young children. For example, a pioneer in the area of spoken-language development, Roger Brown (1973), created transcripts from repeated audio recordings of three children as they developed spoken language. Brown then analyzed the transcripts to determine the order of development of semantic and syntactic aspects, such as classes of words (nouns, verbs, adjectives) and word endings (plurals, present progressive -ing, past tense). Similarly, Mildred Templin (1957) studied the developmental acquisition of speech sounds, creating charts showing which speech sounds developed earliest and at what ages children mastered the various speech sounds or phonemes.

According to this behavioral information, by school age, children were expected to have mastered basic grammatical aspects of spoken language, to have acquired a sufficient lexicon to talk about a variety of concrete and abstract experiences, and to be able to clearly produce all but a few of the latest developing speech sounds. Having learned language, the child was now ready to use language for learning. In school, the child needed to develop knowledge of the vocabulary related to specific subjects introduced in school, develop more mature conversational interaction skills and appropriate verbal behavior for the classroom, and learn to tell stories and give oral presentations and explanations. According to this model, the development of these skills was a matter of experience, teacher expectations, and the use of frameworks that are taught in school, such as story grammars and how to organize a presentation. Little thought was given to the nature of the neural processes that supported these language functions.

Neuroscientists have now gone beyond behavioral measures to examine the development and maturation of the structure and function of the brain related to a number of cognitive skills, including speech and language. These studies indicate that brain development to support the acquisition and refinement of speech and language skills is ongoing until early adulthood (Toga, Thompson, & Sowell, 2006). Therefore, not all children come to school with fully developed speech and language, ready to use these skills for reading, writing, and oral expression. Similarly, not all older children are neurologically ready for higher order or more abstract understanding and production of spoken language. Brain development and experiential learning are interactive processes. The brain structures and functions to support speech and language skills continue to mature as the child grows and develops through the school years. In addition, the experiences that children have during the process of learning appear to result in changes in brain structure and function (Casey, Tottenham, Liston, & Durston, 2005). The brain is not a static entity. Modern neuroscience has revealed that it changes as it unfolds developmentally but, more importantly, in response to environmental input and the experiences of the learner, making the role of the teacher in this process extremely important.

The unfolding of speech and language development is genetically controlled, which means that there may be differences in the rate at which this process occurs. Children in the same class may have very different skills because their brains are at different points of development, not because they lack exposure or opportunity to practice these skills.

> Children in the same class may have very different language skills because their brains are at different points of development.

Behavioral measures are not exact measures of brain function. In fact, behavioral observations may lead to incorrect conclusions about brain function. For example, children may appear to perform some behaviors at the same skill level as an adult, leading to the conclusion that their brains are functioning at a similar level. However, neuroimaging studies that have compared the cortical-activation data of children and adults indicate that children may have a more diffuse pattern of activation than that of adults (Brown et al., 2005). This diffuse pattern appears to become more focused or fine-tuned over time as a child becomes more proficient at a skill (Durston et al., 2006). Neuroimaging studies also indicate that children may recruit more prefrontal areas than adults, a pattern that is thought to represent more controlled processing, meaning that children must devote more effort or cognitive resources to thinking about how to do a task that adults may perform automatically (Casey et al., 2005).

Children may also have a slower time course of brain activation than adults, including activating language areas in the right hemisphere before the left hemisphere language areas (Brauer, Neumann, & Friederici, 2008). Therefore, the neurofunctional data from children suggests that, even if they are exhibiting behavioral performance similar to that of adults, they have different neural patterns that are thought to reflect the use of different cognitive strategies (Amso & Casey, 2006). The more diffuse activation pattern of children, the use of prefrontal brain areas, and the slower time course of brain activation may indicate that children's brains work harder than that of the adults to accomplish the same behavioral result.

Gender Differences in Language Processing

Based on behavioral observations, a common assumption has been that girls are better at language-based learning than boys. This assumption is supported by numerous behavioral studies (Lynn, 1992; Mann, Sasanuma, Sakuma, & Masaki, 1990; Martin & Hoover, 1987). Only a limited number of neuroimaging studies have examined gender differences in language processing in children. The results of these studies have been mixed, with reports of no gender effects (Gaillard et al., 2003) and other reports of small gender effects that only are apparent when also considering age differences (Plante, Schmithorst, Holland, & Byars, 2006).

The results of a recent fMRI study suggest that boys may actually process language differently from girls. Burman, Bitan, and Booth (2008) used functional magnetic resonance imaging with thirty-one girls and thirty-one boys, ages nine to fifteen years. The children performed orthographic judgment (spelling correctness) and rhyming tasks that were presented in both visual and auditory versions. The brain-activation results suggested that the girls processed the language tasks using similar brain regions (left inferior frontal gyrus and left middle temporal/fusiform gyrus) for both the auditory and visual presentations. However, the processing network used by the boys was dependent on the modality of the task. For the auditory task, the boys activated a left inferior frontal area and a left superior temporal area, regions typically involved in auditory and phonological processing. For the visual task, the boys activated visual association cortex and posterior parietal regions. The authors suggested that these results indicated that the boys did not convert sensory information to language as easily as the girls did. This difference has implications for students' classroom performance when receiving auditorily presented information and when learning to read.

> The results of a recent fMRI study suggest that boys may actually process language differently from girls.

The study of individual differences in neurofunction associated with language processing is in the beginning stages (Prat, Keller, & Just, 2007). At this time, the primary attempts to tease apart differences have been based on considerations of age and gender. However, examining the language processing of children based on their age and gender may reveal only part of the story. Like athletic skills, spoken-language skills are determined by the child's genetic makeup and the amount of time and effort spent on practice and development of the skills. Not all children are capable of the same level of verbal expression. Some children are slower processors and some are faster processors of language. Therefore, some children may be verbally fluent while others struggle to put their thoughts into words.

These differences are not related to innate intelligence or motivation; rather, they are related to individual differences in brain development. The faster language processors probably have highly myelinated and refined connections between conceptual and word-generation networks, whereas the slower language processors must allow more time for word-form searching and construction of spoken sentences. Being slower does not necessarily mean that the child knows or understands less; it simply means the child needs more time to express what he or she knows.

Bilingualism

The advantages and disadvantages of learning two or more languages during early childhood have been much debated. The general fear has been that exposure to two languages at once would negatively affect the child's ability to learn language, resulting in a delay in language acquisition and an impoverished model for both languages. The underlying assumption about neural function was that the brain would be confused if exposed to different speech and language systems, causing a disruption in the normal development of language.

Behavioral studies have provided evidence that young children exposed to two languages before the age of seven develop proficiency in both languages (Johnson & Newport, 1989). However, these behavioral studies could not address brain function associated with these behavioral observations. Even though children might have appeared to have no behavioral difficulty, examination of brain function might reveal differences in skills such as the processing of speech sounds that would have implications for learning potential.

According to neuroimaging research with bilingual adults who had been exposed to two languages before age five, these individuals process their languages in overlapping brain areas (Kovelman, Baker, & Petitto, 2008). Furthermore, the brain areas used to process both languages are the same left-hemisphere language areas (left inferior frontal gyrus or Broca's area and superior temporal gyrus) that are observed in neuroimaging studies of language processing in monolingual speakers.

Later development of bilingualism appears to result in the use of different cognitive strategies, as indicated by a different pattern of brain activation. The brain activation of later-exposed bilinguals is more bilateral with more distributed activation of the frontal lobe, including areas that are thought to represent working memory and inhibitory processing (Kim, Relkin, Lee, & Hirsch, 1997; Perani et al., 1996; Wartenburger et al., 2003; Weber-Fox & Neville, 1999). This pattern of activation is thought to be consistent with greater cognitive effort and less automatic processing.

The results of neuroimaging research indicate that, rather than causing confusion in the brain, the brain adaptively uses language areas to process both languages efficiently. More effortful neural processing is required when exposure to a second language occurs after age five, as this later bilingual exposure results in a different pattern of neural organization for language processing. The most efficient use of neural resources occurs when language learning happens early.

Changes in Language in Adolescence and Beyond

There is no doubt that plasticity, or the possibility for change in brain function, is greatest in the earliest years of life (Newport, Bavelier, & Neville, 2001). However, this does not mean that there are no changes in the brain associated with language learning in adolescents and adults. As described earlier, language networks interact with other cortical resources, such as memory, that are associated with continuing changes in neural structure and function. New memories are formed throughout the lifespan and, associated with this process, new neurons are created in the hippocampus—the area responsible for forming memories (Bruel-Jungerman, Laroche, & Rampon, 2005; Eriksson et al., 1998; Gould, Beylin, Tanapat, Reeves, & Shors, 1999).

Additionally, the frontal lobe continues to develop through early adulthood (Giedd et al., 1999; Shaw et al., 2006), making it possible for adolescents to develop metacognitive and metalinguistic skills. These higher-order cognitive skills allow adolescents to use their language for abstract thinking and to communicate and think more flexibly and creatively. Rather than being a time when language skills plateau, adolescence is when more sophisticated forms of communication and language use can develop.

Rather than being a time when language skills plateau, adolescence is when more sophisticated forms of communication and language use can develop.

Implications for Teaching and Learning

Modern neuroscience has led to a greater understanding of the brain bases of speech and language. The left-hemisphere dominance for language processing has been confirmed, but we have new appreciation for the contributions of the right hemisphere for the processing of language. We also have a better understanding of language as a network function with resources that are shared with other cognitive and emotional processes. Educators should consider the following research findings regarding speech and language development in students:

- Structural and functional imaging studies indicate that brain development to support the acquisition and refinement of speech and language is ongoing until early adulthood.

- School-age children do not have fully developed language systems; therefore, their spoken language skills continue to grow and change throughout elementary and secondary school. These changes are not only the result of learning more sophisticated vocabulary and grammar but also are associated with underlying changes in neural structure and function.

- Children have differences in cognitive processing that may not be apparent from behavioral observations; they are less efficient language processors than adults.

- Gender differences in language processing have been observed.

- With respect to language skills, most boys are different from most girls. Boys may have more difficulty with verbal expression, and modality of presentation may make a greater difference to their ability to learn.

- The brain learns a second language most easily before school age; learning additional languages is possible after that time but requires the use of controlled rather than automatic language processing.

- During the school years, children's brains continue to mature and develop with both age and new experiences with language. Teachers must consider whether a child has the maturational readiness to use a language skill for a learning task. If the language skill involves more effortful processing, the cognitive resources needed for the learning task are reduced.

- Children may not be able to coordinate listening to language and writing language. Consideration should be given to the language-processing demands of a task and how proficient a child is in that language task. Lack of proficiency indicates the use of more cognitive resources.

- Simply because a child can behaviorally perform a task does not mean that the brain is efficiently performing that task. If an adult can't tell how hard a child is working by looking at his or her behavior, the adult may inadvertently push the child to do more than they really can. This can lead to unexpected emotional outbursts in some children while others may become frustrated and refuse to continue.

- Age is not a clear indicator of maturity of brain function. Language skills can vary widely in groups of same-age children.

- Children should have options for how they express what they know. Spoken language is not the only means to determine whether a child understands a concept. Showing or demonstrating arises from the same conceptual base as spoken words and may give a clearer indication of where the child is in the learning process.

Neuroscience is helping us to learn more about how language develops throughout childhood and is giving us a new appreciation of underlying differences in brain function that may affect behavioral performance. Language is not simply a tool that children apply to the learning process. It is a growing, changing skill.

References

Amso, D., & Casey, B. J. (2006). Beyond what develops when: Neuroimaging may inform how cognition changes with development. *Current Directions in Psychological Science, 15*(1), 24–29.

Balsamo, L. M., Zu, B., Grandin, C. B., Petrella, J. R., Braniecki, S. H., Elliott, T. K., & Gaillard, W. D. (2002). A functional magnetic resonance imaging study of left hemisphere language dominance in children. *Archives of Neurology, 59*(7), 1168–1174.

Beeman, M. (1993). Semantic processing in the right hemisphere may contribute to drawing inferences during comprehension. *Brain and Language, 44*(2), 80–120.

Beeman, M. (1998). Coarse semantic coding and discourse comprehension. In M. Beeman & C. Chiarello (Eds.), *Right hemisphere language comprehension: Perspectives from cognitive neuroscience* (pp. 255–284). Mahwah, NJ: Erlbaum.

Beeman, M., & Chiarello, C. (1998). *Right hemisphere language comprehension: Perspectives from cognitive neuroscience.* Mahwah, NJ: Lawrence Erlbaum Associates.

Benowitz, L. I., Moya, K. L., & Levine, D. N. (1990). Impaired verbal reasoning and constructional apraxia in subjects with right hemisphere damage. *Neuropsychologia, 28*(3), 231–241.

Bihrle, A. M., Brownell, H. H., Powelson, J. A., & Gardner, H. (1986). Comprehension of humorous and non-humorous materials by left and right brain-damaged patients. *Brain and Cognition, 5,* 399–411.

Bookheimer, S. (2002, March). Functional MRI of language: New approaches to understanding the cortical organization of semantic processing. *Annual Reviews of Neuroscience, 25,* 151–188.

Bottini, G., Corcoran, R., Sterzi, R., Paulescu, E., Schenone, P., Scarpa, P., et al. (1994). The role of the right hemisphere in the interpretation of figurative aspects of language: A positron emission tomography activation study. *Brain, 117*(6), 1241–1253.

Brauer, J., & Friederici, A. D. (2007). Functional neural networks of semantic and syntactic processes in the developing brain. *Journal of Cognitive Neuroscience, 19*(10), 1609–1623.

Brauer, J., Neumann, J., & Friederici, A. D. (2008). Temporal dynamics of perisylvian activation during language processing in children and adults. *NeuroImage, 41*(4), 1484–1492.

Brown, R. (1973). *A first language.* Cambridge, MA: Harvard University Press.

Brown, R., & Fraser, C. (1964). The acquisition of syntax. *Monographs of the Society for Research in Child Development, 29*(1), 43–79.

Brown, T. T., Lugar, H. M., Coalson, R. S., Miezin, F. M., Petersen, S. E., & Schlaggar, B. L. (2005). Developmental changes in human cerebral functional organization for word generation. *Cerebral Cortex, 15*(3), 275–290.

Brownell, H. H., Potter, H. H., Bihrle, A. M., & Gardner, H. (1986, March). Inference deficits in right brain-damaged patients. *Brain and Language, 27*(2), 310–321.

Brownell, H. H., Potter, H. H., Michelow, D., & Gardner, H. (1984, July). Sensitivity to lexical denotation and connotation in brain-damaged patients: A double dissociation? *Brain and Language, 22*(2), 253–265.

Brownell, H. H., Simpson, T. L., Bihrle, A. M., Potter, H. H., & Gardner, H. (1990). Appreciation of metaphoric alternative word meanings by left and right brain-damaged patients. *Neuropsychologia, 28*(4), 375–383.

Bruel-Jungerman, E., Laroche, S., & Rampon, C. (2005). New neurons in the dentate gyrus are involved in the expression of enhanced long-term memory following environmental enrichment. *European Journal of Neuroscience, 21*(2), 513–521.

Burgess, C., & Simpson, G. (1988). Cerebral hemispheric mechanisms in the retrieval of ambiguous word meanings. *Brain and Language, 33*(1), 86–104.

Burman, D. D., Bitan, T., & Booth, J. R. (2008). Sex differences in neural processing of language among children. *Neuropsychologia, 46*(5), 1349–1362.

Cabeza, R., & Nyberg, L. (2000). Imaging cognition II: An empirical review of 275 PET and fMRI studies. *Journal of Cognitive Neuroscience, 12*(1), 1–47.

Caplan, D., Alpert, N., & Waters, G. (1998). Effects of syntactic structure and propositional number on patterns of regional cerebral blood flow. *Journal of Cognitive Neuroscience, 10*(4), 541–552.

Casey, B. J., Tottenham, N., Liston, C., & Durston, S. (2005). Imaging the developing brain: What have we learned about cognitive development? *Trends in Cognitive Sciences, 9*(3), 104–109.

Chein, J. M., Ravizza, S. M., & Fiez, J. A. (2003). Using neuroimaging to evaluate models of working memory and their implications for language processing. *Journal of Neurolinguistics, 16*(4–5), 315–339.

Clark, W. W. (1959). Boys and girls: Are there significant ability and achievement differences? *Phi Delta Kappan, 41*(2), 73–76.

Dehaene-Lambertz, G., Dehaene, S., & Hertz-Pannier, L. (2002). Functional neuroimaging of speech perception in infants. *Science, 298*(5600), 2012–2015.

Durston, S., Davidson, M. C., Tottenham, N. T., Galvan, A., Spicer, J., Fossella, J. A., et al. (2006). A shift from diffuse to focal cortical activity with development. *Developmental Science, 9*(1), 1–8.

Eriksson, P. S., Perfilieva, E., Bjork-Eriksson, T., Alborn, A., Nordborg, C., Peterson, D. A., et al. (1998). Neurogenesis in the adult human hippocampus. *Nature Medicine, 4*(11), 1313–1317.

Fiez, J. (1997). Phonology, semantics, and the role of the left inferior prefrontal cortex. *Human Brain Mapping, 5*(2), 79–83.

Fiez, J., & Petersen, S. E. (1998). Neuroimaging studies of word reading. *Proceedings of the National Academy of Sciences, 95*(3), 914–921.

Fodor, J. A. (1983). *The modularity of mind.* Cambridge, MA: Bradford Books, MIT Press.

Friederici, A. D., Rüschemeyer, S. A., Hahne, A., & Fiebach, C. J. (2003). The role of left inferior frontal and superior temporal cortex in sentence comprehension: Localizing syntactic and semantic processes. *Cerebral Cortex, 13*(2), 170–177.

Gabrieli, J., Poldrack, R., & Desmond, J. (1998). The role of left prefrontal cortex in language and memory. *Proceedings of the National Academy of Sciences, 95*(3), 906–913.

Gaillard, W. D., Sachs, B. C., Whitnah, J. R., Ahmad, Z., Balsamo, L. M., Petrella, J. R., et al. (2003). Developmental aspects of language processing: fMRI of verbal fluency in children and adults. *Human Brain Mapping, 18*(3), 176–185.

Giedd, J. N., Blumenthal, J., Jeffries, N. O., Castellanos, F. X., Liu, H., Zijdenbos, A., et al. (1999). Brain development during childhood and adolescence: A longitudinal MRI study. *Nature Neuroscience, 2*(10), 861–863.

Giraud, A. L., & Price, C. J. (2001). The constraints functional neuroimaging places on classical models of auditory word processing. *Journal of Cognitive Neuroscience, 13*(6), 754–765.

Gould, E., Beylin, A., Tanapat, P., Reeves, A., & Shors, T. J. (1999). Learning enhances adult neurogenesis in the hippocampal formation. *Nature Neuroscience, 2*(3), 260–265.

Hagoort, P. (2003). How the brain solves the binding problem for language: A neurocomputational model of syntactic processing. *NeuroImage, 2*(S1), S18–S29.

Hough, M. S. (1990). Narrative comprehension in adults with right and left hemisphere brain-damage: Theme organization. *Brain and Language, 38*(2), 253–277.

Johnson, J. S., & Newport, E. L. (1989). Critical period effects in second language learning: The influence of maturational state on the acquisition of English as a second language. *Cognitive Psychology, 2*(1), 60–99.

Josse, G., & Tzourio-Mazoyer, N. (2004). Hemispheric specialization for language. *Brain Research Reviews, 44*(1), 1–12.

Just, M. A., Carpenter, P. A., Keller, T. A., Eddy, W. F., & Thulborn, K. R. (1996). Brain activation modulated by sentence comprehension. *Science, 274*(5284), 114–116.

Kim, K. H., Relkin, N. R., Lee, K.-M., & Hirsch, J. (1997). Distinct cortical areas associated with native and second languages. *Nature, 388*(6638), 171–174.

Kovelman, I., Baker, S. A., & Petitto, L. A. (2008). Bilingual and monolingual brains compared: A functional magnetic resonance imaging investigation of syntactic processing and a possible "neural signature" of bilingualism. *Journal of Cognitive Science, 20*(1), 153–169.

Krashen, S. (1973). Lateralization, language, learning, and the critical period: Some new evidence. *Language Learning, 23*(1), 63–74.

Lenneberg, E. H. (1967). *Biological foundations of language.* New York: Wiley.

Lynn, R. (1992). Sex differences on the Differential Aptitude Test in British and American adolescents. *Educational Psychology, 12*(2), 101–106.

Maccoby, E. (1966). *The development of sex differences.* Stanford, CA: Stanford University Press.

Mann, V. A., Sasanuma, S., Sakuma, N., & Masaki, S. (1990). Sex differences in cognitive abilities: A cross-cultural perspective. *Neuropsychologia, 28*(10), 1063–1077.

Martin, A., Haxby, J. V., Lalonde, F. M., Wiggs, C. L., & Ungerleider, L. G. (1995). Discrete cortical regions associated with knowledge of color and knowledge of action. *Science, 270*(5233), 102–105.

Martin, A., Wiggs, C. L., Ungerleider, L. G., & Haxby, J. V. (1996). Neural correlates of category-specific knowledge. *Nature, 379*(6566), 649–652.

Martin, D. J., & Hoover, H. D. (1987). Sex differences in educational achievement: A longitudinal study. *Journal of Early Adolescence, 7*(1), 65–83.

Mason, R. A., & Just, M. A. (2004). How the brain processes causal inferences in text: A theoretical account of generation and integration component processes utilizing both cerebral hemispheres. *Psychological Science, 15*(1), 1–7.

Mason, R. A., & Just, M. A. (2006). Neuroimaging contributions to the understanding of discourse processes. In M. Traxler & M. A. Gernsbacher (Eds.), *Handbook of psycholinguistics* (pp. 765–799). Amsterdam: Elsevier.

McNeill, D. (1970). *The acquisition of language: The study of developmental psycholinguistics.* New York: Harper & Row.

Monetta, L., & Joanette, Y. (2003). Specificity of the right hemisphere's contribution to verbal communication: The cognitive resources hypothesis. *Journal of Medical Speech-Language Pathology, 11*(4), 203–212.

Moro, A., Tettamanti, M., Perani, D., Donati, C., Cappa, S. F., & Fazio, F. (2001). Syntax and the brain: Disentangling grammar by selective anomalies. *NeuroImage, 13*(1), 110–118.

Muma, J. R. (1978). *Language handbook: Concepts, assessment, intervention.* Englewood Cliffs, NJ: Prentice Hall.

Murray, L. L. (2000). The effects of varying attentional demands on the word retrieval skills of adults with aphasia, right hemisphere brain damage, or no brain damage. *Brain and Language, 72*(1), 40–72.

Newport, E. L., Bavelier, D., & Neville, H. J. (2001). Critical thinking about critical periods: Perspectives on a critical period for language acquisition. In E. Dupoux (Ed.), *Language, brain, and cognitive development* (pp. 481–502). Cambridge, MA: MIT Press.

Owen, A. M., McMillan, K. M., Laird, A. R., & Bullmore, E. (2005). N-back working memory paradigm: A meta-analysis of normative functional neuroimaging studies. *Human Brain Mapping, 2*(1), 46–59.

Perani, D., Dehaene, S., Grassi, F., Cohen, L., Cappa, S. F., Dupoux, E., et al. (1996). Brain processing of native and foreign languages. *NeuroReport, 7*(15–17), 2439–2444.

Petitto, L. A. (2009). New discoveries from the bilingual brain and mind across the life span: Implications for education. *Mind, Brain, and Education, 3*(4), 185–197.

Petitto, L. A., Katerelos, M., Levy, B. G., Gauna, K., Tétreault, K., & Ferraro, V. (2001). Bilingual signed and spoken language acquisition from birth: Implications for the mechanisms underlying early bilingual language acquisition. *Journal of Child Language, 28*(2), 453–496.

Plante, E., Schmithorst, V. J., Holland, S. K., & Byars, A. W. (2006). Sex differences in the activation of language cortex during childhood. *Neuropsychologia, 44*(7), 1210–1221.

Prat, C. S., Keller, T. A., & Just, M. A. (2007). Individual differences in sentence comprehension: A functional magnetic resonance imaging investigation of syntactical and lexical processing demands. *Journal of Cognitive Neuroscience, 19*(12), 1950–1963.

Premack, D. G., & Woodruff, G. (1978). Does the chimpanzee have a theory of mind? *Behavioral and Brain Sciences, 1*(4), 515–526.

Price, C. J. (2000). The anatomy of language: Contributions from functional neuroimaging. *Journal of Anatomy, 197*(3), 335–359.

Pujol, J., Deus, J., Losilla, J. M., & Capdevila, A. (1999). Cerebral lateralization of language in normal left-handed people studied by functional MRI. *Neurology, 52*(5), 1038.

Redlinger, W., & Park, T. Z. (1980). Language mixing in young bilingual children. *Journal of Child Language, 7*(1), 24–30.

Ross, E. D., & Mesulam, M.-M. (1979). Dominant language functions of the right hemisphere? Prosody and emotional gesturing. *Archives of Neurology, 36*(3), 144–148.

Ross, E. D., Thompson, R. D., & Yenkosky, J. (1997). Lateralization of affective prosody in brain and the callosal integration of hemispheric language functions. *Brain and Language, 56*(1), 27–54.

Schmithorst, V. J., Holland, S. K., & Plante, E. (2006). Cognitive modules utilized for narrative comprehension in children: A functional magnetic resonance imaging study. *NeuroImage, 29*(1), 254–266.

Shammi, P., & Stuss, D. T. (1999). Humour appreciation: A role of the right frontal lobe. *Brain, 122*(4), 657–666.

Shaw, P., Greenstein, D., Lerch, J., Clasen, L., Lenroot, R., Gogtay, N., et al. (2006). Intellectual ability and cortical development in children and adolescents. *Nature, 440*(7084), 676–679.

St. George, M., Kutas, M., Martinez, A., & Sereno, M. I. (1999). Semantic integration in reading: Engagement of the right hemisphere during discourse processing. *Brain, 12*(7), 1317–1325.

Szaflarski, J. P., Holland, S. K., Schmithorst, V. J., & Byars, A. W. (2006). fMRI study of language lateralization in children and adults. *Human Brain Mapping, 27*(3), 2002–2012.

Templin, M. (1957). *Certain language skills in children.* Minneapolis: University of Minnesota Press.

Toga, A. W., Thompson, P. M., & Sowell, E. R. (2006). Mapping brain maturation. *Trends in Neuroscience, 29*(3), 148–159.

Tompkins, C. A. (1990). Knowledge and strategies for processing lexical metaphor after right or left hemisphere brain damage. *Journal of Speech and Hearing Research, 33*(2), 307–316.

Tompkins, C. A., Baumgaertner, A., Lehman, M. T., & Foassett, T. R. D. (1997). Suppression and discourse comprehension in right brain-damaged adults: A preliminary report. *Aphasiology, 11*(4), 505–519.

Vandenberghe, R. R., Price, C., Wise, R., Josephs, O., & Frackowiak, R. S. (1996). Functional anatomy of a common semantic system for words and pictures. *Nature, 383*(6597), 254–256.

Vannest, J., Karunanayaka, P. R., Schmithorst, V. J., Szaflarski, J. P., & Holland, S. K. (2009). Language networks in children: Evidence from functional MRI studies. *American Journal of Roentgenology, 192*(5), 1190–1196.

Vihman, M. (1985). Language differentiation by the bilingual infant. *Journal of Child Language, 12*(2), 297–324.

Virtue, S., Haberman, J., Clancy, Z., Parrish, T., & Beeman, M. J. (2006). Neural activity of inferences during story comprehension. *Brain Research, 1084*(1), 104–114.

Wada, J., & Rasmussen, T. (1960). Intracarotid injection of Sodium Amytal for the lateralization of cerebral speech dominance: Experimental and clinical observations. *Journal of Neurosurgery, 17*(2), 266–282.

Wagner, A. D., Shannon, B. J., Kahn, I., & Buckner, R. L. (2005). Parietal lobe contributions to episodic memory retrieval. *Trends in Cognitive Sciences, 9*(9), 445–453.

Wartenburger, I., Heekeren, H. R., Abutalebi, J., Cappa, S. F., Villringer, A., & Perani, D. (2003). Early setting of grammatical processing in the bilingual brain. *Neuron, 37*(1), 159–270.

Weber-Fox, C., & Neville, H. J. (1999). Functional neural subsystems are differentially affected by delays in second-language immersion: ERP and behavioral evidence in bilingual speakers. In D. Birdsong (Ed.), *New perspectives on the critical period for second language acquisition* (pp. 23–38). Hillsdale, NJ: Erlbaum.

Wood, A. G., Harvey, A. S., Wellard, R. M., Abbott, D. F., Anderson, M. K., Saling, M. M., et al. (2004). Language cortex activation in normal children. *Neurology, 63*(6), 1035–1044.

Zola-Morgan, S. (1995). Localization of brain function: The legacy of Franz Joseph Gall (1758–1828). *Annual Review of Neuroscience, 18,* 359–383.

John Gabrieli

John Gabrieli, PhD, is professor of Health Sciences and Technology and Cognitive Neuroscience at the Massachusetts Institute of Technology (MIT). He has a dual appointment in the Harvard-MIT Division of Health Sciences and Technology and in the Department of Brain and Cognitive Sciences. He is Director of the Imaging Center at the McGovern Institute for Brain Research and Co-Director of the MIT Clinical Research Center. He has a BA in English from Yale and a PhD in behavioral neuroscience from MIT, and was a postdoctoral fellow in the Psychology Department at Harvard. His area of research is human cognitive neuroscience, in which he studies the brain basis of memory, language, and thought.

Joanna A. Christodoulou

Joanna A. Christodoulou, EdD, is a post-doctoral associate in the Gabrieli Lab in the Department of Brain and Cognitive Sciences at MIT. She has an EdD in human development and psychology from the Harvard Graduate School of Education (HGSE), an EdM in mind, brain, and education from HGSE, and an MA in child development from Tufts University. She works clinically with struggling students and conducts research at the intersection of education and cognitive neuroscience, with a focus on reading development and difficulties.

Tricia O'Loughlin

Tricia O'Loughlin, EdM, is a former Montessori early childhood teacher with a master's degree in mind, brain, and education. She researched reading and dyslexia at the Gabrieli Lab at MIT before becoming a doctoral student at the Harvard Graduate School of Education. She studies human development through the intersection of cognitive neuroscience and education.

Marianna D. Eddy

Marianna D. Eddy, PhD, is a postdoctoral associate in the Gabrieli Lab in the Department of Brain and Cognitive Sciences at the Massachusetts Institute of Technology. She received her PhD from Tufts University in experimental psychology. Her research uses electrophysiological measures to investigate reading development and dyslexia.

In this chapter, John Gabrieli and his colleagues describe their work in looking at the different ways the brain derives meaning from the printed word. Most of us don't recall much about learning how to talk. It just seemed to come naturally. Learning to speak is an innate ability supported by specialized areas of the brain, and is automatic for almost all children raised in typical circumstances (see chapter 5). But for many children, learning to read is a long, complicated task requiring years of conscious effort. Can you remember the first time you encountered printed text and tried to make sense of those letters? Exactly how the brain is able to associate squiggly lines and curves with snippets of sound that are stored in our head had long been a mystery—one that cognitive scientists were eager to investigate with their new brain imaging technologies. Consequently, how the brain learns to read has been one of the areas of human learning extensively explored by research in neuroscience.

Because there are no specialized areas for reading as there are for spoken language, the brain has to recruit certain regions to recognize written text. The authors describe the role of one major region, called the visual word form area, and how it interacts with other regions of the brain as they develop their ability to support reading. Of particular interest is the research that led to a deeper understanding of the brain differences that result in dyslexia and the development of the remarkable interventions that have helped individuals with dyslexia become capable readers.

Chapter 6

The Reading Brain

John Gabrieli, Joanna A. Christodoulou,
Tricia O' Loughlin, and Marianna D. Eddy

The ability to read is one of the most remarkable of our cultural inventions. Reading is a powerful portal to knowledge, from books to the Internet, from authors near and far, alive and deceased. It is initially the focus of formal education (learning to read) and then becomes the medium of formal education (reading to learn). Reading combines in a novel way two amazing abilities of the human brain—vision and language. Human vision and language are so brilliantly constructed through genes and experience in the human mind and brain that a main agenda of psychologists and neuroscientists has been to discover how people see and communicate so well.

Reading is, however, a relatively recent cultural invention; as such, it reflects the capacity of the human brain to create new abilities through the integration of old abilities. The fact that the human brain was not evolved to read may explain why reading must be taught so explicitly and formally (no child receives such instruction on how to see, speak, or hear) and why many children struggle to read (for example, as in the case of dyslexia). In this chapter, we selectively review major research findings and current understandings about how the human brain empowers reading, how the child's brain learns to read, what is different in the brain of a child who struggles to read, and finally how the neuroscience of reading may come to play a role in education. We focus our review on reading in English but also discuss how reading differs across languages, as we recognize that universal principles of the brain organization of vision and language are expressed differently among diverse languages and writing systems.

The Adult Reading Brain

In reading, as in other domains of human ability, much of our most certain knowledge about the functional organization of the brain comes from striking examples of adults with focal brain injuries. These examples offer unexpected lessons about how the human brain works. We learned from Broca's patient Leborgne (also known as "Tan" because he most frequently uttered that word) that language is represented primarily in the left hemisphere of the human brain (Broca, 1865), from the amnesic patient H. M. (Henry Molaison) that formation of a new memory depends on the hippocampus (Milner, Corkin, & Teuber, 1968), and from the case of Phineas Gage that moral reasoning is supported by the lower aspects of the frontal lobes (Macmillan, 1986, 1992). In regard to reading, perhaps the two most influential findings from neurology are that of Mr. C., the first documented case of alexia (the selective inability of an adult reader to read words by sight) (Dejerine, 1892), and a small group of patients with two contrasting patterns of reading impairment that reveal two reading pathways in the brain.

Alexia

In 1892, the French neurologist Joseph Jules Dejerine described the seminal case of Mr. C., a skilled adult reader who suddenly lost the ability to read. Mr. C. had a case of "pure verbal blindness": he could not read words, but he could speak and comprehend speech (his language was intact), he could recognize faces and objects by sight (his vision was intact), and he could even write words (which he then could not read). After Mr. C. died, Dejerine conducted a postmortem examination of Mr. C's brain and discovered an injury, the result of a stroke, in the left posterior (rear) part of the brain. This region appears to play a highly specialized and vital role in reading by beginning the transformation of visual input into letters and words. Subsequent studies with patients and with healthy people in functional neuroimaging studies have supported this existence of a brain area called the visual word form area.

Two Routes for Reading

When readers engage with text, the brain must balance two sometimes competing goals: (1) relating printed words to sounds of words (most children learn to read after they have learned spoken words) and (2) facilitating the fastest possible matching of printed words to meanings (so that skilled adults can read five hundred words per minute; they could read at four times that rate if they did not also have to make four eye movements per second scanning connected text). Two patterns of reading impairment after stroke have taught us that the human brain solves the problem of reading by using two different neural routes.

> The human brain solves the problem of reading by using two different neural routes.

Readers use the *phonological route* to decode a string of letters, translate it into a sound pattern, and then access the meaning of the word from that sound pattern. This route is specialized for words that are regular, rare, or novel; on this neural route, the typical rules for translation from letters to sounds can or must be applied. *Regularity* refers to how certain we are in knowing how to pronounce a word based on the typical correspondence between graphemes (letters or groups of letters) and phonemes (sound constituents of words). A word such as *can* is regular—the *c*, *a*, and *n* are pronounced the usual way. On the other hand, a word such as *yacht* is irregular because *ch* is rarely silent. The phonological route is used to "sound out" rare or novel words because we typically do not know how to pronounce them, so we apply regular rules of letter-sound correspondence (for example, if we see *chiple*, we apply the regular rule that *ch* is pronounced as in *chess* rather than silent as in the irregular *ch* in *yacht*). This is a relatively slow, systematic route that codes the typical rules of pronunciation of words that we read. The phonological route relies on left hemisphere posterior temporoparietal brain regions.

Readers use the other, *direct route* to bypass the sound-pattern stage and attempt to match a printed word directly with its meaning. This route is ideal for very frequently encountered words (termed "sight words") that we know so well that we can jump from sight to meaning (such as *head*), and also for irregular words (such as *yacht*) that we have memorized because regular pronunciation rules would mislead us. This route tends to be faster because of the single-step access to meaning without parsing the letters into component sounds. The direct route relies on left hemisphere posterior occipitotemporal brain regions.

The physical separation of these two reading routes was discovered through two different patterns of reading impairment in patients who suffered left hemisphere strokes. Some patients had injury to the phonological route; they could not read aloud uncommon regular words (for example, *sextant*) or sound out novel words (*cabding*), but they could read frequently encountered words (*head*) or irregular common words (*women*) through their intact direct route.

Thus, the intact direct route in these patients supported reading of very frequent or "sight" words and irregular words whose pronunciation was memorized, but the injured phonological route prevented reading of words that involved "sounding out" the relations of letters to sounds. Other patients exhibited the reverse pattern, with an impaired direct route (from sight to meaning) but an intact phonological route (from sight to sound to meaning). The typical healthy reader is thought to use both routes constantly and interactively.

Functional Imaging of the Reading Brain

Neuroimaging reveals brain organization of reading in healthy people. Functional imaging methods examine brain function during reading (see table 6.1). Functional magnetic resonance imaging (fMRI) and positron emission tomography (PET, which is now used less for reading research) identify which brain regions support specific components of reading—that is, *where* reading operations occur. Event-related potentials (ERP) and magnetoencephalography (MEG) identify with millisecond (msec) accuracy the temporal dynamics of reading—that is, *when* reading operations occur. In combination, these different brain measurement techniques offer new ways to discern the brain basis of reading.

Table 6.1: Description of Functional Neuroimaging Methods

Method	Source	Temporal Resolution	Spatial Resolution
fMRI	Deoxygenated blood flow changes	4 to 6 seconds	2 to 4 millimeters
EEG/ERP	Electric field associated with moving electrical charges from the brain's cortical surfaces	1 millisecond	Cortical structures: 10 to 20 millimeters
MEG	Magnetic field associated with moving electrical charges from the brain's cortical surfaces	1 millisecond	Cortical structures: 5 to 10 millimeters

Visual Word Form Area

Consistent with the location of injury in cases of alexia, fMRI and PET studies have identified a region in the left rear region of the healthy human brain that responds selectively to words and letters (Petersen et al., 1988, 1990)—the visual word form area (Cohen et al., 2000). Despite some debate about the precise operations this area performs, there is general agreement that visually presented words and letters activate this region preferentially compared to auditorily presented words and many other kinds of visual stimuli (such as faces). The brain location of this region is fairly consistent from person to person, although its precise location may be more influenced by experience than genetics (discussed later). The relative consistency of the visual word form area reflects its role in relating visual (occipital-lobe) and language (temporal-lobe) neural systems that develop even before birth, and far before learning to read.

Further support for the role of this region in the initial stage of reading comes from rare invasive studies in which electrodes are placed for clinical purposes directly on the surface of the brain in patients with epilepsy (Allison et al., 1994; Mani et al., 2008). The left posterior occipitotemporal brain region responds selectively to words compared to faces about 180 msecs after a word is seen. Further, the visual word form area responds only to the written language that one has learned. If a person knows English but has not learned Hebrew, the visual word form area responds only to the English letters; if a person knows both written languages, the visual word form area responds to both English and Hebrew (Baker et al., 2007). Thus, the selective response of the visual word form area is education dependent (it depends upon the written language one has learned), but can respond to written words across familiar languages (in this example, English and Hebrew).

Because reading is a recent cultural invention relative to our long evolutionary history, it is unlikely that our brains are genetically predisposed to develop neural systems that support reading-specific processes. Functional neuroimaging has revealed brain regions that are specialized for specific kinds of visual perception, such as for faces or places. However, researchers have hypothesized that primates have long had the survival need to perceive faces (to identify others) and places (to identify one's location), and that the relatively consistent locations of face-selective and place-selective brain regions reflect genetic programming for these vital aspects of vision. The weaker genetic influence on the precise location of the visual word form area is supported by functional neuroimaging studies of identical twins. There is a significant similarity between identical twins for the locations of face and place areas, but not for the visual word form area (Polk, Park, Smith, & Park, 2007). This finding supports the view that specialization for perception of faces and places in the human brain is genetically guided, whereas specialization for letters and words is not.

The visual word form area may reflect an experience-dependent transformation of neocortex that, prior to reading, was part of a larger area devoted to the perception of objects (a process termed "neuronal recycling" by Dehaene, 2005, and Dehaene & Cohen, 2007). The way young children frequently write backward letters and words (a behavior now known to be unrelated to dyslexia) may be an intriguing consequence of this recycling. Visual recognition of objects is known to be independent of which way an object faces: a chair or a dog or a cup remains the same thing whether it faces to the left or to the right. Backward writing by children, remarkable because they have never seen it modeled and it appears normal to their eyes, may be a lingering consequence of the use of visual systems that are typically insensitive to right/left orientation because such insensitivity helps in general object recognition.

Phonological Awareness for Reading

Beginning readers must learn to relate auditory language to print through explicit phonological awareness—that is, knowledge that spoken words are composed of discrete sounds (phonemes) that can be mapped onto letters or syllables (graphemes). Phonological awareness in prereaders predicts later success in learning to read in both alphabetic and nonalphabetic languages (Ziegler & Goswami, 2005), although the precise relationship between phonological awareness and reading acquisition may differ across writing systems (orthographies) (Goswami & East, 2000). Because this mapping of visual language to auditory/spoken language is so fundamental to reading, many studies have examined the brain basis of phonological awareness.

Functional neuroimaging studies have examined the brain basis of phonological awareness by asking people to make judgments about visually presented words that require thinking about the sounds associated with them (Bitan et al., 2007, 2009; Bolger, Hornickel, Cone, Burman, & Booth, 2008; Bolger, Minas, Burman, & Booth, 2008; Booth et al., 2004; Cao, Bitan, Chou, Burman, & Booth, 2006; Hoeft et al., 2006; Shaywitz et al., 2004, 2007; Temple et al., 2001, 2003). Rhyme detection tasks, in which people decide whether two visually presented words or groups of letters rhyme, have been frequently used to identify the neural circuitry associated with phonological awareness for print. These tasks are useful because rhyming judgments require phonological awareness of the constituent sound parts of words or letter names. Studies employing these tasks inform our general understanding of the brain networks recruited for phonological awareness, an important skill for reading. Functional neuroimaging studies identify a circuit that is engaged during phonological analysis of reading, which typically includes several left-side brain regions in frontal, temporal, and parietal lobes where graphemes (print) are matched to phonemes (sounds). Thus, the neural systems identified in functional neuroimaging studies of phonological awareness appear to be those that support reading itself.

Timeline of Reading in the Brain

ERP and MEG research reveals that the processing of words occurs quickly. In adults, visual processing of words cascades through single letter units to whole word units to meaning all within 400 to 500 msecs of seeing a word (Grainger & Holcomb, 2009). In skilled adult readers, specialized visual responses to words occur 150 to 200 msecs after seeing a word (called the N1 component) (Allison, Puce, & McCarthy, 2002). In typical adult readers, the N1 response is left lateralized for words and right lateralized for faces. Thus, there is parallel specialization for rapid visual analysis of words in the left hemisphere and faces in the right hemisphere.

MEG studies demonstrate that word processing is not serial, proceeding step-by-step from a visual analysis of word properties to meaning. Rather, lower- and higher-level cognitive processing occurs early and in tandem. Within about 200 msecs, not only are specialized visual areas engaged for print, but also, nearly simultaneously, areas in higher-order brain regions are engaged in phonological and semantic processing of words (Pammer et al., 2004; Cornelissen et al., 2009). Thus, higher-level brain areas involved in extracting sound and meaning from print do not wait for visual analyses to be completed; instead, an early interaction among vision, sound, and meaning takes place.

Cross-Linguistic Differences

The organization of a written language has an effect on the processing demands of the brain. Alphabetic languages vary in their *orthographical transparency*—how much a single letter or group of letters represents a single sound. Italian and Spanish are highly transparent, with nearly a 1:1 ratio of graphemes to phonemes (that is, if you see how a word is spelled, you know how to say it aloud). English has poor transparency because it is full of exceptions (such as the silent *s* in *island*), with an average of nearly thirty alternative pronunciations for each grapheme. Other languages, such as Japanese and Cherokee, have a syllabary (or syllable-based) system, in which many set syllables combine to form written words. Chinese uses a logographic system that has thousands of symbols that represent entire words. This enormous variation in writing systems has profound effects on education

> The writing system of a language has an enormous effect on how long it takes children to become skilled readers in that language.

and in how the brain has to support reading (Ellis et al., 2004). For example, a child becomes a skilled reader in Italian in about a year, in English in about three years, and in Mandarin Chinese in about ten years.

Readers of alphabetic languages recruit similar brain regions, but the ways they rely on the brain regions vary, depending on the language structure. English and Italian readers share left hemisphere reading networks (Paulesu et al., 2000). However, for reading nonsense words, English readers rely more on brain regions associated with retrieval of memorized words, whereas Italian readers rely more on brain regions associated with phonological processing (Paulesu et al., 2000). These brain differences likely reflect the different strategies that readers learn depending upon the transparency of their written languages. Italian readers learn a very transparent or regular written language, and employ a regular set of phonological processing rules when deciding how to pronounce an unknown letter string (a nonsense word). English readers learn a very irregular language, full of memorized exceptions, and consider these many exceptions when deciding how to pronounce an unknown letter string.

Similarities and differences are found in brain regions engaged by Chinese, English, and Japanese writing systems (Bolger, Perfetti, & Schneider, 2005). All three writing systems engage brain systems associated with visual processing. The Chinese logographic system, however, with its extensive graphical information, activates a wider visual area. The Japanese written system has two forms: *kana* use a consistent mapping between graphemes and spoken syllables, and *kanji* rely on a mapping of single characters to whole words. Frontal regions are activated in reading of all three languages. The temporoparietal region associated with mapping letters to sounds in English is least engaged by the logographic Chinese language. Thus, diverse languages (for example, Italian and English) using a common writing system or alphabet and diverse writing systems (for example, Roman alphabet and Chinese characters) place different demands on the reading brain.

Development of the Reading Brain

Advances in the neuroimaging of children's brains provide insights into how children learn to read. Studies typically compare brain function between children (early readers) and adults (mature readers) or between children of different ages who are progressing towards reading maturity. In general, typical reading development shows (1) increased specialization of the left hemisphere, (2) increased engagement of left posterior (rear) brain regions, and (3) decreased engagement of left anterior (front) brain regions.

Increased Specialization of Left Hemisphere for Reading

A cross-sectional fMRI study examined brain responses to words in individuals ages six to twenty-two (Turkeltaub, Gareau, Flowers, Zeffiro, & Eden, 2003). Across these ages, researchers found decreasing activation in rear right hemisphere regions and increasing activation in left hemisphere regions. Increased left hemisphere specialization for reading across development does not reflect increasing specialization for language in general but may reflect a maturing visual mapping between print and language. Oral language is already strongly lateralized at birth: fMRI reveals strong left-lateralization in three-month-old infants in response to hearing speech (Dehaene-Lambertz, Dehaene, & Hertz-Pannier, 2002). Rather, the shift from right to left hemispheric support for reading print may reflect a transition in how letters are represented in the brain. For the beginning reader, letters are arbitrary visuospatial symbols, and the right hemisphere is specialized for visuospatial perception. With practice, children learn that letters represent sounds. Further, they learn that a wide variety of visuospatial symbols, in print and in handwriting, all represent the same abstract letter. For example, different symbols, such as a, A, a, A, α, A, **a**, A, *a*, *A*, all represent the same category of the letter *a*. Neuroimaging experiments examining how people transition from perceiving particular visuospatial symbols to perceiving visual *categories* find precisely this shift—from right hemisphere dominance in the naïve or beginning participant perceiving visual symbols to left hemisphere dominance in the skilled and advanced participant perceiving meaningful visual categories (Seger et al., 2000). Thus, as children mature, they may no longer see letters as many different visuospatial items, but as twenty-six categories that can be used to access the sounds and meanings of words.

Increased Engagement of Left Posterior Brain Regions and Decreased Engagement of Left Anterior Brain Regions for Reading

The left posterior neocortex includes the brain regions that map print to sound and meaning, including the visual word form area. Neuroimaging studies have found that as children become older and more skilled readers from ages seven to eighteen, these regions become increasingly engaged in reading (Booth et al., 2004; Hoeft, Meyler, Hernandez, et al., 2007; Hoeft, Ueno, Reiss, et al., 2007; Shaywitz et al., 2007; Turkeltaub et al., 2003). Within the left hemisphere posterior regions, readers shift from reliance on the temporoparietal region to the visual word form region, consistent with a shift from effortful phonological decoding to automatic word recognition as reading proficiency increases (Church et al., 2008). The visual, auditory, and semantic interactions in posterior left hemisphere regions may become more automatic and integrated with practice in reading.

The left anterior (front) neocortex includes brain regions that support working-memory operations that allow people to intentionally select, maintain, and manipulate a word in mind. Over the course of development these regions become decreasingly engaged in reading (Hoeft, Meyler, Hernandez, et al., 2007; Shaywitz et al., 2007). It may be that as posterior brain regions mature in their ability to support fluent, automatic reading, there is a corresponding reduction in demands on frontal-lobe areas.

Development of Temporal Aspects of Reading

ERP and MEG studies document how the temporal dynamics of reading change in the developing reader's brain. In general, across typical development, there is increased selectivity in response to print relative to other visual inputs and increased specialization of the left hemisphere.

Unlike adult readers, who show a selective ERP response for words 150 to 200 msecs after a word is presented, nonreading kindergartners do not show a word-selective N1—by this brain measure, words are not perceived differently from meaningless symbols (Maurer et al., 2006). The same children, however, exhibited a word-selective N1 by second grade as readers. Children with a larger difference between words and symbols on the N1 were also faster readers in second grade.

ERP studies also document maturation of mapping from graphemes to phonemes. On a rhyming task, an ERP response associated with phonological processing becomes increasingly left-lateralized with age (Grossi et al., 2001). Indeed, ERP evidence indicates that the automatic integration of print and sound continues to develop in the brain for many years, perhaps into adulthood (Froyen et al., 2009).

Reading Difficulty in the Brain: Developmental Dyslexia

An estimated 5 to 17 percent of school-age children have developmental dyslexia and do not easily develop reading skills (Lyon, Shaywitz, & Shaywitz, 2003; Stanovich, 1986). Beyond dyslexia, readers may struggle to read because of difficulty with executive-function skills, difficulty with second-language learning, or impoverished learning environments. Dyslexia, the most commonly identified reading disability, is defined as difficulty in reading or spelling words accurately and/ or fluently given average or higher cognitive ability (Lyon, Shaywitz, & Shaywitz, 2003). A weakness in phonological processing skills, which involve the manipulation of language sounds and subsequently access to the sounds in printed words, typically underlies dyslexia throughout development (Bradley & Bryant, 1978; Shaywitz, 1998; Shaywitz et al., 1999; Wagner & Torgesen, 1987; Wagner, Torgesen, & Rashotte, 1994). Dyslexia is, however, a heterogeneous disorder that may result from a variety of specific underlying difficulties that vary from child to child (Pennington, 2006), including specific deficits in automaticity or auditory and visual perception (Farmer & Klein, 1995; Wolf et al., 2002).

Functional Brain Differences That Characterize Dyslexia

In contrast to typically developing readers who increase left posterior and decrease left anterior activation with age, readers with dyslexia consistently exhibit decreased or absent activations in the left posterior brain regions when performing tasks that require phonological or orthographic processing when compared to reading-matched and age-matched readers (Brunswick, McCrory, Price, Frith, & Frith, 1999; Hoeft et al., 2006; Hoeft, Meyler, et al., 2007; Horwitz, Rumsey, & Donohue, 1998; Paulesu et al., 1996, 2001; Ruff et al., 2002, 2003; Rumsey et al., 1992, 1997, 1999; Shaywitz, 1998; Shaywitz et al., 2002; Shaywitz, Mody, & Shaywitz, 2006; Simos, Breier, Fletcher, Bergman, & Papanicolaou, 2000; Simos et al., 2000; Temple et al., 2001). Readers with dyslexia often exhibit increased activation in frontal brain regions and the right-hemisphere posterior regions (Brunswick et al., 1999; Georgiewa et al., 2002; Milne, Syngeniotis, Jackson, & Corballis, 2002; Richards et al., 2002; Salmelin, Service, Kiesilä, Uutela, & Salonen, 1996; Shaywitz et al., 2002, 2004). This may reflect compensatory efforts to overcome the weakness of posterior reading networks. Readers with dyslexia and younger reading-matched children do not differ in frontal activations (Hoeft et al., 2006; Hoeft, Meyler, et al., 2007), suggesting that recruitment of frontal regions is related to reading *ability*, not to dyslexia per se. Adolescents with dyslexia who most improve or compensate over time appear to do so by exploiting this atypical use of frontal-lobe regions rather than developing a typical left-posterior reading system (Shaywitz et al., 2003).

Brain differences in readers with dyslexia are similar across alphabetic languages but may differ for nonalphabetic languages. Readers of English, Italian, and French with dyslexia share the characteristic hypoactivation of posterior brain networks (Paulesu et al., 2001). Chinese readers with dyslexia, however, show less activation in left middle frontal gyrus, a region important for processing a logographic language (Siok et al., 2004). Thus, dyslexia has common brain bases across languages, but also varies to some extent across fundamentally different writing systems.

> Brain differences in readers with dyslexia are similar across alphabetic languages but may differ for nonalphabetic languages.

MEG and ERP studies show different temporal patterns of brain activation in children with dyslexia. Children with dyslexia show less word-specific response to print (N1) and less left hemisphere lateralization than typically developing readers (Maurer et al., 2007). Thus, children with dyslexia do not have the same initial brain response to words that allows the words to stand out from other stimuli such as symbols. Further, MEG studies examining the timing of phonological processing during reading find that when typically developing children engage the left temporoparietal cortex, children with dyslexia instead engage the right temporoparietal cortex (Simos, Breier, Fletcher, Bergman, & Papanicolaou, 2000). This is another sign that dyslexia does not have the same pattern of left hemisphere specialization that characterizes the typical maturation of reading networks in the brain.

Structural Brain Differences That Reflect Functional Brain Differences

Structural, as opposed to functional, differences in the brain anatomy of people with dyslexia have been found in the gray matter (composed of neuronal cell bodies) and the white matter (composed of myelinated axon tracts). Readers with dyslexia show less gray matter volume in several regions associated with reading (Kronbichler et al., 2008). Even when compared to a younger reading-matched group, readers with dyslexia show less gray matter volume in the same left posterior (temporoparietal) region in which they show reduced activation (Hoeft, Meyler, Hernandez, et al., 2007). Thus, there is some correspondence between functional and structural brain differences in dyslexia.

White-matter pathways of the brain may be distinguished by diffusion tensor imaging (DTI), which provides a quantitative index of the organization of large myelinated nerve axons constituting the long-range connections of brain networks. Better-organized white matter in the left posterior brain region is associated with better reading skill among healthy individuals (Klingberg et al., 2000). White-matter organization appears to be weaker in the left posterior brain region of adults and children with dyslexia than in typical readers (Klingberg et al., 2000; Deutsch et al., 2005). White-matter tracts in left frontal regions also reflect weaker connections in readers with dyslexia (Rimrodt et al., 2009). DTI studies of dyslexia also report greater-than-normal white-matter connectivity in the corpus callosum, the large white-matter tract connecting regions of the left and right hemispheres (Dougherty et al., 2007). These findings suggest that, in dyslexia, white-matter pathways supporting reading project too weakly within the primary reading pathways of the linguistic left hemisphere, but they project too strongly between hemispheres (which may reflect an atypical reliance on right hemisphere regions for reading).

How Intervention Affects the Struggling Reader's Brain

Neuroimaging studies have investigated how reading interventions change the structure and function of the brain. These studies highlight the plasticity of the reading brain in children and adults with dyslexia. Functional neuroimaging studies have shown that left-hemisphere brain regions that are typically underactivated in dyslexia exhibit a gain in activation after effective intervention, such as intervention with the Lindamood-Bell program in adults with dyslexia (Eden et al., 2004) or the Fast ForWord® language program in children with dyslexia (Temple et al., 2003). For example, children with dyslexia who exhibited the typical hypoactivation in left temporoparietal and frontal brain regions showed gains in activation in those brain regions after effective remediation (Temple et al., 2003).

An MEG study showed that effective interventions using the Phono-Graphix or the Lindamood Phoneme Sequencing programs resulted in a shift from greater activation in the right hemisphere to greater left hemisphere activation (Simos et al., 2002). DTI also reveals normalization of white-matter structure after intervention (Keller & Just, 2009).

> Reading interventions can change the structure and functions of the brain.

Effective interventions with dyslexic readers can also strengthen activation in brain regions not typically engaged in reading. Both adults and children often exhibit increased activation in right-hemisphere regions that are not typically part of the reading network (Eden et al., 2004, Temple et al., 2003; Shaywitz et al., 2004). Thus, effective intervention for dyslexia may involve brain normalization (such that dyslexic readers exhibit changes that approach the typically reading brain) and brain compensation (such that dyslexic readers show changes in brain regions not typically involved in reading).

Brain plasticity induced by effective intervention can be long lasting, may vary in relation to treatment response, and can alter how brain regions interact or coordinate. Brain changes have been seen a year after completion of an effective intervention (Shaywitz et al., 2003; Meyler, Keller, Cherkassky, Gabrieli, & Just, 2008). In one study, children with dyslexia who responded best to intervention (improved to average reading range) were compared to nonresponders (who remained in the below-average range) (Odegard, Ring, Smith, Biggan, & Black, 2008). The responders showed greater right-frontal activation than either typical readers or nonresponders, which suggests that intervention in this case was supported by compensation rather than normalization, although some left hemisphere normalization occurred in both dyslexic groups. Finally, effective intervention can alter functional connectivity between brain regions (measured as the temporal correlation of activation across brain regions), such that the functional connectivity looks more similar to typically reading children (Richards & Berninger, 2008).

Implications for the Future

Neuroscience investigations have revealed for the first time the functional brain organization of reading, how diverse languages and writing systems are differently supported by the brain, the development of the reading brain, and the brain basis of dyslexia and its effective treatment. A fundamental question is how neuroscience methods and knowledge can benefit educational practices and policies. In general, a deep understanding of the brain basis of reading seems likely to be informative, but it will be important to identify precisely how neuroscience can be useful in education.

A near-term goal could be the prediction and prevention of dyslexia (Gabrieli, 2009). Considerable evidence exists to show that preventive or early treatment of dyslexia yields better outcomes than later treatment. Thus, early identification of children at risk for dyslexia is important. Neuroscience methods have shown surprising strength in predicting future reading difficulty. ERPs measured with newborns from families with a risk for reading difficulty have correlated with language and reading scores years later (Guttorm et al., 2005; Guttorm, Leppänen, Richardson, & Lyytinen, 2001; Molfese, 2000). ERPs in prereading children with familial risk not only added significantly to behavioral measures in predicting reading outcomes, but only the ERP measure predicted reading ability five years later (Maurer et al., 2009). Gains in phonological decoding by poor readers across a school year were predicted similarly by behavioral and MRI measures, but the combination of behavioral and brain measures predicted gains significantly better than either measure alone (Hoeft, Ueno, Reiss, et al., 2007). Brain imaging may play a valuable role in predicting future success or difficulty in reading; combined with genetic and familial information, it thus may facilitate preventive intervention and allow more children to succeed at learning to read.

Acknowledgments

Writing of this chapter was supported by the Ellison Medical Foundation, MIT Class of 1976 Funds for Dyslexia Research, and B. Richmond and J. Richmond through the Martin Richmond Memorial Fund. We thank Bianca Levy for assistance with references.

References

Allison, T., Ginter, H., McCarthy, G., Nobre, A. C., Puce, A., Luby, M., et al. (1994). Face recognition in human extrastriate cortex. *Journal of Neurophysiology, 71*(2), 821–825.

Allison, T., Puce, A., & McCarthy, G. (2002). Category-sensitive excitatory and inhibitory processes in human extrastriate cortex. *Journal of Neurophysiology, 88*(5), 2864–2868.

Baker, C. I., Liu, J., Wald, L. L., Kwong, K. K., Benner, T., & Kanwisher, N. (2007). Visual word processing and experiential origins of functional selectivity in human extrastriate cortex. *Proceedings of the National Academy of Sciences, 104*(21), 9087–9092.

Bitan, T., Burman, D. D., Chou, T.-L., Lu, D., Cone, N. E., Cao, F., Bigio, J. D., & Booth, J. R. (2007). The interaction between orthographic and phonological information in children: An fMRI study. *Human Brain Mapping, 28*, 880–891.

Bitan, T., Burman, D. D., Lu, D., Cone, N. E., Gitelman, D. R., Mesulam, M., & Booth, J. R. (2006). Weaker top-down modulation from the left inferior frontal gyrus in children. *Neuroimage, 33*(3), 991–998.

Bitan, T., Cheon, J., Lu, D., Burman, D. D., & Booth, J. R. (2009). Developmental increase in top-down and bottom-up processing in a phonological task: An effective connectivity, fMRI study. *Journal of Cognitive Neuroscience, 21*(6), 1135–1145.

Bolger, D. J., Hornickel, J., Cone, N. E., Burman, D. D., & Booth, J. R. (2008). Neural correlates of orthographic and phonological consistency effects in children. *Human Brain Mapping, 29*(12), 1416–1429.

Bolger, D. J., Minas, J., Burman, D. D., & Booth, J. R. (2008). Differential effects of orthographic and phonological consistency in cortex for children with and without reading impairment. *Neuropsychologia, 46*(14), 3210–3224.

Bolger, D. J., Perfetti, C. A., & Schneider, W. (2005). Cross-cultural effect on the brain revisited: Universal structures plus writing system variation. [Special issue: Meta-analysis in functional brain mapping.]. *Human Brain Mapping, 25*(1), 92–104.

Booth, J. R., Burman, D. D., Meyer, J. R., Gitelman, D. R., Parrish, T. B., & Mesulam, M. M. (2004). Development of brain mechanisms for processing orthographic and phonologic representations. *Journal of Cognitive Neuroscience, 16*(7), 1234–1249.

Bradley, L., & Bryant, P. E. (1978). Difficulties in auditory organisation as a possible cause of reading backwardness. *Nature, 271*(5647), 746–747.

Broca, P. (1865). Sur le siège de la faculté du langage articulé. *Bulletin de la Société d'Anthropologie, 6*, 337–393.

Brunswick, N., McCrory, E., Price, C. J., Frith, C. D., & Frith, U. (1999). Explicit and implicit processing of words and pseudowords by adult developmental dyslexics: A search for Wernicke's Wortschatz? *Brain, 122*, 1901–1917.

Cao, F., Bitan, T., Chou, T. L., Burman, D. D., & Booth, J. R. (2006). Deficient orthographic and phonological representations in developmental dyslexics revealed by brain activation patterns. *Journal of Child Psychology and Psychiatry, 40*(10), 1041–1050.

Church, J., Coalson, R. S., Lugar, H. M., Petersen, S. E., & Schlaggar, B. L. (2008). A developmental fMRI study of reading and repetition reveals changes in phonological and visual mechanisms over age. *Cerebral Cortex, 18*(9), 2054–2065.

Cohen, L., Dehaene, S., Naccache, L., Lehéricy, S., Dehaene-Lambertz, G., Hénaff, M.-A., & Michel, F. (2000). The visual word form area: Spatial and temporal characterization of an initial stage of reading in normal subjects and posterior split-brain patients. *Brain: A Journal of Neurology, 123*(2), 291–307.

Cornelissen, P. L., Kringelbach, M. L., Ellis, A. W., Whitney, C., Holliday, I. E., & Hansen, P. C. (2009). Activation of the left inferior frontal gyrus in the first 200 ms of reading: Evidence from magnetoencephalography (MEG). *PLoS ONE, 4*(4), e5359.

Dehaene, S. (2005). Imaging conscious and subliminal word processing. In U. Mayr, E. Awh, & S. W. Keele (Eds.), *Developing individuality in the human brain: A tribute to Michael I. Posner* (pp. 65–86). Washington, DC: American Psychological Association.

Dehaene, S., & Cohen, L. (2007). Cultural recycling of cortical maps. *Neuron, 56,* 384–398.

Dehaene, S., & Cohen, L. (2010). Neural coding of written words in the visual word form area. In P. L. Cornelissen, P. C. Hansen, M. L. Kringelbach, & K. Pugh (Eds.), *The neural basis of reading* (pp. 111–146). New York: Oxford University Press.

Dehaene-Lambertz, G., Dehaene, S., & Hertz-Pannier, L. (2002). Functional neuroimaging of speech perception in infants. *Science, 298*(5600), 2013–2015.

Dejerine, J. (1892). Contribution a l'etude anatomo-pathologique et clinique des différentes variétés de cécité verbale. *Mémoires de la Société de Biologie, 4,* 61–90.

Deutsch, G., Dougherty, R., Bammer, R., Siok, W. T., Gabrieli, J. D. E., & Wandell, B. (2005). Children's reading performance is correlated with white matter structure measured by tensor imaging. [Special issue: The neurobiology of developmental disorders.]. *Cortex, 41*(3), 354–363.

Dougherty, R. F., Ben-Shachar, M., Deutsch, G. K., Hernandez, A., Fox, G. R., & Wandell, B. A. (2007). Temporal-callosal pathway diffusivity predicts phonological skills in children. *Proceedings of the National Academy of Sciences, 104*(20), 8556–8561.

Eden, G. F., Jones, K. M., Cappell, K., Gareau, L., Wood, F. B., & Zeffiro, T. A. (2004). Neural changes following remediation in adult developmental dyslexia. *Neuron, 44*(3), 411–422.

Ellis, N. C., Natsume, M., Stavropoulou, K., Hoxhallari, L., Van Daal, V. H. P., Polyzoe, N., et al. (2004). The effects of orthographic depth on learning to read alphabetic, syllabic, and logographic scripts. *Reading Research Quarterly, 39*(4), 438–468.

Farmer, M., & Klein, R. (1995). The evidence for a temporal processing deficit linked to dyslexia: A review. *Psychonomic Bulletin & Review, 2*(4), 460–493.

Froyen, D. J. W., Bonte, M. L., van Atteveldt, N., & Blomert, L. (2009). The long road to automation: Neurocognitive development of letter-speech sound processing. *Journal of Cognitive Neuroscience, 21*(3), 567–580.

Gabrieli, J. D. E. (2009). Dyslexia: A new synergy between education and cognitive neuroscience. *Science, 325*(5938), 280–283.

Georgiewa, P., Rzanny, R., Gaser, C., Gerhard, U. J., Vieweg, U., Freesmeyer, D., et al. (2002). Phonological processing in dyslexic children: A study combining functional imaging and event related potentials. *Neuroscience Letters, 318,* 5–8.

Goswami, U., & East, M. (2000). Rhyme and analogy in beginning reading: Conceptual and methodological issues. *Applied Psycholinguistics, 21,* 63–93.

Grainger, J., & Holcomb, P. J. (2009). Watching the word go by: On the time-course of component processes in visual word recognition. *Language and Linguistics Compass, 3*(1), 128–156.

Grossi, G., Coch, D., Coffey, S., Holcomb, P. J., & Neville, H. J. (2001). Phonological processing visual rhyming: A developmental ERP study. *Journal of Cognitive Neuroscience, 13*(5), 610–625.

Guttorm, T. K., Leppänen, P. H. T., Poikkeus, A.-M., Eklund, K. M., Lyytinen, P., & Lyytinen, H. (2005). Brain event-related potentials (ERPs) measured at birth predict later language development in children with and without familial risk for dyslexia. *Cortex, 41*(3), 291–303.

Guttorm, T. K., Leppänen, P. H. T., Richardson, U., & Lyytinen, H. (2001). Event-related potentials and consonant differentiation in newborns with familial risk for dyslexia. *Journal of Learning Disabilities, 34*(6), 534–544.

Hoeft, F., Hernandez, A., McMillon, G., Taylor-Hill, H., Martindale, J. L., Meyler, A., et al. (2006). Neural basis of dyslexia: A comparison between dyslexic and nondyslexic children equated for reading ability. *Journal of Neuroscience, 26*(42), 10700–10708.

Hoeft, F., Meyler, A., Hernandez, A., Juel, C., Taylor-Hill, H., Martindale, J. L., et al. (2007). Functional and morphometric brain dissociation between dyslexia and reading ability. *Proceedings of the National Academy of Sciences, 104*(10), 4234–4239.

Hoeft, F., Ueno, T., Reiss, A. L., Meyler, A., Whitfield-Gabrieli, S., Glover, G. H., et al. (2007). Prediction of children's reading skills using behavioral, functional, and structural neuroimaging measures. *Behavioral Neuroscience, 121*(3), 602–613.

Horwitz, B., Rumsey, J. M., & Donohue, B. C. (1998). Functional connectivity of the angular gyrus in normal reading and dyslexia. *Proceedings of the National Academy of Sciences, 95,* 8939–8944.

Keller, T. A., & Just, M. A. (2009). Altering cortical connectivity: Remediation-induced changes in the white matter of poor readers. *Neuron, 64*(5), 624–631.

Klingberg, T., Hedehus, M., Temple, E., Salz, T., Gabrieli, J. D. E., Moseley, M. E., et al. (2000). Microstructure of temporo-parietal white matter as a basis for reading ability: Evidence from diffusion tensor magnetic resonance imaging. *Neuron, 25*(2), 493–500.

Kronbichler, M., Wimmer, H., Staffen, W., Hutzler, F., Mair, A., & Ladurner, G. (2008). Developmental dyslexia: Gray matter abnormalities in the occipi-totemporal cortex. *Human Brain Mapping, 29*(5), 613–625.

Lyon, G. R., Shaywitz, S. E., & Shaywitz, B. A. (2003). A definition of dyslexia. *Annals of Dyslexia, 53*(1), 1–14.

Macmillan, M. (1992). Inhibition and control of behavior: From Gall to Freud via Phineas Gage and the frontal lobes. *Brain & Cognition, 19,* 72–104.

Macmillan, M. B. (1986). A wonderful journey through skull and brains: The travels of Mr. Gage's tamping iron. *Brain & Cognition, 5,* 67–107.

Mani, J., Diehl, B., Piao, Z., Schuele, S. S., LaPresto, E., Liu, P., et al. (2008). Evidence for a basal temporal visual language center: Cortical stimulation producing pure alexia. *Neurology, 71*(20), 1621–1627.

Maurer, U., Brem, S., Bucher, K., Kranz, F., Benz, R., Steinhausen, H.-C., et al. (2007). Impaired tuning of a fast occipito-temporal response for print in dyslexic children learning to read. *Brain, 130*(12), 3200–3210.

Maurer, U., Brem, S., Kranz, F., Buchera, K., Benza, R., Haldera, P., et al. (2006). Coarse neural tuning for print peaks when children learn to read. *NeuroImage, 33*(2), 749–758.

Maurer, U., Bucher, K., Brem, S., Benz, R., Kranz, F., Schulz, E., et al. (2009). Neurophysiology in preschool improves behavioral prediction of reading ability throughout primary school. *Biological Psychiatry, 66*(4), 341–348.

Meyler, A., Keller, T. A., Cherkassky, V. L., Gabrieli, J. D., & Just, M. A. (2008). Modifying the brain activation of poor readers during sentence comprehension with extended remedial instruction: A longitudinal study of neuroplasticity. *Neuropsychologia, 46*(10), 2580–2592.

Milne, R. D., Syngeniotis, A., Jackson, G., & Corballis, M. C. (2002). Mixed lateralization of phonological assembly in developmental dyslexia. *Neurocase, 8,* 205–209.

Milner, B., Corkin, S., & Teuber, H. L. (1968). Further analysis of the hippocampal amnesic syndrome: 14-year followup study of H. M. *Neuropsychologia, 6,* 215–234.

Molfese, D. L. (2000). Predicting dyslexia at 8 years of age using neonatal brain responses. *Brain and Language, 72*(3), 238–245.

Odegard, T. N., Ring, J., Smith, S., Biggan, J., & Black, J. (2008). Differentiating the neural response to intervention in children with developmental dyslexia. *Annals of Dyslexia, 58*(1), 1–14.

Pammer, K., Hansen, P. C., Kringelbach, M. L., Holliday, I., Barnes, G., Hillebrand, A., et al. (2004). Visual word recognition: The first half second. *NeuroImage, 22*(4), 1819–1825.

Paulesu, E., Démonet, J. F., Fazio, F., McCrory, E., Chanoine, V., Brunswick, N., et al. (2001). Dyslexia: Cultural diversity and biological unity. *Science, 291*(5511), 2165–2167.

Paulesu, E., Frith, U., Snowling, M., Gallagher, A., Morton, J., Frackowiak, R. S., et al. (1996). Is developmental dyslexia a disconnection syndrome? Evidence from PET scanning. *Brain, 119,* 143–157.

Paulesu, E., McCrory, E., Fazio, F., Menoncello, L., Brunswick, N., Cappa, S. F., et al. (2000). A cultural effect on brain function. *Nature Neuroscience, 3*(1), 91–96.

Pennington, B. (2006). From single to multiple deficit models of developmental disorders. *Cognition, 101*(2), 385–413.

Petersen, S. E., Fox, P. T., Posner, M. I., Mintun, M., & Raichle, M. E. (1988). Positron emission tomographic studies of the cortical anatomy of single-word processing. *Nature, 331*(6157), 585–589.

Petersen, S. E., Fox, P. T., Snyder, A. Z., & Raichle, M. E. (1990). Activation of extrastriate and frontal cortical areas by visual words and word-like stimuli. *Science, 249*(4972), 1041–1044.

Polk, T. A., Park, J., Smith, M. R., & Park, D. C. (2007). Nature versus nurture in ventral visual cortex: A functional magnetic resonance imaging study of twins. *Journal of Neuroscience, 27*(51), 13921–13925.

Richards, T. L., & Berninger, V. W. (2008). Abnormal fMRI connectivity in children with dyslexia during a phoneme task: Before but not after treatment. *Journal of Neurolinguistics, 21*(4), 294–304.

Richards, T. L., Berninger, V. W., Aylward, E. H., Richards, A. L., Thomson, J. B., Nagy, W. E., et al. (2002). Reproducibility of Proton MR Spectroscopic Imaging (PEPSI): Comparison of dyslexic and normal-reading children and effects of treatment on brain lactate levels during language tasks. *American Journal of Neuroradiology, 23*, 1678–1685.

Rimrodt, S. L., Clements-Stephens, A. M., Pugh, K. R., Courtney, S. M., Gaur, P., Pekar, J. J., et al. (2009). Functional MRI of sentence comprehension in children with dyslexia: Beyond word recognition. *Cerebral Cortex, 19*(2), 402–413.

Ruff, S., Cardebat, D., Marie, N., & Démonet, J. F. (2002). Enhanced response of the left frontal cortex to slowed down speech in dyslexia: An fMRI study. *Neuroreport, 13*, 1285–1289.

Ruff, S., Marie, N., Celsis, P., Cardebat, D., & Démonet, J. F. (2003). Neural substrates of impaired categorical perception of phonemes in adult dyslexics: An fMRI study. *Brain and Cognition, 53*, 331–334.

Rumsey, J. M., Andreason, P., Zametkin, A. J., Aquino, T., King, A. C., Hamburger, S. D., et al. (1992). Failure to activate the left temporoparietal cortex in dyslexia: An oxygen 15 positron emission tomographic study. *Archives of Neurology, 49*(5), 527–534.

Rumsey, J. M., Horwitz, B., Donohue, B. C., Nace, K. L., Maisog, J. M., & Andreason, P. (1999). A functional lesion in developmental dyslexia: Left angular gyral blood flow predicts severity. *Brain and Language, 70*, 187–204.

Rumsey, J. M., Nace, K., Donohue, B., Wise, D., Maisog, J. M., & Andreason, P. (1997). A positron emission tomographic study of impaired word recognition and phonological processing in dyslexic men. *Archives of Neurology, 54*(5), 562–573.

Salmelin, R., Service, E., Kiesilä, P., Uutela, K., & Salonen, O. (1996). Impaired visual word processing in dyslexia revealed with magnetoencephalography. *Annals of Neurology, 40,* 157–162.

Seger, C. A., Poldrack, R. A., Prabhakaran, V., Zhao, M., Glover, G. H., & Gabrieli, J. D. (2000). Hemispheric asymmetries and individual differences in visual concept learning as measured by functional MRI. *Neuropsychologia, 38*(9), 1316–1324.

Shaywitz, B. A., Shaywitz, S. E., Blachman, B. A., Pugh, K. R., Fulbright, R. K., Skudlarski, P., et al. (2004). Development of left occipitotemporal systems for skilled reading in children after a phonologically-based intervention. *Biological Psychiatry, 55*(9), 926–933.

Shaywitz, B. A., Shaywitz, S. E., Pugh, K. R., Mencl, W. E., Fulbright, R. K., Skudlarksi, P., et al. (2002). Disruption of posterior brain systems for reading in children with developmental dyslexia. *Biological Psychiatry, 52*(2), 101–110.

Shaywitz, B. A., Skudlarski, P., Holahan, J. M., Marchione, K. E., Constable, R. T., Fulbright, R. K., et al. (2007). Age-related changes in reading systems of dyslexic children. *Annals of Neurology, 61*(4), 363–370.

Shaywitz, S. E. (1998). Dyslexia. *New England Journal of Medicine, 338*(5), 307–312.

Shaywitz, S. E., Fletcher, J. M., Holahan, J. M., Shneider, A. E., Marchione, K. E., Stuebing, K. K., et al. (1999). Persistence of dyslexia: The Connecticut Longitudinal Study at adolescence. *Pediatrics, 104*(6), 1351–1359.

Shaywitz, S. E., Mody, M., & Shaywitz, B. A. (2006). Neural mechanisms in dyslexia. *Current Directions in Psychological Science, 15,* 278–281.

Shaywitz, S. E., Shaywitz, B. A., Fulbright, R. K., Skudlarski, P., Mencl, W. E., Constable, T., et al. (2003). Neural systems for compensation and persistence: Young adult outcome of childhood reading disability. *Biological Psychiatry, 54*(1), 25–33.

Shaywitz, S. E., Shaywitz, B. A., Pugh, K. R., Fulbright, R. K., Constable, R. T., Mencl, W. E., et al. (1998). Functional disruption in the organization of the brain for reading in dyslexia. *Proceedings of the National Academy of Sciences, 95,* 2636–2641.

Simos, P. G., Breier, J. I., Fletcher, J. M., Bergman, E., & Papanicolaou, A. C. (2000). Cerebral mechanisms involved in word reading in dyslexic children: A magnetic source imaging approach. *Cerebral Cortex, 10*(8), 809–816.

Simos, P. G., Breier, J. I., Fletcher, J. M., Foorman, B. R., Bergman, E., Fishbeck, K., et al. (2000). Brain activation profiles in dyslexic children during non-word reading: A magnetic source imaging study. *Neuroscience Letters, 290,* 61–65.

Simos, P. G., Fletcher, J. M., Bergman, E., Breier, J. I., Foorman, B. R., Castillo, E. M., Davis, R. N., et al. (2002). Dyslexia-specific brain activation profile becomes normal following successful remedial training. *Neurology, 58*(8), 1203–1213.

Siok, W. T., Perfetti, C. A., Jin, Z., & Tan, L. H. (2004). Biological abnormality of impaired reading is constrained by culture. *Nature, 431*(7004), 71–76.

Stanovich, K. E. (1986). Matthew effects in reading: Some consequences of individual differences in the acquisition of literacy. *Reading Research Quarterly, 21*(4), 360–406.

Temple, E., Deutsch, G. K., Poldrack, R. A., Miller, S. L., Tallal, P., Merzenich, M., et al. (2003). Neural deficits in children with dyslexia ameliorated by behavioral remediation: Evidence from functional MRI. *Proceedings of the National Academy of Sciences, 100*(5), 2860–2865.

Temple, E., Poldrack, R. A., Salidis, J., Deutsch, G. K., Tallal, P., Merzenich, M. M., et al. (2001). Disrupted neural responses to phonological and orthographic processing in dyslexic children: An fMRI study. *Neuroreport, 12*(2), 299–307.

Turkeltaub, P. E., Gareau, L., Flowers, D. L., Zeffiro, T. A., & Eden, G. F. (2003). Development of neural mechanisms for reading. *Nature Neuroscience, 6*(7), 767–773.

Wagner, R. K., & Torgesen, J. K. (1987). The nature of phonological processing and its causal role in the acquisition of reading skills. *Psychological Bulletin, 101*(2), 192–212.

Wagner, R. K., Torgesen, J. K., & Rashotte, C. A. (1994). Development of reading-related phonological processing abilities: New evidence of bidirectional causality from a latent variable longitudinal study. *Developmental Psychology, 30*(1), 73–87.

Wolf, M., Goldberg O'Rourke, A., Gidney, C., Lovett, M., Cirino, P., & Morris, R. (2002). The second deficit: An investigation of the independence of phonological and naming-speed deficits in developmental dyslexia. *Reading and Writing, 15*(1–2), 43–72.

Ziegler, J. C., & Goswami, U. (2005). Reading acquisition, developmental dyslexia, and skilled reading across languages: A psycholinguistic grain size theory. *Psychological Bulletin, 131*(1), 3–29.

Donna Coch

Donna Coch, EdD, is an assistant professor in the Department of Education at Dartmouth College and graduate faculty in the Psychological and Brain Sciences Graduate Program at Dartmouth. She majored in cognitive science as an undergraduate at Vassar College, earned master's and doctoral degrees in human development and psychology from Harvard University Graduate School of Education, and conducted postdoctoral research at the University of Oregon Brain Development Lab.

Using a noninvasive brain wave recording technique (the recording of event-related potentials, or ERPs) in combination with standardized behavioral measures, her research focuses on what happens in the brain as children learn how to read. Undergraduate students, including students in the teacher certification program at Dartmouth, are involved in all aspects of her research. A goal of both her research and her teaching is to make meaningful connections between the fields of developmental cognitive neuroscience and education.

In this chapter, Dr. Coch discusses the complex processes involved as the young brain learns to read. She explains what neuroscience has revealed about the interaction of the visual and auditory processing systems, the development of the alphabetic principle, semantics, and comprehension. She also suggests ways this information can help parents and teachers of reading design successful learning activities.

Chapter 7

Constructing a Reading Brain

Donna Coch

Despite numerous cautions about making connections between neuroscience and education—perhaps the most often quoted being Bruer's (1997) warning of "a bridge too far"—many educators may still believe that neuroscience can tell teachers what to do in the classroom (see Goswami, 2006). I believe that expectations for neuroscience-based, easy-to-follow recipes for classroom practice are unrealistic. The power of neuroscience is not that it will provide direct instruction for teachers but that, in combination with what we know from the cognitive, developmental, and other learning sciences, neuroscience can provide a new perspective on education (see Ansari & Coch, 2006; Fischer et al., 2007). In the case of reading, neuroscience has helped to unmask the myth of the reading brain and begun to reveal the astonishing complexity of the process of constructing a brain that can read.

Contrary to popular belief, there is no "reading brain." There is no single part of the brain that "does reading," whether in the infant brain, the fluently reading college student brain, or the aging brain. Yet you are reading the words on this page; if there is no part of the brain that does reading, how is that so? Contrary to another popular belief, reading is not natural (Goodman & Goodman, 1979). The brain simply is not designed for reading, which is a relatively recent cultural invention highly valued by our education system and society. As we learn to read, we are borrowing from and building on multiple neural systems with their own specializations, actively constructing a brain that can read (Dehaene & Cohen, 2007). You are able to read the words on this page because you have, over time, painstakingly cobbled together a complex of neural systems that accomplish reading. Learning to read involves both developing each of the constituent systems and connecting those systems so that they work in concert automatically and fluently. This process does not just happen in the early elementary grades. The time course for learning to read begins well before formal schooling and extends throughout the school years (Biancarosa & Snow, 2004; Snow, Burns, & Griffin, 1998).

A lengthy developmental time course for learning to read is not surprising when we consider some of the key constituent systems of the brain that reads. These include an orthographic system, based on visual processing of text. Certainly, most children are exposed to letters and print well before they enter school—on road signs and cereal boxes as well as on paper (Burns & Snow, 1999). Constituent systems also include a phonological system, based on auditory processing of the sounds of language. Again, most children are exposed to speech well before they enter school, but language development extends well into adolescence (Nippold, 1998). Another constituent system is a semantic system, based on understanding the meanings of words. Similarly, most children know the meanings of at least a small set of words before entering formal education, and their vocabulary expands throughout the school years (Cunningham, Perry, & Stanovich, 2001; Hart & Risley, 1995). Perhaps most importantly, students must be able to comprehend what they read.

In the next sections, I take a closer look at each of these systems in turn and consider some of what we know from the neurosciences as well as the developmental and learning sciences, and how that knowledge informs and is informed by what we know from education.

Visual Processing: Orthography

The task of a reader is to make meaning of marks on a page. The orthography of a language has to do with what those marks look like—how a language is written. Learning orthography begins with recognizing the orthographic symbols of the language—in the case of English, the letters of the Roman alphabet. This in itself is a difficult task because the symbols in alphabetic languages such as English are arbitrary, abstract, and, in some cases, easily confused (Gervais, Harvey, & Roberts, 1984; Gibson, 1965). Consider, for example, the slight differences between the capitals G and C in some fonts. Children must recognize that a very small horizontal line makes all the difference. Thus, distinguishing between letters requires a highly sensitive visual system.

For the most part, perceptual processing of the visual elements that make up the letters of our alphabet occurs in the visual cortex in the occipital lobes (the most posterior part of the brain). The visual cortex is specialized for such processing, and recordings from the occipital lobes of cats indicate that even neurons in the cat visual cortex are tuned to many of the elements—lines, curves, angles, terminals, and junctions—that comprise our letters (Crair, Gillespie, & Stryker, 1998). But clearly (as far as we know, cats do not read), additional processing is required. The visual elements must be combined into meaningful groups that make up letters, and those letters must be combined into meaningful groups that make up words.

From the occipital lobes, the cortical visual processing stream divides into two. One pathway, the ventral (or "what") pathway, continues down through the temporal lobes while the other, the dorsal (or "where") pathway, continues up through the parietal lobes (Ungerleider & Mishkin, 1982). The ventral visual pathway is specialized for processing color, form, texture, pattern, and fine detail (Livingstone & Hubel, 1988). Not surprisingly, the patterns, forms, and fine detail that characterize letters and strings of letters are further processed along this visual pathway, similarly to other visual information that is characterized by pattern, form, and detail. The detailed features of letters appear to be processed simultaneously, within about 150 milliseconds of presentation (Cole & Haber, 1980; Petit, Midgley, Holcomb, & Grainger, 2006). Given that one millisecond is 1/1000th of one second, such processing is very fast and eventually highly automatic as it taps into the basic visual processing strengths of the ventral pathway. In adults, letters appear to be processed as letters, with special abstract letter identities, just a few milliseconds later within a subregion of an area called the fusiform gyrus (Flowers et al., 2004; James, James, Jobard, Wong, & Gauthier, 2005; Mitra &

Coch, 2009; Petit et al., 2006). How such specialization develops, and when, are potentially educationally relevant questions.

Another subregion within the fusiform gyrus has received much more attention in the research literature on orthography. Petersen and colleagues (Petersen, Fox, Posner, Mintun, & Raichle, 1988) first reported on this region in a positron emission tomography study comparing the processing of real words, made-up words, unpronounceable strings of letters, and strings of letter-like symbols. In this study, they noticed an area that was activated only by stimuli that were legitimately word-like (words and made-up words that followed the rules of English) and called it the visual word form area. Since this original report, others have replicated the finding of specialized processing for word-like stimuli in the visual word form area (Cohen & Dehaene, 2004; McCandliss, Cohen, & Dehaene, 2003; Price & Devlin, 2004). Interestingly, recent clinical work with an adult patient suggests that this region plays a causal role in reading because surgical removal resulted in loss of reading ability (Gaillard et al., 2006).

How does the visual word form area develop? Many researchers believe that the visual word form area becomes specialized for word processing progressively, over time, and with experience with words (McCandliss, Cohen, & Dehaene, 2003). But is the development of such specialized processing within the visual system related more to maturation and chronological age or to experience and practice (that is, education)? Maurer and colleagues have reported that a brain wave index of visual word form processing (a specific brain wave component called N1 that was more responsive to words than symbols) is absent in kindergartners, present in second graders, and continues to develop through adolescence (Brem et al., 2006; Maurer et al., 2006). Shaywitz and colleagues (Shaywitz et al., 2002) have reported that activation in the visual word form area is correlated with decoding ability even after controlling for age, strongly suggesting that experience plays the more important role.

Interestingly, for adults who are not experts at reading—adults with dyslexia, for example—there is evidence that the visual word form area is not activated during reading (Paulesu et al., 2001). The advantage of a visual word form area, lacking in beginning and dyslexic readers, is instant recognition of familiar letter patterns, also known as automaticity in processing, which frees resources for higher-level processing of the text (LaBerge & Samuels, 1974). Overall, learning to read appears to involve adapting and specializing the ventral visual stream through practice with printed words (McCandliss, Cohen, & Dehaene, 2003; Polk & Farah, 1998).

It is clear that the ventral visual pathway is a crucial component of the brain that can read, particularly in terms of orthographic processing. Can the same be said of the dorsal visual pathway, the visual processing stream that projects from the occipital lobes up through the parietal lobes? How could the "where" system be involved in reading, given that words on the page are localized and do not move through space? Although the words on the page do not move, the reader's eyes must move across the page in a complicated series of fixations (short periods during which the eyes are relatively still) and saccades (brief jumps across the text) (Rayner, Foorman, Perfetti, Pesetsky, & Seidenberg, 2001).

Not surprisingly, beginning readers have longer fixations, shorter saccades, and far more regressions (eye movements from right to left in reading English) than fluent readers (Rayner et al., 2001). Thus, carefully watching a reader's eyes as she reads might reveal something about her visual fluency with words. The dorsal stream is involved in controlling eye movements, and dorsal stream deficits have been associated with reading difficulties (Boden & Giaschi, 2007; Stein, 2001). For example, two functional magnetic resonance imaging studies have shown no or much reduced activation in dorsal stream regions in adults with dyslexia as compared to typically reading adults (Demb, Boynton, & Heeger, 1997; Eden et al., 1996).

Neuroscience studies on the development of the visual "what" and "where" streams indicate that basic visual processing systems are not yet adult-like by the age of eight (Coch, Skendzel, Grossi, & Neville, 2005). Building a brain that reads involves developing these visual systems, fostering the growth of specializations for reading within these systems, and connecting these systems to the others that, together, make reading possible. Children who are learning how to read and teachers who are teaching how to read are truly changing the brain by building multiple visual systems specialized for orthographic processing of text.

Auditory Processing: Phonology

Whereas orthography involves visual processing, phonology involves the sound system of a language. The sounds of a language are called phonemes. One of the language skills that is key to reading is phonological awareness—the understanding that spoken words come apart into smaller bits of sound, such as phonemes. For example, the spoken word *fox* is composed of four phonemes: /f/, /o/, /k/, /s/. If the four sounds in *fox* surprised you, that would be consistent with research showing that many teachers of reading are not explicitly aware of phonemes and, in order to teach children to become phonemically aware, need some retraining themselves (Stainthorp, 2003). In fact, most adults "never have analyzed language at the level required for explaining and teaching it" (Moats, 2000, p. 7).

Many teachers of reading are not explicitly aware of phonemes and, in order to teach children to become phonemically aware, need some retraining themselves.

Phonological awareness occurs at multiple levels of sound analysis. Many teachers are aware of larger chunks of sound, such as rhymes like *train* and *cane* (Stainthorp, 2003). Brain wave recording studies reveal similar neural responses to auditory rhymes in six- and seven-year-olds and adults, confirming that phonological processing systems related to rhyme develop early (Coch, Grossi, Coffey-Corina, Holcomb, & Neville, 2002; Coch, Grossi, Skendzel, & Neville, 2005). Activities that emphasize the sound structure of language, such as rhyming games, reciting nursery rhymes or poetry, or phoneme-deletion tasks (for example, saying *cat* without the /k/), help to develop phonological awareness (Adams, 1990; MacLean, Bryant, & Bradley, 1987). Developing phonological awareness is of interest because behavioral studies have shown that measures of phonological awareness are positively correlated with reading skill from preschool through high school (Adams, 1990). Furthermore, children with poor phonological awareness in the early grades are at risk not only for poor reading, but also for generally poor academic outcomes in later grades (called the "Matthew effect" in Stanovich, 1986).

At the neural level, speech appears to afford specialized processing separate from general auditory processing of other sounds, tones, and noise. The region associated with speech processing is called the superior temporal sulcus and is a folded-in part of the brain at the top of the temporal lobe (Binder, 2000). Strikingly, the results of functional magnetic resonance imaging studies with five-year-olds and even three-month-olds suggest that this region is sensitive to speech very early in the course of typical development (Ahmad, Balsamo, Sachs,

Children with poor phonological awareness in the early grades are at risk not only for poor reading, but also for generally poor academic outcomes in later grades.

Xu, & Gaillard, 2003; Dehaene-Lambertz et al., 2006). But why might such an early-developing speech processing system be important for reading? Unless a child is reading aloud, reading does not seem to be an auditory skill. However, the superior temporal region, with its specialized processing for phonology, is used in both spoken and written language processing. Many studies clearly show that silent reading involves activation of the superior temporal region (for example, Joubert et al., 2004; Simos, Breier, Wheless, et al., 2000).

Building a brain that reads involves not only using speech circuits specialized for phonological processing in the service of reading but also developing new phonological networks. In a remarkable study with literate and illiterate women, Castro-Caldas and colleagues asked the women to repeat real and made-up words while the researchers recorded brain activations using positron emission tomography (Castro-Caldas, Petersson, Reis, Stone-Elander, & Ingvar, 1998). There were no brain activation differences for real-word repetition between the literate and illiterate women, but an extensive network of activation was seen only in the literate women during repetition of made-up words. Repeating made-up words requires remembering and articulating a sequence of phonemes never heard before. Learning to read apparently develops phonological processing systems that change the way speech is analyzed and phonemes are remembered (Castro-Caldas, 2004). That is, learning to read, according to Frith (1998), affects "all speech processing, as now whole word sounds are automatically broken up into sound constituents. Language is never the same again. This is not cause for regret, since a benefit of this sort of 'brainwashing' is an improvement in memory—by keeping track of phoneme constituents, novel word sounds are remembered more accurately" (p. 1011). Thus, children who are learning how to read and teachers who are teaching how to read are truly changing the brain by building specialized phonological systems.

Connectivity: Mapping Orthography to Phonology

In combination, the visual/orthographic and auditory/phonological systems are crucial to learning to read. The two best predictors of reading achievement in early elementary school are letter identification (knowing the orthographic symbols or graphemes) and phonological awareness (knowing the sounds of the language or phonemes) (Scarborough, 2005; Treiman, 2000). These same skills often are lacking in children who struggle to develop reading ability in the early elementary grades and beyond (Adams, 1990; Snow et al., 1998; Vellutino, Fletcher, Snowling, & Scanlon, 2004). The alphabetic principle involves understanding that these two sets of knowledge map onto one another—that is, there is a connection between the letters on the page and the sounds of spoken language. Learning those mappings—the grapheme-to-phoneme correspondence rules—is learning the process of decoding words.

Learning to decode English is difficult for many students, in part because English has a "deep orthography," meaning that the mappings between letter and sound are not one to one. A famous example of this, often attributed to George Bernard Shaw, is the made-up word *ghoti*. Before reading further, think about how you would pronounce this if it were a real word. Here are some rules from English to help you: take the *gh* sound from *rough*, the *o* sound from *women*, and the *ti* sound from *caution*. I doubt that your first pronunciation of *ghoti* was "fish." These pronunciations all follow grapheme-to-phoneme correspondence rules in English, but their application in the context is incorrect. This illustrates why learning to read (and spell) in a language with a deep orthography is difficult. You might recognize these connections between orthography and phonology as the focus of the phonics method for teaching reading (Adams, 1990; Ehri et al., 2001).

There is evidence for neural specialization related to mapping orthography to phonology within multiple systems (Joubert et al., 2004; van Atteveldt, Formisano, Goebel, & Blomert, 2004). For example, Joubert and colleagues recorded brain activations using functional magnetic resonance imaging as participants silently read high-frequency words, made-up words, and low-frequency words (Joubert et al., 2004). They hypothesized that reading very familiar, high-frequency words would not require effortful phonological analysis, whereas reading made-up words and low-frequency words would require a more effortful process of assembling phoneme-to-grapheme mappings. They observed two different brain activation patterns that supported their hypothesis. Activation in a more posterior system was related to easy, familiar orthographic-to-phonological mapping, while activation in a more anterior system was related to more effortful, articulated assembly of such mappings (see also Shaywitz, Mody, & Shaywitz, 2006).

Other studies have shown greater activation in regions associated with automatic mapping in adults or older children as compared to younger children, suggesting that automatic mapping develops over time (Booth et al., 2004; Froyen, Bonte, van Atteveldt, & Blomert, 2009). Also educationally relevant, a lack of activation in the left posterior system has been related to reading disability (Pugh et al., 2001; Pugh et al., 2000; Shaywitz et al., 1998; Simos, Breier, Fletcher, Bergman, & Papanicolaou, 2000; Temple et al., 2001). Intensive phonologically based interventions focusing on letter-sound mappings have been shown both to increase activation in this system and to improve reading in children with reading disabilities (Shaywitz et al., 2004; Simos et al., 2002; Temple et al., 2001).

As noted, it is not enough to develop each of these neural systems in order to construct a brain that can read; these systems must be connected to work as an efficient system of systems that accomplishes the task of reading. There are few neuroscientific studies investigating this connectivity, but some have produced tantalizing findings. For example, Horwitz and colleagues reported that blood-flow levels within a portion of the left posterior system (specifically, the angular gyrus) were correlated with blood-flow levels in visual areas (specifically, the visual word form area) and temporal lobe regions during a reading task in fluent readers (Horwitz, Rumsey, & Donohue, 1998). These correlations suggested that these regions were working in concert, in a coordinated fashion, to perform the reading task (generally, greater blood flow is considered a marker

> Intensive phonologically based interventions focusing on letter-sound mappings can improve reading in children with reading disabilities.

of greater neural activity). In contrast, blood-flow levels in the left angular gyrus were not correlated with levels within the other regions in a comparison group of participants with dyslexia (Horwitz et al., 1998). Other findings also suggest that functional and structural disconnection among neural areas that are typically involved in reading—that is, uncoordinated processing—may be characteristic of poor reading (Cao, Bitan, & Booth, 2008; Deutsch et al., 2005; Klingberg et al., 2000; Niogi & McCandliss, 2006).

Meaning Processing: Semantics

Like orthographic and phonological knowledge, building knowledge about words and their meanings begins well before children enter school. By age three, 86 to 98 percent of a child's vocabulary consists of words in his or her caregivers' vocabulary (Hart & Risley, 1995). Children who grow up in low-income households in which they are not spoken to extensively and are not exposed to a variety of words begin school with many fewer words than their peers from higher-income households in which speech to children is more frequent (Hart & Risley, 1995, 1999). In these classic studies, children in professional families heard about eleven million words per year while children in families receiving welfare heard just three million, and this vocabulary gap remained in follow-up studies years later (Hart & Risley, 1995).

Recently, the weaker language skills of children growing up in low-income households have been related to a pattern of reduced neural specialization, both functionally and structurally (Hackman & Farah, 2009; Noble, Wolmetz, Ochs, Farah, & McCandliss, 2006; Raizada, Richards, Meltzoff, & Kuhl, 2008). Taking time to teach children vocabulary in the preschool years establishes a base on which to build when the children enter school. Without that foundational vocabulary, which often is assumed in curricula and instruction, children are at risk for both reading and school failure.

That spoken-vocabulary knowledge, sometimes called the lexicon, allows children to make meaning when they begin reading. In decoding the word *dog*, a child might sound out the three phonemes /d/ /o/ /g/. If there is no entry in the mental lexicon that maps onto that string of phonemes, the child might be considered a decoder but not a reader.

However, if the child has heard that word before, sounding out the string of phonemes mapped to those letters will activate the lexical entry for *dog*, and all of the information that the child knows about *dog* (four legs, furry, wags tail,

> Time spent reading is the best predictor of vocabulary knowledge after about third grade.

Fido . . .) will become available to make sense of what the child is reading. By the third grade, there is a shift from spoken to written language as the source of most new entries in the lexicon. In fact, time spent reading is the best predictor of vocabulary knowledge after about third grade (Adams, 1990; Nippold, 1998). Obviously this does not mean that parents and teachers should stop talking to their children after the third grade. But the vocabulary available in print is critical to children's further development of an elaborated, dense lexicon. Not incidentally, this lexicon appears to be *the* lexicon, as spoken and written words are processed for meaning in the same brain regions (Barsalou, 2008; Booth et al., 2002).

How is lexical information stored in the brain? Some data from studies of patients with brain damage have suggested that specific categories of semantic information (for example, tools, famous people, animals) are stored in different regions, primarily within the temporal lobe (Damasio, Grabowski, Tranel, Hichwa, & Damasio, 1996; Shallice, 1988). Other data have suggested that semantic information is distributed throughout the brain (Binder et al., 2003; Goldberg, Perfetti, & Schneider, 2006; Martin & Chao, 2001). For example, what we know about a word such as *telephone* includes action-oriented, kinesthetic, tactile, visual, auditory, and orthographic and phonological elements (Allport, 1985; Thompson-Schill, 2003). In the distributed view, it is likely that regions of the brain that are typically activated by picking up a telephone (action), the feel of a telephone in one's hand (touch), what a telephone looks like (vision), and so forth are partly reactivated when reading the word *telephone* as part of what readers know about the word (Goldberg et al., 2006; Mitchell et al., 2008). Although these studies have not focused on instructional strategies, it is not difficult to speculate about how such findings might be translated into the world of vocabulary instruction and development in terms of multisensory approaches and deep knowledge of words well beyond dictionary definitions (Birsh, 2005).

In addition to being distributed throughout the brain, vocabulary knowledge appears to be organized into semantic networks—that is, words conceptually related to one another are linked (Bower, 1970; Collins & Loftus, 1975; Goldberg et al., 2006). The richer your vocabulary, the richer your semantic networks, the more connections you can make among lexical items, and the fuller your understanding of what you are reading (Cunningham & Stanovich, 1998). This is true even for children who have difficulty reading. In a fascinating study, highly successful adults with dyslexia who still struggled with reading reported having read deeply in an area of passionate interest as children (Fink, 1995/1996), speculatively building a dense semantic network related to that topic that helped to ease and motivate further reading on that topic. Thus, word-level vocabulary knowledge has consequences for comprehension (Perfetti, 2007).

Vocabulary and conceptual knowledge are also organized in terms of schemata (Anderson & Pearson, 1984). For example, if you were reading a paragraph that began, "When Mary arrived at the restaurant," reading the word *restaurant* might prime your restaurant schema—your knowledge of what happens in a restaurant, including what words typically go with *restaurant* in your semantic network (Anderson et al., 1985). Without reading further into the paragraph, you might predict (either consciously or unconsciously) that words such as *table, menu, eat, waiter, meal, main course, bill,* and *paid* would appear in the rest of the text. When those words do occur in the text as you continue reading, making meaning will be faster and easier. The predictable texts used by advocates of the whole-language approach often make use of such schemata and the repetitive experiences that help to build schemata.

Accessing a schema when reading might be considered an instance of using context to boost understanding while reading. Stanovich (1993/1994) has shown that poor readers tend to depend heavily on context to figure out the meaning of unknown words. If readers have not developed dense semantic networks and rich schemata, their strategies for determining meaning are limited. Brain research has shown that the effects of context, even in fluently reading adults, are fast and powerful (Kutas & Hillyard, 1980; Nieuwland & van Berkum, 2006). In a classic study, Kutas and Hillyard (1980) presented adults with meaningful (for example, *He spread the warm bread with butter.*) and senseless (*He spread the warm bread with socks.*) sentences. They recorded brain waves at the final words in the sentences and found that words that did not make sense in the context elicited a specific response within only 400 milliseconds of presentation; that is, the brain determined the nonsensical nature of the misfit words within less than half of one second. Remarkably, a similar study showed that the brains of children as young as seven years old respond to semantic anomalies in the same way (Holcomb, Coffey, & Neville, 1992). Overall, building a brain that reads involves building an efficient, elaborated semantic system in the service of reading.

Making Sense of It All: Comprehension

Decoding and developing vocabulary may be necessary but are not sufficient prerequisites and correlates to comprehension (Best, Floyd, & McNamara, 2008). The goal and purpose of reading are to make meaningful connections with the text. In this view, reading is active, interactive, and thoughtful—a dynamic transaction between reader and text in which both process and product matter (Kintsch, 1988; Perfetti, Van Dyke, & Hart, 2001; Rapp & van den Broek, 2005). It is through this interaction between text and reader that comprehension develops. The critical, inferential abilities that support comprehension, such as using prior knowledge (tapping into the semantic network and schemata), generating and answering questions, imaging, predicting, clarifying, and summarizing, have been documented in the education literature. Often they need to be modeled and explicitly taught, although many curricula do not include these components (Biancarosa & Snow, 2004; Dewitz, Jones, & Leahy, 2009; Keene & Zimmerman, 2007). Deficits in these skills can be observed in middle and high school students (Biancarosa & Snow, 2004), but there is no need to wait until middle school to start building a brain that can comprehend text (Snow, Griffin, & Burns, 2005). Indeed, developing comprehension skills can begin even before children enter school. For example, consider the method of reading picture books with prereaders known as dialogic reading (Arnold, Lonigan, Whitehurst, & Epstein, 1994; Whitehurst et al., 1998). In dialogic reading, "rather than simply reading the text, the adult provides models of language, asks the child questions, provides the child with feedback, and elicits increasingly sophisticated descriptions from the child" (Arnold et al., 1994, p. 236). Asking questions, providing feedback to clarify and summarize, describing based on current and prior knowledge, and interacting with the text are all skills that are critical to comprehension in reading. Modeling and developing these skills—and the systems in the brain that undergird comprehension—is possible throughout the preschool and school years.

Comprehension involves a complex set of processes characterized by many skills and individual differences (Cutting, Eason, Young, & Alberstadt, 2009). Thus, what we call comprehension is difficult to investigate using standardized tests (Cutting & Scarborough, 2006) or brain-imaging technologies. Despite this complexity, one finding from one neuroimaging study seems particularly relevant to teachers of reading. This was a positron emission tomography study in which adult participants were asked to read passages that they could not comprehend and then were given a context clue that allowed for comprehension when they reread the passages (Maguire, Frith, & Morris, 1999). Numerous regions in the brain were more active during reading with comprehension than without comprehension, including a region called the medial ventral orbitofrontal cortex (the middle, lower part of the frontal cortex just behind the eyes). Other studies have shown that processing within this region is part of a reward network (Krawczyk, 2002). Speculatively and wonderfully, it appears that reading with comprehension is a rewarding experience.

A New Science of Reading

Particularly if you are a parent or teacher, I hope that this chapter has given you a new—or renewed—appreciation for the remarkable plasticity and complexity of the brain that can read. A number of systems need to be developed and connected. Practice and experience—that is, education—must focus on all of these systems in order to create a brain that can read (see also Berninger & Richards, 2002; Schlaggar & McCandliss, 2007). From this dynamic complexity, it follows that there are a number of ways that a child might have difficulty with reading (Spear-Swerling, 2004). Understanding how the system is put together should help us to understand the ways in which the system might break down. Although these breakdowns have not been the focus of this chapter, they are a pressing educational concern, as national statistics indicate that slightly fewer than one-third of both fourth graders and eighth graders are reading proficiently (Lee, Grigg, & Donahue, 2007).

I have focused on some of the key components of the brain that can read but have neglected others (for example, morphology, syntax, and fluency) because of space limitations. Even so, it is clear that to really understand the brain that can read and to use that understanding in developing brains that can read requires expert knowledge from multiple perspectives and fields. Evidence-based practice demands both understanding of and critical thinking about the evidence. Particularly in terms of assessment and intervention, educators must understand and consider strengths and weaknesses across a number of reading subskills and systems, in addition to educational opportunity (Vellutino et al., 2004). In this sense, teaching reading really *is* rocket science (Moats, 1999). Indeed, we are in a new era for the science of reading, a science that draws from multiple disciplines in order to understand the complexity of reading and put that understanding to good use in our classrooms—a science that is not often taught in schools of education (Ansari & Coch, 2006; Lyon & Chhabra, 2004; McCandliss, Kalchman, & Bryant, 2003; McCardle & Chhabra, 2004; Snowling & Hulme, 2005; Walsh, Glaser, & Wilcox, 2006).

The neuroscience studies reviewed in this chapter have not provided a recipe for practice or a prescription for a certain curriculum. However, I hope that they have encouraged you to think about developing reading in new and different ways. Just as comprehension involves a transaction between reader and text, using neuroscientific findings in education requires meaningful transactions between neuroscientists and educators, labs and classrooms (Ansari & Coch, 2006; Fischer et al., 2007; McCandliss, Kalchman, et al., 2003). I hope that this chapter has demonstrated some of the promise of a mind, brain, and education perspective on constructing a brain that can read, especially for those of you who work with children learning to read.

> We are in a new era for the science of reading—a science that is not often taught in schools of education.

References

Adams, M. J. (1990). *Beginning to read: Thinking and learning about print.* Cambridge, MA: MIT Press.

Ahmad, Z., Balsamo, L. M., Sachs, B. C., Xu, B., & Gaillard, W. D. (2003). Auditory comprehension of language in young children. *Neurology, 60*(10), 1598–1605.

Allport, D. A. (1985). Distributed memory, modular systems, and dysphasia. In S. K. Newman & R. Epstein (Eds.), *Current perspectives in dysphasia* (pp. 32–60). Edinburgh, United Kingdom: Churchill Livingstone.

Anderson, R. C., Hiebert, E. H., Scott, J. A., Wilkinson, I. A. G., & Commission on Reading. (1985). *Becoming a nation of readers: The report of the Commission on Reading.* Champaign: University of Illinois.

Anderson, R. C., & Pearson, P. D. (1984). A schema-theoretic view of basic processes in reading comprehension. In P. D. Pearson, R. Barr, M. L. Kamil, & P. B. Mosenthal (Eds.), *Handbook of reading research* (pp. 255–291). Cambridge: Cambridge University Press.

Ansari, D., & Coch, D. (2006). Bridges over troubled waters: Education and cognitive neuroscience. *Trends in Cognitive Sciences, 10*(4), 146–151.

Arnold, D. H., Lonigan, C. J., Whitehurst, G. J., & Epstein, J. N. (1994). Accelerating language development through picture book reading: Replication and extension to a videotape training format. *Journal of Educational Psychology, 86*(2), 235–243.

Barsalou, L. W. (2008). Cognitive and neural contributions to understanding the conceptual system. *Current Directions in Psychological Science, 17*(2), 91–95.

Berninger, V. W., & Richards, T. L. (2002). *Brain literacy for educators and psychologists.* Boston: Academic Press.

Best, R. M., Floyd, R. G., & McNamara, D. S. (2008). Differential competencies contributing to children's comprehension of narrative and expository texts. *Reading Psychology, 29*(2), 137–164.

Biancarosa, G., & Snow, C. (2004). *Reading next: A vision for action and research in middle and high school literacy—A report to the Carnegie Corporation of New York.* Washington, DC: Alliance for Excellent Education.

Binder, J. (2000). The new neuroanatomy of speech perception. *Brain, 123*(12), 2371–2372.

Binder, J. R., McKiernan, K. A., Parsons, M. E., Westbury, C. F., Possing, E. T., Kaufman, J. N., et al. (2003). Neural correlates of lexical access during visual word recognition. *Journal of Cognitive Neuroscience, 15*(3), 372–393.

Birsh, J. R. (Ed.). (2005). *Multisensory teaching of basic language skills* (2nd ed.). Baltimore: Paul H. Brookes.

Boden, C., & Giaschi, D. (2007). M-stream deficits and reading-related visual processes in developmental dyslexia. *Psychological Bulletin, 133*(2), 346–366.

Booth, J. R., Burman, D. D., Meyer, J. R., Gitelman, D. R., Parrish, T. B., & Mesulam, M. M. (2002). Modality independence of word comprehension. *Human Brain Mapping, 16*(4), 251–261.

Booth, J. R., Burman, D. D., Meyer, J. R., Gitelman, D. R., Parrish, T. B., & Mesulam, M. M. (2004). Development of brain mechanisms for processing orthographic and phonologic representations. *Journal of Cognitive Neuroscience, 16*(7), 1234–1249.

Bower, G. H. (1970). Organizational factors in memory. *Cognitive Psychology, 1*(1), 18–46.

Brem, S., Bucher, K., Halder, P., Summers, P., Dietrich, T., Martin, E., et al. (2006). Evidence for developmental changes in the visual word processing network beyond adolescence. *NeuroImage, 29*(3), 822–837.

Bruer, J. T. (1997). Education and the brain: A bridge too far. *Educational Researcher, 26*(8), 4–16.

Burns, M. S., & Snow, C. E. (Eds.). (1999). *Starting out right: A guide to promoting children's reading success.* Washington, DC: National Academies Press.

Cao, F., Bitan, T., & Booth, J. R. (2008). Effective brain connectivity in children with reading difficulties during phonological processing. *Brain and Language, 107*(2), 91–101.

Castro-Caldas, A. (2004). Targeting regions of interest for the study of the illiterate brain. *International Journal of Psychology, 39*(1), 5–17.

Castro-Caldas, A., Petersson, K. M., Reis, A., Stone-Elander, S., & Ingvar, M. (1998). The illiterate brain: Learning to read and write during childhood influences the functional organization of the adult brain. *Brain, 121*(6), 1053–1063.

Coch, D., Grossi, G., Coffey-Corina, S., Holcomb, P. J., & Neville, H. J. (2002). A developmental investigation of ERP auditory rhyming effects. *Developmental Science, 5*(4), 467–489.

Coch, D., Grossi, G., Skendzel, W., & Neville, H. (2005). ERP nonword rhyming effects in children and adults. *Journal of Cognitive Neuroscience, 17*(1), 168–182.

Coch, D., Skendzel, W., Grossi, G., & Neville, H. J. (2005). Motion and color processing in school-age children and adults: An ERP study. *Developmental Science, 8*(4), 372–386.

Cohen, L., & Dehaene, S. (2004). Specialization within the ventral stream: The case for the visual word form area. *NeuroImage, 22*(1), 466–476.

Cole, R. A., & Haber, R. N. (1980). Reaction time to letter name or letter case. *Acta Psychologica, 44*(3), 281–285.

Collins, A. M., & Loftus, E. F. (1975). A spreading-activation theory of semantic processing. *Psychological Review, 82*(6), 407–428.

Crair, M. C., Gillespie, D. C., & Stryker, M. P. (1998). The role of visual experience in the development of columns in the cat visual cortex. *Science, 279*(5350), 566–570.

Cunningham, A. E., Perry, K. E., & Stanovich, K. E. (2001). Converging evidence for the concept of orthographic processing. *Reading and Writing, 14*(5–6), 549–568.

Cunningham, A. E., & Stanovich, K. E. (1998). What reading does for the mind. *American Educator, 22*(1–2), 8–15.

Cutting, L. E., Eason, S. H., Young, K. M., & Alberstadt, A. L. (2009). Reading comprehension: Cognition and neuroimaging. In K. Pugh & P. McCardle (Eds.), *How children learn to read: Current issues and new directions in the integration of cognition, neurobiology, and genetics of reading and dyslexia research and practice* (pp. 195–213). New York: Psychology Press.

Cutting, L. E., & Scarborough, H. S. (2006). Prediction of reading comprehension: Relative contributions of word recognition, language proficiency, and other cognitive skills can depend on how comprehension is measured. *Scientific Studies of Reading, 10*(3), 277–299.

Damasio, H., Grabowski, T. J., Tranel, D., Hichwa, R. D., & Damasio, A. R. (1996). A neural basis for lexical retrieval. *Nature, 380,* 499–505.

Dehaene, S., & Cohen, L. (2007). Cultural recycling of cortical maps. *Neuron, 56*(2), 384–398.

Dehaene-Lambertz, G., Hertz-Pannier, L., Dubois, J., Mériaux, S., Roche, A., Sigman, M., et al. (2006). Functional organization of perisylvian activation during presentation of sentences in preverbal infants. *Proceedings of the National Academy of Sciences, 103*(38), 14240–14245.

Demb, J. B., Boynton, G. M., & Heeger, D. J. (1997). Brain activity in visual cortex predicts individual differences in reading performance. *Proceedings of the National Academy of Sciences, 94*(24), 13363–13366.

Deutsch, G. K., Dougherty, R. F., Bammer, R., Siok, W. T., Gabrieli, J. D. E., & Wandell, B. A. (2005). Children's reading performance is correlated with white matter structure measured by diffusion tensor imaging. *Cortex, 41*(3), 354–363.

Dewitz, P., Jones, J., & Leahy, S. (2009). Comprehension strategy instruction in core reading programs. *Reading Research Quarterly, 44*(2), 102–126.

Eden, G. F., VanMeter, J. W., Rumsey, J. M., Maisog, J. M., Woods, R. P., & Zeffiro, T. A. (1996). Abnormal processing of visual motion in dyslexia revealed by functional brain imaging. *Nature, 382,* 66–69.

Ehri, L., Nunes, S. R., Willows, D. M., Schuster, B. V., Yaghoub-Zadeh, Z., & Shanahan, T. (2001). Phonemic awareness instruction helps children learn to read: Evidence from the National Reading Panel's meta-analysis. *Reading Research Quarterly, 36*(3), 250–287.

Fink, R. P. (1995/1996). Successful dyslexics: A constructivist study of passionate interest reading. *Journal of Adolescent & Adult Literacy, 39*(4), 268–280.

Fischer, K. W., Daniel, D. B., Immordino-Yang, M. H., Stern, E., Battro, A., & Koizumi, H. (2007). Why mind, brain, and education? Why now? *Mind, Brain, and Education, 1*(1), 1–2.

Flowers, D. L., Jones, K., Noble, K., VanMeter, J., Zeffiro, T. A., Wood, F. B., et al. (2004). Attention to single letters activates left extrastriate cortex. *NeuroImage, 21*(3), 829–839.

Frith, U. (1998). Literally changing the brain. *Brain, 121*(6), 1011–1012.

Froyen, D. J. W., Bonte, M. L., van Atteveldt, N., & Blomert, L. (2009). The long road to automation: Neurocognitive development of letter-speech sound processing. *Journal of Cognitive Neuroscience, 21*(3), 567–580.

Gaillard, R., Naccache, L., Pinel, P., Clémenceau, S., Volle, E., Hasboun, D., et al. (2006). Direct intracranial, fMRI, and lesion evidence for the causal role of left inferotemporal cortex in reading. *Neuron, 50*(2), 191–204.

Gervais, M. J., Harvey, L. O., & Roberts, J. O. (1984). Identification confusions among letters of the alphabet. *Journal of Experimental Psychology: Human Perception and Performance, 10*(5), 655–666.

Gibson, E. J. (1965). Learning to read. *Science, 148*(3673), 1066–1072.

Goldberg, R. F., Perfetti, C. A., & Schneider, W. (2006). Distinct and common cortical activations for multimodal semantic categories. *Cognitive, Affective, & Behavioral Neuroscience, 6*(3), 214–222.

Goodman, K. S., & Goodman, Y. M. (1979). Learning to read is natural. In L. B. Resnick & P. A. Weaver (Eds.), *Theory and practice of early reading* (Vol. 1, pp. 137–154). Hillsdale, NJ: Erlbaum.

Goswami, U. (2006). Neuroscience and education: From research to practice? *Nature Reviews Neuroscience, 7,* 406–413.

Hackman, D. A., & Farah, M. J. (2009). Socioeconomic status of the developing brain. *Trends in Cognitive Sciences, 13*(2), 65–73.

Hart, B., & Risley, T. R. (1995). *Meaningful differences in the everyday experience of young American children.* Baltimore: Paul H. Brookes.

Hart, B., & Risley, T. R. (1999). *The social world of children learning to talk.* Baltimore: Paul H. Brookes.

Holcomb, P. J., Coffey, S. A., & Neville, H. J. (1992). Visual and auditory sentence processing: A developmental analysis using event-related brain potentials. *Developmental Neuropsychology, 8*(2&3), 203–241.

Horwitz, B., Rumsey, J. M., & Donohue, B. C. (1998). Functional connectivity of the angular gyrus in normal reading and dyslexia. *Proceedings of the National Academy of Sciences, 95*(15), 8939–8944.

James, K. H., James, T. W., Jobard, G., Wong, A. C.-N., & Gauthier, I. (2005). Letter processing in the visual system: Different activation patterns for single letters and strings. *Cognitive, Affective, & Behavioral Neuroscience, 5*(4), 452–466.

Joubert, S., Beauregard, M., Walter, N., Bourgouin, P., Beaudoin, G., Leroux, J.-M., et al. (2004). Neural correlates of lexical and sublexical processes in reading. *Brain and Language, 89*(1), 9–20.

Keene, E. O., & Zimmerman, S. (2007). *Mosaic of thought: The power of comprehension strategy instruction* (2nd ed.). Portsmouth, NH: Heinemann.

Kintsch, W. (1988). The role of knowledge in discourse comprehension: A construction-integration model. *Psychological Review, 95*(2), 163–182.

Klingberg, T., Hedehus, M., Temple, E., Salz, T., Gabrieli, J. D. E., Moseley, M. E., et al. (2000). Microstructure of temporo-parietal white matter as a basis for reading ability: Evidence from diffusion tensor magnetic resonance imaging. *Neuron, 25*(2), 493–500.

Krawczyk, D. C. (2002). Contributions of the prefrontal cortex to the neural basis of human decision making. *Neuroscience and Biobehavioral Reviews, 26*(6), 631–664.

Kutas, M., & Hillyard, S. A. (1980). Reading senseless sentences: Brain potentials reflect semantic incongruity. *Science, 207*(4427), 203–204.

LaBerge, D., & Samuels, S. J. (1974). Toward a theory of automatic information processing in reading. *Cognitive Psychology, 6*(2), 293–323.

Lee, J., Grigg, W. S., & Donahue, P. L. (2007). *The nation's report card: Reading 2007* (No. NCES 2007496). Washington, DC: U.S. Department of Education, Institute of Education Sciences, National Center for Education Statistics, National Assessment of Educational Progress.

Livingstone, M., & Hubel, D. (1988). Segregation of form, color, movement, and depth: Anatomy, physiology, and perception. *Science, 240*(4853), 740–749.

Lyon, G. R., & Chhabra, V. (2004). The science of reading research. *Educational Leadership, 61*(6), 13–17.

MacLean, M., Bryant, P., & Bradley, L. (1987). Rhymes, nursery rhymes, and reading in early childhood. *Merrill-Palmer Quarterly, 33*(3), 255–281.

Maguire, E. A., Frith, C. D., & Morris, R. G. M. (1999). The functional neuroanatomy of comprehension and memory: The importance of prior knowledge. *Brain, 122*(10), 1839–1850.

Martin, A., & Chao, L. L. (2001). Semantic memory and the brain: Structure and processes. *Current Opinion in Neurobiology, 11*(2), 194–201.

Maurer, U., Brem, S., Kranz, F., Bucher, K., Benz, R., Halder, P., et al. (2006). Coarse neural tuning for print peaks when children learn to read. *NeuroImage, 33*(2), 749–758.

McCandliss, B. D., Cohen, L., & Dehaene, S. (2003). The visual word form area: Expertise for reading in the fusiform gyrus. *Trends in Cognitive Sciences, 7*(7), 293–299.

McCandliss, B. D., Kalchman, M., & Bryant, P. (2003). Design experiments and laboratory approaches to learning: Steps toward collaborative exchange. *Educational Researcher, 32*(1), 14–16.

McCardle, P., & Chhabra, V. (Eds.). (2004). *The voice of evidence in reading research*. Baltimore: Paul H. Brookes.

Mitchell, T. M., Shinkareva, S. V., Carlson, A., Chang, K.-M., Malave, V. L., Mason, R. A., et al. (2008). Predicting human brain activity associated with the meanings of nouns. *Science, 320*(5880), 1191–1195.

Mitra, P., & Coch, D. (2009). A masked priming ERP study of letter processing using single letters and false fonts. *Cognitive, Affective, & Behavioral Neuroscience, 9*(2), 216–228.

Moats, L. C. (1999). *Teaching reading is rocket science: What expert teachers of reading should know and be able to do* (No. 372). Washington, DC: American Federation of Teachers.

Moats, L. C. (2000). *Speech to print: Language essentials for teachers.* Baltimore: Paul H. Brookes.

Nieuwland, M. S., & van Berkum, J. J. A. (2006). When peanuts fall in love: N400 evidence for the power of discourse. *Journal of Cognitive Neuroscience, 18*(7), 1098–1111.

Niogi, S. N., & McCandliss, B. (2006). Left lateralized white matter microstructure accounts for individual differences in reading ability and disability. *Neuropsychologia, 44*(11), 2178–2188.

Nippold, M. A. (1998). *Later language development: The school-age and adolescent years* (2nd ed.). Austin, TX: Pro-Ed.

Noble, K. G., Wolmetz, M. E., Ochs, L. G., Farah, M. J., & McCandliss, B. D. (2006). Brain-behavior relationships in reading acquisition are modulated by socioeconomic factors. *Developmental Science, 9*(6), 642–654.

Paulesu, E., Démonet, J.-F., Fazio, F., McCrory, E., Chanoine, V., Brunswick, N., et al. (2001). Dyslexia: Cultural diversity and biological unity. *Science, 291*(5511), 2165–2167.

Perfetti, C. A. (2007). Reading ability: Lexical quality to comprehension. *Scientific Studies of Reading, 11*(4), 357–383.

Perfetti, C. A., Van Dyke, J., & Hart, L. (2001). The psycholinguistics of basic literacy. *Annual Review of Applied Linguistics, 21,* 127–149.

Petersen, S. E., Fox, P. T., Posner, M. I., Mintun, M., & Raichle, M. E. (1988). Positron emission tomographic studies of the cortical anatomy of single-word processing. *Nature, 331,* 585–589.

Petit, J.-P., Midgley, K. J., Holcomb, P. J., & Grainger, J. (2006). On the time course of letter perception: A masked priming ERP investigation. *Psychonomic Bulletin & Review, 13*(4), 674–681.

Polk, T. A., & Farah, M. J. (1998). The neural development and organization of letter recognition: Evidence from functional neuroimaging, computational modeling, and behavioral studies. *Proceedings of the National Academy of Sciences, 95*(3), 847–852.

Price, C. J., & Devlin, J. T. (2004). The pro and cons of labelling a left occipito-temporal region: "The visual word form area." *NeuroImage, 22*(1), 477–479.

Pugh, K. R., Mencl, W. E., Jenner, A. R., Lee, J. R., Katz, L., Frost, S. J., et al. (2001). Neuroimaging studies of reading development and reading disability. *Learning Disabilities Research & Practice, 16*(4), 240–249.

Pugh, K. R., Mencl, W. E., Shaywitz, B. A., Shaywitz, S. E., Fulbright, R. K., Constable, R. T., et al. (2000). The angular gyrus in developmental dyslexia:

Task-specific differences in functional connectivity within posterior cortex. *Psychological Science, 11*(1), 51–56.

Raizada, R. D. S., Richards, T. L., Meltzoff, A., & Kuhl, P. K. (2008). Socioeconomic status predicts hemispheric specialisation of the left inferior frontal gyrus in young children. *NeuroImage, 40*(3), 1392–1401.

Rapp, D. N., & van den Broek, P. (2005). Dynamic text comprehension: An integrative view of reading. *Current Directions in Psychological Science, 14*(5), 276–279.

Rayner, K., Foorman, B. R., Perfetti, C. A., Pesetsky, D., & Seidenberg, M. S. (2001). How psychological science informs the teaching of reading. *Psychological Science in the Public Interest, 2*(2), 31–74.

Scarborough, H. S. (2005). Developmental relationships between language and reading: Reconciling a beautiful hypothesis with some ugly facts. In H. W. Catts & A. G. Kamhi (Eds.), *The connections between language and reading disabilities* (pp. 3–24). Mahwah, NJ: Lawrence Erlbaum.

Schlaggar, B. L., & McCandliss, B. D. (2007). Development of neural systems for reading. *Annual Review of Neuroscience, 30*, 475–503.

Shallice, T. (1988). Specialisation within the semantic system. *Cognitive Neuropsychology, 5*(1), 133–142.

Shaywitz, B. A., Shaywitz, S. E., Blachman, B. A., Pugh, K. R., Fulbright, R. K., Skudlarski, P., et al. (2004). Development of left occipitotemporal systems for skilled reading in children after a phonologically-based intervention. *Biological Psychiatry, 55*(9), 926–933.

Shaywitz, B. A., Shaywitz, S. E., Pugh, K. R., Mencl, E., Fulbright, R. K., Skudlarski, P., et al. (2002). Disruption of posterior brain systems for reading in children with developmental dyslexia. *Biological Psychiatry, 52*(2), 101–110.

Shaywitz, S. E., Mody, M., & Shaywitz, B. A. (2006). Neural mechanisms in dyslexia. *Current Directions in Psychological Science, 15*(6), 278–281.

Shaywitz, S. E., Shaywitz, B. A., Pugh, K. R., Fulbright, R. K., Constable, R. T., Mencl, W. E., et al. (1998). Functional disruption in the organization of the brain for reading in dyslexia. *Proceedings of the National Academy of Sciences, 95*(5), 2636–2641.

Simos, P. G., Breier, J. I., Fletcher, J. M., Bergman, E., & Papanicolaou, A. C. (2000). Cerebral mechanisms involved in word reading in dyslexic children: A magnetic source imaging approach. *Cerebral Cortex, 10*(8), 809–816.

Simos, P. G., Breier, J. I., Wheless, J. W., Maggio, W. W., Fletcher, J. M., Castillo, E. M., et al. (2000). Brain mechanisms for reading: The role of the superior temporal gyrus in word and pseudoword naming. *NeuroReport, 11*(11), 2443–2447.

Simos, P. G., Fletcher, J. M., Bergman, E., Breier, J. I., Foorman, B. R., Castillo, E. M., et al. (2002). Dyslexia-specific brain activation profile becomes normal following successful remedial training. *Neurology, 58*(8), 1203–1213.

Snow, C. E., Burns, M. S., & Griffin, P. (Eds.). (1998). *Preventing reading difficulties in young children*. Washington, DC: National Academies Press.

Snow, C. E., Griffin, P., & Burns, M. S. (Eds.). (2005). *Knowledge to support the teaching of reading*. San Francisco: Jossey-Bass.

Snowling, M. J., & Hulme, C. (Eds.). (2005). *The science of reading: A handbook*. Malden, MA: Blackwell Publishing.

Spear-Swerling, L. (2004). A road map for understanding reading disability and other reading problems: Origins, prevention, and intervention. In R. B. Ruddell & N. J. Unrau (Eds.), *Theoretical models of processes of reading* (5th ed., pp. 517–573). Newark, DE: International Reading Association.

Stainthorp, R. (2003, March). Use it or lose it. *Literacy Today, 34,* 16–17.

Stanovich, K. E. (1986). Matthew effects in reading: Some consequences of individual differences in the acquisition of literacy. *Reading Research Quarterly, 21*(4), 360–407.

Stanovich, K. E. (1993/1994). Romance and reality. *The Reading Teacher, 47*(4), 280–291.

Stein, J. (2001). The neurobiology of reading difficulties. In M. Wolf (Ed.), *Dyslexia, fluency, and the brain* (pp. 3–21). Timonium, MD: York Press.

Temple, E., Deutsch, G. K., Poldrack, R. A., Miller, S. L., Tallal, P., Merzenich, M. M., et al. (2003). Neural deficits in children with dyslexia ameliorated by behavioral remediation: Evidence from functional MRI. *Proceedings of the National Academy of Sciences, 100*(5), 2860–2865.

Thompson-Schill, S. L. (2003). Neuroimaging studies of semantic memory: Inferring "how" from "where." *Neuropsychologia, 41*(3), 280–292.

Treiman, R. (2000). The foundations of literacy. *Current Directions in Psychological Science, 9*(3), 89–92.

Ungerleider, L. G., & Mishkin, M. (1982). Two cortical visual systems. In D. Ingle, M. Goodale, & R. Monsfield (Eds.), *Analysis of visual behavior* (pp. 549–586). Cambridge, MA: MIT Press.

van Atteveldt, N., Formisano, E., Goebel, R., & Blomert, L. (2004). Integration of letters and speech sounds in the human brain. *Neuron, 43*(2), 271–282.

Vellutino, F. R., Fletcher, J. M., Snowling, M., & Scanlon, D. M. (2004). Specific reading disability (dyslexia): What have we learned in the past four decades? *Journal of Child Psychology and Psychiatry, 45*(1), 2–40.

Walsh, K., Glaser, D., & Wilcox, D. D. (2006). *What education schools aren't teaching about reading—and what elementary teachers aren't learning.* Washington, DC: National Council on Teacher Quality.

Whitehurst, G. J., Falco, F. L., Lonigan, C. J., Fischel, J. E., DeBaryshe, B. D., Valdez-Menchaca, M. C., et al. (1998). Accelerating language development through picture book reading. *Developmental Psychology, 24*(4), 552–559.

Keith Devlin

Keith Devlin, PhD, is a cofounder and Executive Director of Stanford University's H-STAR institute, a cofounder of the Stanford Media X research network, and Senior Researcher at the university's Center for the Study of Language and Information. He is a World Economic Forum Fellow and a Fellow of the American Association for the Advancement of Science. His current research is focused on the use of different media to teach and communicate mathematics to diverse audiences. He also works on the design of information/reasoning systems for intelligence analysis.

Dr. Devlin's other research interests include theory of information, models of reasoning, applications of mathematical techniques in the study of communication, and mathematical cognition. He has written twenty-eight books and over eighty published research articles. He is the recipient of the Pythagoras Prize, the Peano Prize, the Carl Sagan Award, and the Joint Policy Board for Mathematics Communications Award. In 2003, he was recognized by the California State Assembly for his "innovative work and longtime service in the field of mathematics and its relation to logic and linguistics." He is "the Math Guy" on National Public Radio.

In this chapter, Dr. Devlin discusses what we know to date about how the young brain uses innate number sense to learn to process numbers and eventually become efficient at arithmetic operations. He suggests that the brain's strength as a pattern-seeker accounts for many of the difficulties people have with basic arithmetic operations. The mental processes required for algebra and beyond are also examined, and he offers some proposals to educators on instructional approaches in mathematics based on recent neuroscience research.

Chapter 8

The Mathematical Brain

Keith Devlin

Mathematics teachers—at all education levels—face two significant obstacles:

1. We know almost nothing about how people do mathematics.

2. We know almost nothing about how people learn how to do mathematics.

Even professional mathematicians, who spend most waking hours of every day thinking about mathematics, are not aware of what is going on in their minds when they solve a problem. One minute the problem seems intractable, the next everything has miraculously fallen into place and the answer seems obvious. Never again will they truly understand why they had been unable to see it earlier. It follows that mathematics teaching remains largely an art—with good teachers relying heavily on tradition, instinct, experience, and "received wisdom" gained from other teachers—rather than a practice based on established scientific theory and evidence.

This situation is somewhat reminiscent of the state of medicine in the nineteenth century. It remains to be seen whether our understanding of the human brain and the human mind will develop to a point that the field of education reaches a level comparable to today's medical practice. Cognitive neuroscience and cognitive psychology, the equivalents of the chemistry, biology, and physiology on which modern medicine is based, are still relatively young disciplines. In the meantime, we have to rely on hypotheses and speculative theories based on what little we do know about how the brain works—or more precisely, how the mind works, because our knowledge of brain function is actually fairly significant. However, it is important not to confuse hypotheses and speculative theories with guesses. We may not yet have firm conclusions based on hard evidence, but we know a lot more than we did just a few decades ago.

What We Know

The greatest advances in our understanding of mathematical ability have undoubtedly been in the acquisition of the whole number concept and its arithmetic. Starting with Karen Wynn's breakthrough discoveries at MIT in the early 1990s (Wynn, 1992) and continuing with work of Stanislas Dehaene (Dehaene, 1997), Brian Butterworth (Butterworth, 1999), and others, we have learned that:

- The brain of humans and some other species has a "number sense," a seemingly analog sense of relative sizes of collections.

- The brain of humans and some other species has a capacity to form a concept of (discrete) whole number.

- The brain of humans and some other species can distinguish a correct answer from an incorrect one when presented with a scenario involving arithmetic of small whole numbers (1, 2, and 3).

- Numbers and arithmetic beyond 3 require the use of language.

> The greatest advances in our understanding of mathematical ability have been in the acquisition of whole number concept and its arithmetic.

Studies using fMRI indicate that these number capacities appear to be localized in (or at least depend on) particular brain areas. Moreover, damage to certain regions of the brain can impair or destroy any sense of number, leaving other capacities intact, such as language or logical reasoning.

Number Sense

The number sense exhibits what is often referred to as a *logarithmic* nature, in that the speed and accuracy with which a subject can distinguish the larger of two collections (or two numerals in the case of human adults) diminishes as the size of the two collections increases relative to their difference. For example, selecting the larger of two collections of five and eight objects is faster and more accurate than for two collections of nineteen and twenty-two, even though the difference in each case is three.

Small Numbers

Human babies as young as two days after birth exhibit an innate knowledge of the basic arithmetic facts: $1 + 1 = 2$, $1 + 2 = 3$, $1 - 1 = 0$, $2 - 1 = 1$, $3 - 1 = 2$, $3 - 2 = 1$, $2 - 2 = 0$, $3 - 3 = 0$. The general strategy for testing this capacity is, first, to present the subject with a visual depiction of objects being added to and taken away from a collection in such a way that the final outcome is initially hidden from the subject's view and, second, to measure the surprise the subject exhibits when the outcome is revealed. (Hiding the final step allows for manipulation of the result unseen by the subject.) The surprise response can be measured by eye dilation, facial expression, and body reaction captured on video, or by the sucking reflex on a nipple attached by a transponder to a computer.

> Human babies as young as two days after birth exhibit an innate knowledge of basic arithmetic facts.

A child subject will exhibit greater surprise when presented with a wrong answer, such as $1 + 2 = 2$, as opposed to the correct answer of $1 + 2 = 3$. In the first series of such experiments, Karen Wynn (1992) showed her young subjects puppets being put onto and taken from a small puppet theater. The subject first saw the stage empty and then a screen was raised in front of the stage, behind which puppets were visibly introduced and removed. Variations of this procedure eliminated any possibility that the subject's reactions were based on anything other than number.

Beyond 3

The innate precision shown for addition and subtraction for whole numbers up to and including 3 does not extend to greater numbers. Arithmetic ability beyond 3 seems to involve language (at least the ability to assign symbolic names to objects and to carry out binary symbolic reasoning) and requires training.

In particular, mental storage of numbers and access to them appears to be by way of the symbolic names used during the initial learning process. If so, this has two significant implications for learning arithmetic:

1. Children being taught mathematics in a language other than the one in which they first learned the basic number facts (in particular, number names and the multiplication tables) are likely to be at a disadvantage.

2. Asian children enjoy a considerable advantage over their counterparts growing up in the West. The basic number words in Chinese, Japanese, and Korean are a single syllable and combine in a way parallel to the symbolic rules of the decimal number system. For example, 21 would be expressed as "two-ten-one." In English, French, Spanish, and other Western languages, the naming system is more complex, with the need to master special words each time a multiple of ten is reached—eleven, twelve, thirteen, twenty, thirty, and so on—and in some languages special constructions, such as "quatre vingt trois" (literally "four-twenty and three") for 83 in French (see Dehaene, 1997).

Implications for Teaching

To summarize, the picture of arithmetic learning that seems to emerge from the research is that:

1. Humans are born with an innate number sense, accurate in the range 1 to 3, increasingly less accurate and of a more analog nature beyond three.

2. With training, humans can make use of their language capacity to handle with precision numbers beyond 3—indeed, well beyond.

Mathematics educators sometimes disagree as to the most effective way to provide the training referred to in the second item. The disagreement arises from the fact that learning about numbers and how to do arithmetic involves both bottom-up and top-down components. Both of these are required and must mesh in order for successful learning to take place.

First, we have an innate number sense on which we build our formal number concept (bottom-up), and yet we have to use language to impose precision and generate numbers (top-down). Second, the basic operations of arithmetic—addition, subtraction, multiplication, and division—correspond to things we witness and experience in the world and to activities we do in the world (such as combining collections of objects together, scaling, sharing out, and so forth). Thus, arithmetic can be seen to build on our experience of the world—a bottom-up process. But in order to perform the calculations required to reach precise answers about those activities in the world, we have to use symbolic procedures (algorithms) invented by humans—a top-down process.

The familiar system we use to write numbers, using the ten digits 0, 1, 2, . . . , 9, and the algorithms we use to perform basic arithmetic calculations with numbers so written, is known as the Hindu-Arabic decimal number system. It was developed in India during the first six or seven centuries CE and refined by Arabic-speaking scholars before finding its way into Western Europe in the 13th century. It is neither innate nor naturally occurring; it is a human invention and is built on several essentially arbitrary conventions. It became the dominant system, replacing several others, because of its simplicity and efficiency.

Arguably the greatest drawback of the Hindu-Arabic system is that it takes a considerable effort to learn it before you can use it efficiently. First, you have to learn how to read and write numbers in the decimal place-value system. Then you have to commit to memory

> The greatest drawback to our system of numbers is that it takes considerable effort to learn it before you can use it efficiently.

several basic number facts, most notably the multiplication tables. Then you have to learn the algorithms used to compute.

Some of the controversy surrounding mathematics education involves the need for rote learning. At one extreme are those who argue that mathematics education should focus entirely on conceptual understanding, and that there is no place for rote learning. At the other extreme are those who say that mathematics education should concentrate on rote learning the basic number facts and practice repeatedly the procedures—an approach often referred to by proponents as "drill and skill" and by opponents as "drill and kill." The evidence suggests that the best (and in my view the only viable) approach lies somewhere in between these extremes.

Neuroscience has shown us that learning involves the creation or strengthening of various neural pathways in the brain, and that this is achieved by repetition. In fact, as far as we know, repetition is the only way the brain can learn (Deacon, 1997). This understanding provides strong support for those who argue that basic arithmetic education must include rote learning. Without rote learning, no one would ever learn the multiplication tables. On the other hand, numerous studies have shown that rote learning alone produces a narrow and brittle form of knowledge, whereby the individual can reproduce—or recite—what has been learned (and thus can pass the test) but does not necessarily understand the new information and is unable to make practical use of it.

> To produce applicable knowledge and generate useful skills, rote learning must be accompanied by understanding.

To produce applicable knowledge and generate useful skills, rote learning must be accompanied by understanding. Note: *accompanied* by understanding, not replaced by it. Mathematics is an activity—you do it. Like driving a car or skiing, it depends on mastery of basic skills. The necessary understanding needs to be in addition to, indeed coupled with, rote learning. Neither can succeed without the other.

Learning Basic Number Facts

Because of the way the brain works and the way it creates and handles numbers through language, learning the multiplication tables is essentially a linguistic task, not a mathematical one. Even today, more than fifty-five years after I "learned my tables," I still recall the product of any two single-digit numbers by reciting that entry in the table in my head. I remember the sound of the number words spoken, not the numbers themselves. Indeed, I believe the pattern I hear in my head is *precisely* the one I learned when I was seven years old!

Understanding how we handle numbers can explain why, despite many hours of practice, most people encounter great difficulty with the multiplication tables. Ordinary adults of average intelligence make mistakes roughly 10 percent of the time. Some multiplications, such as 8 × 7 or 9 × 7, can take up to two seconds, and the error rate goes up to 25 percent. (Common wrong answers are 8 × 7 = 54 and 9 × 7 = 64.)

Why do we have such difficulty? Discounting the times tables for 1 and 10 as presenting no difficulty, the entire collection of multiplication tables amounts to only sixty-four separate facts (each one of 2, 3, 4, . . . , 9 multiplied by each one of 2, 3, 4, . . . , 9). Most people have little problem with the times tables for 2 or 5. Further discounting those tables leaves only thirty-six single-digit multiplications that take some effort to memorize. In fact, because you can swap the order in multiplication (4 × 7 is the same as 7 × 4), the real total is only half of that, or eighteen.

To put that figure of eighteen simple facts in perspective, consider that by the age of six, a typical American child will have learned to use and recognize between 13,000 and 15,000 words. An American adult has a comprehension vocabulary of about 100,000 words and makes active and fluent use of 10,000 to 15,000. Then there are all the other things we remember: people's names, phone numbers, addresses, book titles, movie titles, and so forth. Moreover, we learn these facts with hardly any difficulty. We certainly don't have to recite words and their meanings over and over the way we do our multiplication tables. In short, most of the time there is nothing wrong with our memories. Not so when it comes to the eighteen key facts of multiplication. Why?

The Brain as Pattern-Seeker

The human mind is a pattern recognizer. Human memory works by association—one thought leads to another. The ability to see patterns and similarities is one of the greatest strengths of the human mind. This is very different from the way a digital computer works. Computers are good at precise storage and retrieval of information and exact calculation. A modern computer can perform billions of multiplications in a single second, getting each one right. But despite an enormous investment in money, talent, and time over fifty years, attempts to develop computers that can recognize faces or indeed make much sense at all of a visual scene have largely failed. Humans, on the other hand, recognize faces and scenes with ease, because human memory works by pattern association. For the same reason, however, we can't do some things that computers do with ease, including remembering multiplication tables.

The reason we have such trouble is that we remember the tables linguistically, and as a result, many of the different entries interfere with one another. A computer is so dumb that it treats $7 \times 8 = 56$, $6 \times 9 = 54$, and $8 \times 8 = 64$ as distinct from each other. But the human mind sees similarities between these three multiplications, particularly linguistic similarities in the rhythm of the words when we recite them aloud. Our difficulty in trying to keep these three equations separate does not indicate a weakness of our memory but of one of its major strengths—its ability to see similarities. When we see the pattern 7×8, it activates several other patterns, among which are likely to be 48, 56, 54, 45, and 64.

Stanislas Dehaene makes this point brilliantly in *The Number Sense* (Dehaene, 1997) with the following example. Suppose you had to remember the following three names and addresses:

- Charlie David lives on Albert Bruno Avenue.
- Charlie George lives on Bruno Albert Avenue.
- George Ernie lives on Charlie Ernie Avenue.

Remembering just these three facts looks like quite a challenge. There are too many similarities, and as a result, each entry interferes with the others. But these are just entries from the multiplication tables. Let the names Albert, Bruno, Charlie, David, Ernie, Fred, and George stand for the digits 1, 2, 3, 4, 5, 6, and 7, respectively, and replace the phrase "lives on" by the equals sign, and you get these multiplications:

- $3 \times 4 = 12$
- $3 \times 7 = 21$
- $7 \times 5 = 35$

It's the pattern interference that causes our problems.

Pattern interference is also the reason why it takes longer to realize that 2 × 3 = 5 is false than to realize that 2 × 3 = 7 is wrong. The
former equation is correct for addition (2 + 3 = 5), and so the pattern
"2 and 3 make 5" is familiar to us. There is no familiar pattern of
the form "2 and 3 make 7." We see this kind of pattern interference
in the learning process of young children. By the age of seven, most
children know by heart many additions of two digits. But as they start
to learn their multiplication tables, the time it takes them to answer
a single-digit addition sum increases, and they start to make errors,
such as 2 + 3 = 6.

Linguistic pattern similarities also interfere with retrieval from
the multiplication table when we are asked for 5 × 6 and answer 36
or 56. Somehow, reading the 5 and the 6 brings to mind both incorrect
answers. People do not make errors such as 2 × 3 = 23 or 3 × 7 = 37.
Because the numbers 23 and 37 do not appear in any multiplication
table, our associative memory does not bring them up in the context
of multiplication. But 36 and 56 are both in the table, so when our
brain sees 5 × 6, both numbers are activated. In other words, much
of our difficulty with multiplication comes from two of the most
powerful and useful features of the human mind: pattern recognition
and associative memory.

To put it another way, millions of years
of evolution have equipped us with a brain
that has particular survival skills. Part of that
endowment is that our minds are very good at
recognizing patterns, seeing connections, and
making rapid judgments and inferences. All of
these modes of thinking are essentially "fuzzy."
Our brains are not at all suited to the kinds of
precise manipulations of information that arise in arithmetic—they
did not evolve to do arithmetic. To do arithmetic, we have to marshal
mental circuits that developed (or were selected during evolution)
for quite different reasons. It's like using the edge of a small coin to
turn a screw. Sure, you can do it, but it's slow, and the outcome is not
always perfect.

> Much of our difficulty
> with multiplication comes
> from two of the most
> powerful and useful
> features of the human
> mind: pattern recognition
> and associative memory.

How Our Brains Store and Access Numbers

We learn the multiplication tables by using our ability to remember patterns of sound. So great is the effort required to learn the tables (because of the interference effects) that people who learn a second language generally continue to do arithmetic in their first language. No matter how fluent they become in their second language (and many people reach the stage of thinking entirely in whichever language they are conversing in), it's easier to slip back into their first language to calculate and then translate the result back to the second language than to try to relearn the multiplication table in the second language. This idea formed the basis of an ingenious experiment that Dehaene and his colleagues performed in 1999 to confirm that we use our language faculty to do arithmetic.

The hypothesis they set out to establish was this: that arithmetical tasks that require an exact answer depend on our linguistic faculty. In particular, such tasks use the verbal representations of numbers, whereas tasks that involve estimation or require an approximate answer do not make use of the language faculty. To test this hypothesis, the researchers assembled a group of English-Russian bilinguals and taught them some new two-digit addition facts in one of the two languages. The subjects were then tested in one of the two languages. For questions that required an exact answer, when both the instruction and the question were in the same language, subjects answered in 2.5 to 4.5 seconds but took a full second longer when the languages were different. The experimenters concluded that the subjects used the extra second to translate the question into the language in which the facts had been learned. However, when the question asked for an approximate answer, the language of questioning did not affect the response time.

The researchers also monitored the subjects' brain activity throughout the testing process. When the subjects were answering questions that asked for approximate answers, the greatest brain activity was in the two parietal lobes—the regions that house number sense and support spatial reasoning. Questions requiring an exact answer, however, elicited far more activity in the frontal lobe, where speech is controlled.

Algebra

Beginning with algebra, most mathematics beyond arithmetic presents the human mind with an additional challenge: abstraction. The basic building blocks of arithmetic, numbers, are abstractions, but abstractions that are tied closely to concrete things in the world in which we live. We count things, measure things, buy things, make things, use the telephone, go to the bank, check the baseball scores, and so on. With algebra, however, the level of abstraction is greater.

Algebraic thinking is not just arithmetic with letters standing for numbers. It is a different kind of thinking. Algebra is thinking logically about numbers rather than computing with numbers. Those x's and y's usually denote numbers in general, not particular numbers. In algebra, we use analytic, *qualitative* reasoning *about* numbers, whereas in arithmetic we use numerical, *quantitative* reasoning *with* numbers.

> Algebra is thinking logically about numbers; arithmetic is computing with numbers.

For example, you need to use algebra if you want to write a macro to calculate the cells in a spreadsheet such as with Microsoft Excel. It doesn't matter whether the spreadsheet is for calculating scores in a sporting competition, keeping track of your finances, running a business, or figuring out the best way to equip your character in World of Warcraft. You need to think algebraically, rather than arithmetically, to set up the spreadsheet to do what you want.

When students start to learn algebra, they inevitably try to solve problems by thinking arithmetically. That's a natural thing to do, given all the effort they have put into mastering arithmetic. And at first, when the algebra problems they meet are particularly simple (that's the teacher's classification), this approach works. In fact, the stronger a student is at arithmetic, the further he or she can progress in algebra using arithmetical thinking. (Many students can solve the quadratic equation $x^2 = 2x + 15$ using basic arithmetic rather than algebra.) Paradoxically, or so it may seem, those better students may thus find it harder to learn algebra. To do algebra, for all but the most basic examples, students must stop thinking arithmetically and learn to think algebraically.

For most students, algebra is their first encounter with the kind of thinking that is typical of modern mathematics—precise, logical, analytical thinking about pure abstractions. Although experienced mathematicians find such thinking "natural," that is a result of training and practice. The brain does not find such thinking at all natural. It has to be learned, and the only known way to do so is top-down, by first learning the rules and allowing meaning and understanding to emerge in due course—as it will, because of the way the human brain seeks meaning and understanding in everything it experiences.

This does not mean that teachers should not try to provide rationales and explanations for those rules. But the real understanding can come only after students have practiced and mastered the rules. Like the training wheels used to help small children learn to ride a bicycle, the explanations teachers provide to students learning abstract mathematics are there primarily to maintain the learner's confidence. Indeed, leaving aside the psychological aspect, there is some evidence that they actually hinder the learning process! A notorious example (within arithmetic) is the common practice among U.S. and British mathematics teachers to introduce multiplication of whole numbers as repeated addition. This practice can cause the students problems throughout the remainder of their mathematical education, and often throughout their adult lives. To cite just one of many studies that have highlighted the problems that result from this approach, see Park & Nunes, 2001.

A number of studies in the United States and elsewhere, plus an entire curriculum developed and studied in the Soviet Union by the mathematics educator Vasily Davydov in the second half of the 20th century, suggest that a top-down approach to teaching mathematics is always better in the long run (see Davydov, 1975a, 1975b; Schmittau, 2004). What these studies indicate is that the most efficient way to teach mathematics is to begin by exposing students to issues that will in due course provide examples of a new concept or method, give the students time to explore those examples with guidance, and then teach the new mathematical ideas in a purely abstract, formal, rule-based fashion. Only afterward should teachers show how the issues explored earlier provide examples of what has just been learned formally. This of course is a systematic approach to the need to merge bottom-up and top-down thinking, which advances in our understanding of the brain have indicated is required to learn mathematics. (There is some controversy about aspects of these curricula, but the overall need for a combination of top-down and bottom-up approaches that they embody is generally accepted.)

Beyond Algebra

When we go from arithmetic to higher mathematics, our understanding of the learning process becomes even less grounded in scientific certainty. To date I am aware of only two attempts to provide scientific theses about the way we learn and do mathematics. Lakoff and Nunez (2000) provide a cognitive science–based theory for the way we learn and understand new mathematics. My own book, *The Math Gene* (Devlin, 2000), uses the technique of rational reconstruction to provide an evolutionary account of our acquisition of mathematical ability.

The Lakoff and Nunez theory is based on the idea of a cognitive metaphor: the individual learning some new mathematics does so by constructing—perhaps unconsciously—an interpretive mapping to the new information from what is already known. Although this thesis is not without problems, at a very basic brain level something like this must be going on.

In my theory, I show how mathematical ability is an amalgam of nine basic capacities that our ancestors acquired through natural selection over hundreds of thousands of years:

1. Number sense

2. Numerical ability

3. Spatial-reasoning ability

4. A sense of cause and effect

5. The ability to construct and follow a causal chain of facts or events

6. Algorithmic ability

7. The ability to handle abstraction

8. Logical-reasoning ability

9. Relational-reasoning ability

All of these nine capacities were in place by about 75,000 years ago, many much earlier than that. I argue that the key capacity, the ability to handle abstraction, is equivalent to having language.

Implications for Teaching

Both theories have implications for how mathematics should be taught. However, although some corroborative evidence has been obtained for each theory, further work is required before they can be viewed as in any way definitive. What is of value now is to keep asking the questions that lay behind both of those investigations:

- How did the human brain acquire the capacity to do mathematics?

- Given a physical brain that is a product of natural selection in the environment of our ancestors, just how can it do mathematics?

What makes the first question particularly intriguing is that mathematics is at most a few thousand years old, which is a mere eye-blink on the timescale of evolution. Thus, the capacity for doing mathematics must have been in place long before the brain started to do mathematics.

The brain's capacity for doing mathematics must have been in place long before it started to do mathematics.

The two questions point to the key issue in learning mathematics: the brain must be able to master new abstractions and to reason at new levels of abstraction. What little evidence there is suggests that this can be done only by a combination of a bottom-up process of reflection about what is already known (meaning giving rise to new rules) and a top-down process of gaining familiarity with formal rules (rules giving rise to new meanings). Different learners seem to fall at different points on a spectrum between these two extremes and so require different forms of teaching.

References

Butterworth, B. (1999). *The mathematical brain*. Basingstoke, United Kingdom: Macmillan.

Davydov, V. V. (1975a). Logical and psychological problems of elementary mathematics as an academic subject. In L. P. Steffe (Ed.), *Children's capacity for learning mathematics: Soviet studies in the psychology of learning and teaching mathematics* (Vol. 7, pp. 55–107). Chicago: University of Chicago Press.

Davydov, V. V. (1975b). The psychological characteristics of the "prenumerical" period of mathematics instruction. In L. P. Steffe (Ed.), *Children's capacity for learning mathematics: Soviet studies in the psychology of learning and teaching mathematics* (Vol. 7, pp. 109–205). Chicago: University of Chicago Press.

Deacon, T. (1997). *The symbolic species: The co-evolution of language and the brain*. London: Allen Lane.

Dehaene, S. (1997). *The number sense: How the mind creates mathematics*. New York: Oxford University Press.

Devlin, K. (2000). *The math gene: How mathematical thinking evolved and why numbers are like gossip*. New York: Basic Books.

Lakoff, G., & Nunez, R. (2000). *Where mathematics comes from: How the embodied mind brings mathematics into being*. New York: Basic Books.

Park, J.-H., & Nunes, T. (2001, July–September). The development of the concept of multiplication. *Cognitive Development, 16,* 763–773.

Schmittau, J. (2004). Vygotskian theory and mathematics education: Resolving the conceptual-procedural dichotomy. *European Journal of Psychology of Education, 19*(1), 19–43.

Wynn, K. (1992). Addition and subtraction by human infants. *Nature, 358,* 749–750.

Stanislas Dehaene

Stanislas Dehaene, PhD, was initially trained in mathematics at the École Normale Supérieure before receiving his doctorate in cognitive psychology at the École des Hautes Études en Sciences Sociales, under the direction of psycholinguist Jacques Mehler. He simultaneously developed neuronal models of cognitive functions with molecular neurobiologist Jean-Pierre Changeux. After a postdoctoral stay with Michael Posner at the University of Oregon, he oriented his interests toward cognitive neuroscience of human abilities, using neuroimaging methods.

His current research investigates the neural bases of human cognitive functions such as reading, calculation, and language, with a particular interest for the differences between conscious and unconscious processing. Since 2005, he teaches at the Collège de France, where he holds the chair of Experimental Cognitive Psychology. He also directs the INSERM-CEA Cognitive Neuroimaging Unit at NeuroSpin in Saclay, just south of Paris—France's advanced neuroimaging research center.

In this chapter, Dr. Dehaene discusses our innate ability to approximate number and how children display this ability at a very early age. He explains how neuroimaging has helped us to understand the three networks our brain uses to evaluate the number of a set of objects. For educators, he suggests ways this information can be used to help students learn arithmetic and mathematics.

Chapter 9

The Calculating Brain

Stanislas Dehaene

Among the three big R's of our school education—reading, 'riting, and 'rithmetic—the knowledge of mathematics is perhaps the most complex. Calculation is easy to test, but what does it mean to master the concept of "number"? When can a child be said to "grasp" a mathematical notion? And do scientific studies help in understanding how mathematics should be taught?

In recent years, child psychology and neuroscience have finally begun to shed light on the nature of one of the most elementary components of mathematical knowledge, the concept of number, and how it develops with school experience. This understanding, while still fragmentary, has many implications for teaching. We can begin to understand some of the determinants that make some children thrive in arithmetic while others strain. Above all, we can propose some practical remediation tools that, when used early, have a significant impact on children with dyscalculia or other difficulties in elementary mathematics.

Are We Born Without Number?

Piaget's influential research, summarized in *The Child's Conception of Number* (Piaget, 1952), initially suggested that preschoolers do not have any stable, invariant representation of number and that knowledge of arithmetic emerges slowly as a logical construction. Piaget's experiments seemed to provide a solid empirical foundation for the conclusion that young children initially lack any understanding of arithmetic. His best known finding is the failure of "number conservation" in children before the age of four or five. Before that age, children do not appear to understand that number is a property of sets that remains stable across various changes. To test number conservation, Piaget would show a child two equally spaced rows of, say, six vases and six flowers in one-to-one correspondence. When asked, the child would readily say that the rows had "the same number." However, when Piaget spread the row of flowers so that it appeared longer than the row of vases, the child would answer that there were more flowers than vases. The child did not seem to realize that moving the objects around left their number unchanged; in Piagetian terminology, he did not "conserve number."

In Piaget's work, even when children succeeded at number conservation at a later age, around seven, they still failed on other logical mathematical tests. For instance, if shown six roses and two tulips, and asked, "Are there more roses or more flowers?" most of them responded that the roses were more numerous than the flowers. It appeared as though they ignored some of the most basic premises of set theory—namely, that any proper subset cannot have more elements than the full set.

According to Piaget's theory, mathematical knowledge is a slow construction. Infants start in life without any concept of objects, sets, cardinal numbers, addition, or subtraction. Each of those ideas, Piaget proposed, was a conquest of the child's logical mind, as he or she progressively abstracted away from sensorimotor interactions with a structured environment and identified increasingly refined logical rules underlying them.

Piaget's constructivism remains quite popular among teachers, and there is no doubt that some of mathematics involves a slow induction process (although its cerebral basis remains unknown). However, Piaget's starting point was wrong. Children do not start life without any mathematical concepts. Further research demonstrates that several of Piaget's tests were biased because they involved a sophisticated verbal dialogue that simply was beyond the child's age. Furthermore, the tests often misled children by requiring inhibition of a prepotent response (for example, having to respond that two rows had the same number of objects even though one row was physically much longer than the other). Thus, the children probably failed because they were lacking the required higher-level executive and inhibition skills—but not necessarily the relevant concepts. Indeed, when simpler nonverbal tests were used, even two- or three-year-olds succeeded in number conservation (for review, see Dehaene, 1997). For instance, when the rows of objects were replaced by rows of M&M candies and the children were allowed to reach for one of the two rows, they were no longer fooled by changes in row length but reached for the larger number—suggesting that even a two-year-old might understand the constancy of number in the face of irrelevant changes.

Even Infants Understand Number

In the 1970s, Rochel Gelman and Randy Gallistel's work, summarized in *The Child's Understanding of Number* (1978), played an instrumental role in overturning the Piagetian view. Gelman and Gallistel showed that even preschoolers had intuitions in arithmetic. During simple "magic shows," in which, say, a plate holding two objects suddenly lost one of them without any apparent cause, the preschoolers readily reacted to these unexpected changes by showing surprise.

Indeed, the surprise response turned out to be extremely useful in moving towards experiments with even younger children, including infants in the first year of life. At that age, surprise can be quantified empirically by measuring how long an infant looks at a display. If infants find a display novel or unexpected, they react by looking longer at it. With this simple test, even few-month-olds could show numerical skills. A large set of behavioral studies using habituation and violation-of-expectancy paradigms have now revealed a clear sensitivity to numbers in infants. For instance, six-month-old infants discriminate when the numerosity of a set unexpectedly changes from eight to sixteen dots or vice versa (Xu & Spelke, 2000). In these experiments, a variety of experimental controls ensured that the discrimination was not based on nonnumerical

Even six-month-old infants can discriminate when the numerosity of a set unexpectedly changes.

parameters such as object size, density, or total surface—only sensitivity to number explains the findings.

In other experiments, infants even detected violations of approximate addition and subtraction events. For instance, on seeing five objects being hidden behind a screen, then another five objects being added, they expected ten objects and reacted with surprise when the screen collapsed to reveal only five objects (McCrink & Wynn, 2004).

A Foundational Concept: Approximate Number

The key variable that allows infants to succeed in such tests is the ratio of the expected and unexpected numbers. The ratio has to be large enough—for instance, eight versus sixteen objects—for infants to notice that something is wrong and that the quantity has changed or is unexpected. Six-month-old infants require a 2:1 ratio, while a few months later, at the age of nine months, a 1.5:1 ratio suffices (for example, eight versus twelve). Thus, and crucially, these experiments reveal an understanding of only approximate number in infants.

The precision of this system is initially quite coarse, but it improves during childhood until it reaches the adult level of about 15 percent accuracy—meaning that, as adults, we can distinguish numbers such as twelve versus fourteen or 100 versus 115 without counting. Refined precision of the approximate number system seems to play an essential role in numerical development. When measured in teenagers, numerical estimation accuracy predicts how well children will perform on standard tests of mathematical achievement (Halberda, Mazzocco, & Feigenson, 2008). Children with lifelong difficulties in learning arithmetic, in the absence of other sensory or cognitive impairment, show a drastically impaired precision of the approximate number system. For example, at age ten, they discriminate numbers only at the level of an average four-year-old child (Piazza et al., in press).

These observations support a simple hypothesis: the approximate number system lays the foundation for subsequent construction of higher-level arithmetical concepts (Dehaene, 1997). We all start in life with a foundational ability to estimate the numerical quantity of objects in a set, and to combine such approximate numbers through simple operations of addition, subtraction, and comparison. These foundational abilities are, in fact, inherited from our evolution. During our evolutionary past, the ability to quantify all sorts of sets (of food items, friends, foes, and so on) was useful to our survival. This ability is also demonstrably present in several other animal species, from dolphins to rats, pigeons, lions, and monkeys. For example, without any training, wild lions that encounter another group of lions readily evaluate the size of the group (the number of potential opponents), and decide whether to attack or to retreat by comparing these two numbers.

One proof that the approximate number system grants children an early intuition of number that is essential to their later school-based understanding of arithmetic comes from a study of preschoolers. Gilmore, McCarthy, and Spelke (2007) gave five- and six-year-olds problems such as, "Sarah has twenty-one candies, and she gets thirty more. John has thirty-four candies. Who has more?" The preschoolers had never received instruction with numbers of that size nor with concepts of addition or subtraction. Nevertheless, they spontaneously performed much better than chance (60 to 75 percent) in these complex arithmetic tests, regardless of their socioeconomic origins. Performance was approximate and depended on the ratio of the two numbers, a clear signature of reliance on the approximate number system. Importantly, variability in performance among the children was predictive of their achievement in the school's curriculum. Thus, the ability to approximate gives children an "intuition" for problems they have never experienced before and therefore a head start in arithmetic.

Even as adults, we continue to rely on the approximate number system for various arithmetic tasks that involve a quick evaluation or "number sense." For example, when we decide which of two Arabic numerals is larger, our speed and even our errors depend on the distance between the numbers. We are faster to compare, say, 31 with 65 than 59 with 65. When we check an arithmetic operation, such as 24 + 13 = 97, we can quickly tell that it is false without calculating, as long as the degree of falsehood is easily detected by simple approximation. And when we evaluate prices, our

> The innate ability to approximate gives children an intuition for problems they have never experienced before and therefore a head start in arithmetic.

judgments are also approximate and based on percentages. In short, the approximate number system is essential whenever we call on our fast intuition of numerical size.

A Brain System for Approximate Number

Since 2000, scientists have made considerable progress in understanding the brain systems that support the foundational approximate number system. Thanks to brain imaging techniques, a crucial area for number sense has been identified. It lies in the top back of both hemispheres, within the parietal lobe, in a cortical fissure called the intraparietal sulcus. One reason that this region is viewed as crucial is that it is active whenever we think of a number, whether spoken or written, as a word or as an Arabic digit, or even when we merely inspect a set of objects and think about its cardinality. It also activates regardless of the task that we have to perform with the number: addition, subtraction, multiplication, or comparison. Merely looking at an Arabic numeral or a set of objects suffices to trigger it. Figure 9.1 shows where the intraparietal sulcus is in humans and in monkeys. In humans, this region systematically activates whenever we calculate (top left). As we shall see next, the same region in the monkey contains neurons tuned to number (top right), and disorganization in its neighborhood can cause dyscalculia in adults and children (bottom).

Another reason to think that the intraparietal region is central to number processing is that the intensity of the activation is directly related to the difficulty of the arithmetic task at hand. For example, by making the numbers larger, we can increase the difficulty of addition, subtraction, or multiplication problems—and the activation of the intraparietal region also thereby increases. Similarly, by bringing two numbers closer together, such as 59 and 61, we can make it harder for participants to decide which is the larger, and again the intraparietal activation increases in direct relation to response times. The intraparietal region can even activate to a *subliminal* number, one that is presented so fast that it is not even seen by the participants. Thus, this brain region seems to provide us with an unconscious evaluation of number size that underlies our spontaneous ability to recognize at once that something is wrong in the equation $24 + 13 = 97$.

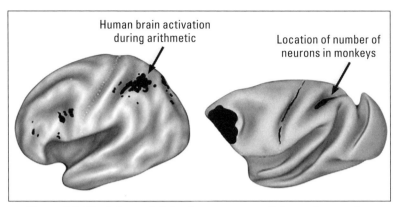

Human brain activation during arithmetic

Location of number of neurons in monkeys

Figure 9.1: The intraparietal sulcus, an essential area for number processing, in humans compared to monkeys.

Research in monkeys has led to a refined understanding of how number is encoded in this brain region. A remarkable discovery is that individual neurons fire preferentially to a given number (Nieder & Miller, 2004). For example, one can find a neuron that prefers the sight of three objects or the hearing of three sounds and fires optimally whenever the monkey sees or memorizes the quantity of three. The same neuron fires much less when presented with only one object or with five objects. Furthermore, these neurons exhibit an approximate tuning curve—that is, our example neuron fires maximally to three objects, somewhat less to two or four, and much less to one and five. Of course, our concept of the quantity of three does not rely on a single such neuron. There seem to be hundreds of thousands of these neurons, distributed in several centimeters of cortex. Collectively, they form a "population code" for approximate numbers—meaning that the number is encoded by which fraction of neurons is firing at a given time.

> A remarkable discovery is that individual neurons fire preferentially to a given number.

A final reason why we think of this area as playing a foundational role is that, when it is impaired by a brain lesion, drastic difficulties with number processing can ensue (particularly when the lesion is in the left hemisphere). In adults, this syndrome is known as acalculia and can be severe enough to prevent simple calculation or the decision that, say, six is larger than five. Strikingly, a similar syndrome of developmental dyscalculia exists in some children. Such children may well be of normal intelligence, yet they seem to lack any intuition of what numbers mean and, therefore, lag behind others in several measures of number discrimination, arithmetic intuition, and automaticity of understanding Arabic numerals. There are several varieties of dyscalculia, including difficulties with memorizing multiplication tables or computing multidigit operations. At least one subtype includes a clear conceptual difficulty with granting a quantity meaning to Arabic numerals. Brain imaging has revealed that several of the children who exhibit this difficulty suffer from reduced activation or impaired gray matter in the left or right intraparietal region, at the precise location that activates during arithmetic in normal subjects (for review, see Dehaene, Molko, Cohen, & Wilson, 2004). Prenatal or perinatal brain injuries, whether due to a genetic cause, to prematurity, or to brain suffering during birth, seem to induce disorganization in this brain region—an early deficit that may have a cascading effect on subsequent numerical development.

Multiple Cortical Representations of Number

It would be wrong, however, to think of arithmetic as relying entirely on a single brain region that acts as a module dedicated just to number. There are no modules in the cortex. Even at that hot spot in the intraparietal cortex, the density of neurons coding for number never exceeds about 15 percent. Other neurons, intermixed within the same area, care about motion, touch, object size, location, and other variables. (As we shall see later, this factor can explain the interactions and confusions that occur between number and size or place.)

A Triple-Code Organization

Although the intraparietal area plays a foundational role in arithmetic development, it would never be able to operate without the support of many other brain circuits. When we view a set of objects and evaluate their number, a chain of cortical areas, leading from the primary visual cortex up to the intraparietal cortex, are involved in the progressive extraction of number and the abstraction away from irrelevant parameters such as object size, shape, or location. When we see a spelled-out numeral, such as *fifteen,* other areas that belong to the left hemisphere's language system are involved in the ortho-graphic, lexical, and phonological decoding of the word. Only after the word has been identified within this learned alphabetic system can it be mapped onto a specific quantity within the intraparietal cortex. Similarly, when we see an Arabic numeral, such as *15,* yet other visual areas decode its digital content before mapping it onto the corresponding quantity. Thus, there is a "triple code" organiza-tion, in which three distinct brain networks for quantities, verbal numerals (written and spoken words), and Arabic numerals commu-nicate with each other, so that as adults we can quickly convert from one representation to the other (see fig. 9.2).

> It would be wrong to think of arithmetic as relying entirely on a single brain region that acts as a module dedicated just to number.

This triple-code organization has all-important consequences for our understanding of numerical development. There is evidence

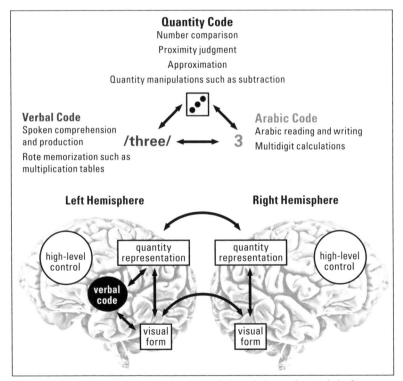

Figure 9.2: A schematic view of the triple-code model of number processing.

Three distinct brain networks for quantities, verbal numerals, and Arabic numerals communicate with each other when we evaluate the number of a set of objects.

that the approximate quantity system is present very early on, particularly in the right intraparietal region, where even three-month-olds exhibit activation during simple number tests. This evidence strongly supports the view that number sense does not rely on a slow process of induction or Piagetian constructivism, but rather is largely defined on a genetic basis. However, the other two systems for verbal or Arabic numerals cannot be inherited; they are recent cultural inventions, specific to our Western world, that need to be learned.

Thus, according to this view, numerical development consists largely of establishing firm, efficient, and automatized links between the cortical representations of numbers in various forms. As adults, we quickly move back and forth between the written, spoken, or approximate form of a given number without even noticing that we are switching between different brain systems. In children, however, the connections are much less efficient and take years to automatize. At the brain level, imaging methods indicate that arithmetic training develops the approximate quantity system, particularly in the left intraparietal region, as well as the other symbolic representations of numbers that recognize their verbal forms. An important goal of arithmetic education should be to increase the fluency with which information flows across the different cortical representations of numbers, until intuitions of, for example, 3 + 4 or 16 - 8 become as quick and efficient as they are when an infant is presented with corresponding sets of objects.

Developing Recipes for Calculation

An important goal of arithmetic education should be to increase the fluency of numerical intuitions.

Another important goal of arithmetic education consists of developing efficient recipes, or algorithms, for calculation. At the brain level, different types of calculation appear to rely on partially distinct brain systems within the triple-code architecture. For instance, when retrieving a multiplication fact such as 3 × 9 = 27, we mostly use the verbal code that stores this and similar facts as verbal associations ("three times nine is twenty-seven"), much like poems or prayers. As a result, they are encoded in a specific language, do not easily transfer to another language (in bilingual speakers), and can be erased by left-hemisphere lesions that render a patient aphasic or linguistically disabled. Conversely, when computing a subtraction problem such as 12 – 5 = 7, we rely on the Arabic system for spatial processing of the symbols and on the quantity system for retrieving the corresponding quantity. Thus, lesions to the intraparietal cortex can cause a deficiency in subtraction while sparing multiplication facts.

The implication for arithmetic education is that many different brain systems, as well as their interlinking pathways, must be trained before a child becomes fluent in arithmetic. Training in multiplication need not generalize to subtraction or comparison. Furthermore, for each given problem, the child must discover which cognitive strategy and cerebral system is most useful. A number of shortcuts must also be identified (for example, to discover the answer to 6 + 3 - 3 = ? without calculating).

Initially, calculation is an extremely effortful process that requires intense concentration, strategy choice, and working memory resources. These factors are reflected in a very intense activation of the prefrontal cortex—the large expanse of cortex just behind the forehead that is particularly expanded in humans compared to other primates. Prefrontal cortex is a recently developed brain area that plays an essential role in our ability to devise and follow novel nonroutine strategies. Crucially, it acts as a single central resource that cannot be shared between tasks and is therefore largely responsible for the observation that we cannot perform several effortful operations at once. The automatization of arithmetic operations frees up the central resource of prefrontal cortex. As children or adults become more expert at a task, the amount of prefrontal cortex activity decreases and is progressively replaced by the activation of more automatic brain systems in the back of the head. Before such automatization takes place, the child's prefrontal resources are totally absorbed by the mechanics of calculation

Another goal of education is to free the child's mind for more complex problems by helping the child to attain a high degree of fluency in basic number operations.

and cannot be devoted to other important aspects, such as checking the relevance of the solution or the meaning of the whole problem. Thus, a third important goal of education is to free the child's mind for more complex problems by helping the child to attain a high degree of fluency and automaticity in basic arithmetic operations.

Constructing Exact Number

Exposure to number symbols, such as the word *seventeen* or the symbol *17,* does much more than just interconnect pre-existing brain systems. Remember that in infants as in animals, the quantity system is only approximate—that is, it discriminates numbers based on their ratios, and therefore cannot discriminate very close numbers such as 17 and 18. Only humans appear to understand the categorical difference that exists between consecutive numbers, however large. This knowledge is evidently essential in mathematics, for instance, to decide that 17 is prime while 18 is not.

The understanding of exact number does not emerge spontaneously but depends on education. The demonstration of this claim relies on psychological studies of adults from remote cultures in the Amazon, such as the Munduruku people (Pica, Lemer, Izard, & Dehaene, 2004). The Munduruku language has very few number words (up to five). These words are not used for counting and cannot be recited as a counting series. Furthermore, they do not seem to have precise meanings. The word for five, for example, can be used for quantities from four to about nine objects, suggesting that it means something like "five-ish" or "a handful" (which is its literal translation). In the absence of an exact counting system, the Munduruku seem to rely exclusively on the approximate number system that we share with other animal species. They do have elaborate arithmetical intuitions and can perform approximate calculations with large numbers of objects, way beyond their naming range, but they cannot anticipate the result of exact operations such as 7 - 5.

Munduruku adults remind us of how our arithmetic system would look were it not for the many devices that our cultures have invented, such as count words, finger counting, or the abacus. Without these devices, we would have only an approximate arithmetic, not an exact one. In their first few years of life, Western children behave like the Munduruku, but they quickly overcome these limitations and move to an exact system of number when they are exposed to a counting system. This important developmental transition takes place slowly between the ages of two-and-a-half and four, when children begin to acquire the counting routine. The understanding of count words comes in a serial manner: first the word *one,* then the word *two,* and so on. Thus, for several months, a child may know the meaning of the word *one,* for instance, by showing an ability to provide just one object or to name a set with one object. Yet the very same child may not know the meaning of other numbers and may grab a random number of objects when asked to provide two (Wynn, 1992).

Children slowly learn to map number words *one, two, three,* and *four* onto their corresponding quantities, one word after the other, until at some point they suddenly realize that each word maps onto a different number. It may take them at least another six months before they understand that large number words such as *six, eight,* and *ten* map onto distinct quantities. Then they begin to grasp their order relations (Le Corre & Carey, 2007). It is not until the age of five that children usually understand that a word such as *eight,* if it applies to a set, continues to apply after the objects are shuffled but ceases to apply if the set is increased by one, doubled, or halved. Thus, children's verbal knowledge initially lags behind their number sense (as suggested, indeed, by the children's failure on many verbal Piagetian tests). However, once they master the full correspondence between verbal numbers and quantities, their concept of number seems to be radically changed. They now conceptualize numbers as discrete entities, each categorically distinguishable from the next in the series.

The Transition to Exact Numbers

At the time of this writing, nobody understands the mechanisms underlying this transition to exact numbers. The dominant theory is that the ability to track individual objects plays an essential role. I am referring here to yet another system of representation, the object file system, which is also available to infants and can encode very small numbers of objects in an implicit but exact manner. Even young children appear to be able to track up to three objects in space and thus categorically distinguish whether one, two, or three objects are present in a display, without suffering from the ratio limit that characterizes the approximate number system (Feigenson, Dehaene, & Spelke, 2004). Our visual system, in infants and adults alike, appears to incorporate a filing system that tracks the features of up to three objects.

Because this system is exact, although only available for very small numbers, it may help children infer the exact meaning of all numbers. As a child counts, he may be able to discover that each additional count word maps onto an additional file and so increases the quantity represented in the approximate quantity system. Somehow, the understanding of these mappings triggers an induction over all numbers: the child suddenly realizes that to each count word, there will always correspond a different quantity. How this conceptual change translates into a cerebral change within the brain's neuronal networks is not fully understood either, but the current theory is that the educated human brain may contain precise number-coding neurons sharply tuned to an exact number, instead of the coarsely tuned neurons that are found in other primates.

Putting Together Number and Space

A final aspect of human numerical intuition that seems to be heavily influenced by education and cultural background is the linking of numbers with space. This mapping plays an essential role in mathematics. Whenever we measure a length, we assume that numbers can be applied to spatial extensions. Geometry, literally the measure of the earth, is founded on this premise, and so are many higher-level mathematical concepts, such as irrational numbers, Cartesian coordinates, the real number line, and the complex plane.

Psychological and neurobiological research indicates that the concept of a "space of numbers" or "number line" has very deep roots in the brain. In most human adults, the mere presentation of an Arabic numeral automatically elicits a spatial bias in both motor responding and attention orienting (Dehaene, Bossini, & Giraux, 1993). Even when we perform a task as simple as deciding whether a digit is odd or even, or whether it is larger or smaller than five, we respond faster when small numbers are mapped onto a left-hand response and large numbers onto a right-hand response than when the converse mapping is used. This association of large numbers to the right side of space is entirely unconscious, although it can become conscious in rare individuals who literally "see" numbers as extending in two- or three-dimensional space, a phenomenon known as number-space synesthesia.

The direction of the number-space mapping is culturally determined. It varies with the direction of writing, such that the mental number line goes from left to right in Western participants, but from right to left in Arabic or Hebrew participants. The concept that number is like a space, however, has much deeper and universal roots. Even the Munduruku, who live in the Amazon jungle and have very reduced access to education, spontaneously understand that numbers map onto space in a regular manner (Dehaene, Izard, Spelke, & Pica, 2008).

> The concept of number line has very deep roots in the brain.

When we calculate, intuitions of the number line enhance and even bias our understanding of addition and subtraction operations. A spatial code and a sense of motion are automatically activated during mental arithmetic (Knops, Thirion, Hubbard, Michel, & Dehaene, 2009). When subjects approximate the sum or difference of two numbers, their estimates overshoot the correct outcomes, as if they moved "too far" toward large numbers during addition and toward small numbers during subtraction. Furthermore, when picking one of several plausible results displayed on a computer screen, participants are spatially biased toward selecting choices that appear on the top-right side of the screen during addition and on the top-left side during subtraction.

These interactions between number and space appear to originate from the parietal cortex. The quantity system, in the intraparietal region of the cortex, lies remarkably close to or overlaps other brain regions that are engaged in the coding of spatial dimensions such as size, location, and gaze direction (Hubbard, Piazza, Pinel, & Dehaene, 2005). When a number is presented, the parietal activation that its quantity induces spreads to areas involved in spatial coding, and it does so in a consistent way: small numbers cause greater activation in the right hemisphere, which codes for left space, while large numbers cause greater activation in the left hemisphere, which codes for right space. When we do addition, activation appears to move towards the cortex coding for the right-hand side of space, as if we were literally moving our attention from the initial number towards a rightward region of the number line (Knops et al., 2009).

The reason to stress these number-space relations is that they betray a universal aspect of human learning: the recycling of evolutionarily older brain circuits in the service of novel cultural devices. We literally reuse cortical components that are already structured by evolution and put them to a novel but related use. Here, concepts of number and arithmetic expand into older circuitry for space and eye movements. In *Reading in the Brain* I described how the acquisition of reading also makes uses of ancient circuits for object recognition (Dehaene, 2009). In both cases, we can understand not only the extent of children's intuitions, but also some of the difficulties that they face in learning: they are trying to fit new concepts into older shoes. For them, the idea that number is like space is intuitive. Other ideas, such as that a fraction (two numbers) is also a number, can be very counterintuitive because such ideas do not fit with any pre-existing concept and require significantly more recycling.

Even the mapping of number onto space appears to undergo a considerable change in the course of arithmetic development—one that is, again, critical to a deep understanding of arithmetic. Although number-space mappings are present in all humans, even without education, the form of this mapping changes in the course of education (Siegler & Opfer, 2003). When asked to point toward the correct location for a spoken number word on a line segment labeled with 1 at left and 100 at right, even kindergartners understand the task and systematically place smaller numbers at left and larger numbers at right. However, they do not distribute the numbers evenly in a linear manner. Rather, they devote more space to small numbers, thus imposing a compressed mapping. For instance, they place 10 near the middle of the 1-to-100 interval, as if they were responding using a logarithmic scale. This scale is, of course, exactly what one expects from an approximate system based on number ratio: the same ratio exists between 1 and 10 as between 10 and 100. My colleagues and I recently observed the same phenomenon in the Munduruku, even in adult subjects and even in the range 1 to 10 (Dehaene et al., 2008). The Munduruku have strong intuitions of number-space mappings because they can systematically map numbers onto a segment. However, their responses are logarithmically spaced, such that they place number 3 or 4 in the middle of 1 to 10. Only children who are exposed to mathematical culture and education show a striking shift from logarithmic to linear mapping. Suddenly, the children understand that consecutive numbers should be equally spaced, and they begin to respond with the classic linear scale (the only one that allows for easy measurement). This conceptual change takes place quite late in development, between first and fourth grade, depending on experience and the range of numbers tested. Such an understanding goes hand in hand with the understanding of exact numbers. Indeed, linear understanding correlates with standardized school tests of mathematics achievement, and training with one improves the other. Thus, it seems that conceptualizing numbers as a kind of space, and understanding the linearity of that space, are essential steps in the cognitive development of arithmetic.

Educational Implications

I have emphasized how a child's competence for arithmetic is grounded on a foundational representation of approximate number, which is inherited from our evolutionary past and relies on the intraparietal region of the brain's cortex. However, I have also stressed that arithmetic development relies to a large extent on the ability to connect this quantity representation with other representations of the linguistic or Arabic symbols for number, as well as on the recycling of nearby cortical regions involved in representing space. Achieving highly fluent and automatized interactions between these representations is an essential goal of education, both in itself (notably because it refines our concepts and leads to a representation of exact, linear number) and because it frees the all-purpose working memory resource of our prefrontal cortices for other purposes.

All sorts of devices can be used to enhance this developmental cross-linking of mental representations. Playing games, such as count games, abacus games, or simple board games (such as Snakes and Ladders), can be highly efficient in training the number system. Controlled experiments have shown that children who are trained with such games benefit from an earlier understanding of the linear relations between number and space and show generalized and last-ing gains in school-based arithmetic (Siegler & Ramani, 2008). Such games seem to be particularly helpful when they are used at a very early age and with children from impoverished backgrounds, who seem to be particularly at risk of arithmetic deficits. With these find-ings in mind, my laboratory developed and tested a free, open-source computer game, *The Number Race* (www.unicog.org/NumberRace), which is specifically designed to cement the links between the three cardinal representations of numbers (quantity, verbal, Arabic) and enhance the spatial understanding of numbers (Wilson, Revkin, Cohen, Cohen, & Dehaene, 2006). The game has been successfully shown to enhance numerical cognition, particularly in preschoolers at risk of developing difficulties in arithmetic (Wilson, Dehaene, Dubois, & Fayol, 2009).

In conclusion, we are now reaching an exciting time when fundamental research on the brain mechanisms of calculation is being bridged together with applied research on the development of effective tools for teaching arithmetic in elementary school. Much work remains to be done, however, in order to address higher-level concepts which are often the true source of difficulties in older children, such as base-10 notation, fractions, and algebraic notation.

References

Dehaene, S. (1997). *The number sense: How the mind creates mathematics.* New York: Oxford University Press.

Dehaene, S. (2009). *Reading in the brain: The science and evolution of a human invention.* New York: Penguin Viking.

Dehaene, S., Bossini, S., & Giraux, P. (1993). The mental representation of parity and numerical magnitude. *Journal of Experimental Psychology: General, 122*(3), 371–396.

Dehaene, S., Izard, V., Spelke, E., & Pica, P. (2008). Log or linear? Distinct intuitions of the number scale in Western and Amazonian indigene cultures. *Science, 320*(5880), 1217–1220.

Dehaene, S., Molko, N., Cohen, L., & Wilson, A. J. (2004). Arithmetic and the brain. *Current Opinion in Neurobiology, 14*(2), 218–224.

Feigenson, L., Dehaene, S., & Spelke, E. (2004). Core systems of number. *Trends in Cognitive Science, 8*(7), 307–314.

Gelman, R., & Gallistel, C. R. (1978). *The child's understanding of number.* Cambridge, MA: Harvard University Press.

Gilmore, C. K., McCarthy, S. E., & Spelke, E. S. (2007). Symbolic arithmetic knowledge without instruction. *Nature, 447*(7144), 589–591.

Halberda, J., Mazzocco, M. M., & Feigenson, L. (2008). Individual differences in non-verbal number acuity correlate with maths achievement. *Nature, 455*(7213), 665–668.

Hubbard, E. M., Piazza, M., Pinel, P., & Dehaene, S. (2005). Interactions between number and space in parietal cortex. *Nature Reviews Neuroscience, 6*(6), 435–448.

Knops, A., Thirion, B., Hubbard, E. M., Michel, V., & Dehaene, S. (2009). Recruitment of an area involved in eye movements during mental arithmetic. *Science, 324*(5934), 1583–1585.

Le Corre, M., & Carey, S. (2007). One, two, three, four, nothing more: An investigation of the conceptual sources of the verbal counting principles. *Cognition, 105*(2), 395–438.

McCrink, K., & Wynn, K. (2004). Large-number addition and subtraction by 9-month-old infants. *Psychological Science, 15*(11), 776–781.

Nieder, A., & Miller, E. K. (2004). A parieto-frontal network for visual numerical information in the monkey. *Proceedings of the National Academy of Sciences, 101*(19), 7457–7462.

Piaget, J. (1952). *The child's conception of number.* New York: Norton.

Piazza, M., Facoetti, A., Trussardi, A. N., Berteletti, I., Conte, S., Lucangeli, D., et al. (in press). Developmental trajectory of number acuity reveals a severe impairment in developmental dyscalculia. *Cognition.*

Pica, P., Lemer, C., Izard, V., & Dehaene, S. (2004). Exact and approximate arithmetic in an Amazonian indigene group. *Science, 306*(5695), 499–503.

Siegler, R. S., & Opfer, J. E. (2003). The development of numerical estimation: Evidence for multiple representations of numerical quantity. *Psychological Science, 14*(3), 237–243.

Siegler, R. S., & Ramani, G. B. (2008). Playing linear numerical board games promotes low-income children's numerical development. *Developmental Science, 11*(5), 655–661.

Wilson, A. J., Dehaene, S., Dubois, O., & Fayol, M. (2009). Effects of an adaptive game intervention on accessing number sense in low-socioeconomic-status kindergarten children. *Mind, Brain and Education, 3*(4), 224–234.

Wilson, A. J., Revkin, S. K., Cohen, D., Cohen, L., & Dehaene, S. (2006). An open trial assessment of "The Number Race," an adaptive computer game for remediation of dyscalculia. *Behavior and Brain Function, 2*(1), 20.

Wynn, K. (1992). Children's acquisition of the number words and the counting system. *Cognitive Psychology, 24,* 220–251.

Xu, F., & Spelke, E. S. (2000). Large number discrimination in 6-month-old infants. *Cognition, 74*(1), B1–B11.

Daniel Ansari

Daniel Ansari, PhD, MSc, received his undergraduate degree in psychology at the University of Sussex and his doctorate at the Institute of Child Health, University College of London. His thesis was on the numerical and mathematical abilities of children with Williams syndrome. During his doctoral studies, he became increasingly interested in neuroscience, receiving an MSc in neuroscience at the University of Oxford.

Dr. Ansari was an assistant professor of education at Dartmouth College, where he was part of an education department whose principal mission was educational neuroscience. Since 2006, he has been Canada Research Chair in Developmental Cognitive Neuroscience at the University of Western Ontario in Canada, where he heads the Numerical Cognition Laboratory. He and his team explore the developmental trajectory underlying both the typical and atypical development of numerical and mathematical skills, using both behavioral and neuroimaging methods.

In this chapter, Dr. Ansari reviews what is currently known about how the brain computes—that is, how the brain represents numerical quantity (the number of items in a set) and how it transforms quantities in the process of calculation. He pays particular attention to the brain processes involved in enumerating and calculating, and how these change over the course of learning and development. Moreover, he discusses how the brains of individuals with and without mathematical difficulties differ both functionally and structurally. At several points throughout his chapter, Dr. Ansari suggests ways in which the evidence reviewed may inform both the thinking and practice of educational professionals.

Chapter 10

The Computing Brain

Daniel Ansari

Basic numerical and mathematical skills are essential for navigating our everyday lives and have been shown to be critical determinants of professional success. Recent studies support the notion that mathematical fluency is essential by suggesting that achievement levels in numeracy and mathematics in childhood are a better predictor of later academic achievement and life success than are literacy skills (Bynner & Parsons, 1997; Duncan et al., 2007).

A striking example of the importance of numerical and mathematical skills is the finding that these skills are a crucial predictor of the ability of both patients and health professionals to use healthcare-related information, such as dosage of medicine (Ancker & Kaufman, 2007). Thus, a lack of basic numerical and mathematical skills among health professionals can have detrimental effects on the well-being of their patients. This is merely one of many examples that illustrate the dramatic influence that basic numerical and mathematical competencies have on our lives.

Despite the fact that basic numerical and mathematical skills play such a crucial role in modern society, international comparison studies have repeatedly shown that the achievement levels of children in many Western countries, such as the United States and Germany, fall significantly below the international average (OECD, 2004). Furthermore, conservative estimates suggest that between 3 and 5 percent of the population (estimated from studies conducted in Europe, North America, and Israel) have a specific learning difficulty in numeracy and mathematics, commonly referred to as developmental dyscalculia (Shalev, Auerbach, Manor, & Gross-Tsur, 2000). Although developmental dyscalculia is estimated to be as frequent as developmental dyslexia, there has been significantly less research into the impairment of numerical and mathematical competence (Berch & Mazzocco, 2007). In general, research into the psychological and brain mechanisms underlying our ability to enumerate and calculate lag significantly behind the impressive progress that has been made in our understanding of the typical and atypical development of reading skills.

Estimates are that between 3 and 5 percent of the population have a specific learning difficulty in numeracy, referred to as developmental dyscalculia.

A growing number of studies have investigated how numbers are represented in the brain, what brain regions underlie calculation abilities, and how these brain regions develop. Noninvasive brain imaging methods, such as functional magnetic resonance imaging (fMRI), have revealed differences in both the functioning and structure of the brains of individuals with and without developmental dyscalculia.

The aim of this chapter is to review what is currently known about "the computing brain" in both adults and children and how such data might inform the thinking and practice of educational professionals. The chapter will also provide an overview of recent insights into the mechanisms and their development that underlie our ability to enumerate (determining how many items are in a set or comparing which of two sets of objects is numerically larger) and calculate (being able to solve mental arithmetic problems).

The chapter opens with an overview of research into the brain mechanisms underlying numerical and mathematical skills in adults. This review will serve as a basis for exploring the development of the brain circuits for computing. In addition, the chapter will explore what neuroscientific investigations now reveal about the brains of individuals with mathematical difficulties and what role is played by individual differences in both competence and strategy use. Finally, the chapter will close with a discussion of future directions and how tighter connections between neuroscientific studies of the computing brain and mathematics education can be made.

It should be pointed out that the primary intent of this chapter is to inform educators about the current state of the neuroscience of computation rather than to provide direct links between what is known about the brain and the direct application of this knowledge to the mathematics classroom. I would contend that the most effective way of bringing neuroscience into the classroom is to provide teachers with access to the knowledge that neuroscientific studies are yielding. This knowledge will inform teachers' conceptualization of the learning child and therefore their pedagogical approaches (Ansari, 2005; Ansari & Coch, 2006). I hope that readers of this and other chapters in this volume will contribute to the design of novel neuroscientific studies that seek to answer educationally relevant empirical questions by collaborating with neuroscientists.

The Computing Brain in Adulthood

One of the four lobes of the brain, the parietal lobe (see fig. 10.1, page 204), has been associated with numerical and mathematical processing since the beginning of the last century. This link between the parietal cortex and numerical cognition was initially uncovered through the study of adult brain-damaged patients (Henschen, 1919, 1925). Patients with damage to the parietal cortex resulting from a stroke or an accident were found to suffer from calculation deficits. Perhaps most prominent among these investigations are those of Josef Gerstmann; he described a group of patients with lesions to the angular gyrus (see fig. 10.2, page 204) who presented with calculation deficits in addition to agraphia (deficiency in the ability to write), finger agnosia (inability to distinguish fingers on the hand), and left-right disorientation. This group of symptoms has become known as Gerstmann syndrome (Gerstmann, 1940, 1957). These findings provided the first insights into which brain regions were important for numerical and mathematical abilities and pointed to the parietal cortex as a critical region for calculation. Since these pioneering studies, much research has been conducted to further understand the computing brain.

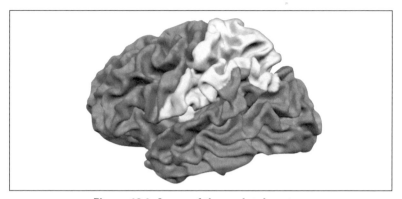

Figure 10.1: Areas of the parietal cortex.

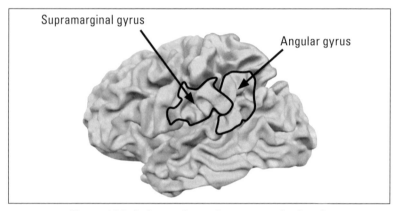

Figure 10.2: Left angular and supramarginal gyri.

With the advent of functional neuroimaging methods since the early 1990s, it has become possible to study the neural correlates of numerical and mathematical processing in the healthy human brain. Studies using positron emission tomography (PET) and functional magnetic resonance imaging (fMRI) have consistently shown that areas of both the parietal and frontal cortex are activated when participants calculate (Burbaud et al., 1995; Dehaene, Spelke, Pinel, Stanescu, & Tsivkin, 1999; Gruber, Indefrey, Steinmetz, & Kleinschmidt, 2001; Rueckert et al., 1996).

Moreover, through the use of data from both neuropsychological patients and functional neuroimaging studies of the healthy adult human brain, investigators have started to differentiate between a variety of numerical and mathematical tasks and their underlying brain processes. Specifically, researchers distinguish, on one hand, between the basic processing of numerical quantity, which is typically measured by tasks such as number comparison (deciding which of two numbers represents a larger quantity) and estimation (guessing how many dots are presented on a screen). On the other hand, researchers investigate the neuronal processes related to arithmetic problem solving and calculation. Thus, processing numerical quantity and calculating are two different aspects of the computing brain.

In a seminal study, Dehaene and colleagues (1999) used fMRI to show that exact, verbal calculation and approximate, nonverbal calculation lead to different patterns of brain activation. More specifically, these researchers asked participants to solve arithmetic problems either exactly or approximately. In the exact condition, participants saw a problem (such as 4 + 5 = ?) followed by two possible solutions, of which one was the correct solution (9) and the other (distractor) an incorrect solution (such as 7). In the approximate condition, the presentation of the problem was followed by two incorrect solutions with one being closer to the correct solution than the other. For example, if the problem was 4 + 5 = ?, the two possible solutions could have been 8 and 3. The "correct" choice would be 8, as it is closer to the correct answer (9) than the alternative solution of 3. A comparison of the brain activation (as measured by fMRI) correlated with exact and approximate calculation revealed that bilateral regions of the intraparietal sulcus (IPS, shown in fig. 10.3) were more activated in approximate than exact problems, while the reverse comparison (exact more than approximate) revealed a network comprising the left angular gyrus and regions of the left frontal cortex.

Because participants could presumably retrieve the exact answers to most problems from memory, engagement of left frontal and temporoparietal regions was consistent with the prediction that these areas are generally engaged in the verbal processing of number and, more specifically, in the retrieval of arithmetic facts. On the other hand, in the approximate condition, participants had to activate and mentally manipulate numerical quantities in order to judge which of the two solutions was closer to the correct answer. The greater parietal engagement during this condition, then, is consistent with a role of the IPS in the semantic representation of numerical quantity.

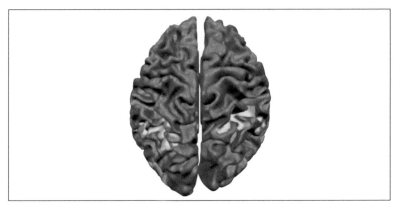

Figure 10.3: Left and right intraparietal sulcus.

Evidence from other fMRI studies has also associated the IPS with numerical quantity processing. Many of these studies have measured the activation of the brain while participants perform a number comparison task, such as judging which of two numbers is larger. It has been known for more than forty years that when participants compare numerical quantities, the difference (or distance) between the numbers affects the speed and accuracy with which their judgments of relative quantity are made. The greater the numerical difference (or distance) between two numbers, the faster and more accurate participants are at comparing their relative quantity (Moyer & Landauer, 1967).

In other words, there is an inverse relationship between the numerical distance between two numbers and the participants' reaction times in number-comparison tasks. This effect is typically referred to as the *numerical distance effect* (NDE). It has been argued that this NDE indicates an analog (approximate, rather than digital) representation of numerical quantity, whereby the overlap between representational features increases as the numerical distance decreases. Put differently, numbers that are closer together share more representational variance than those that are relatively far apart (Dehaene, 1992). This effect of distance on brain activation patterns has been measured in functional neuroimaging studies. Researchers have found that bilateral areas of the IPS exhibit a distance effect. The greatest activation of these regions is observed when numerical quantities that are separated by a relatively small distance are compared (Ansari, Fugelsang, Dhital, &

Venkatraman, 2006; Pinel, Dehaene, Riviere, & Le Bihan, 2001). All of these findings suggest that the IPS is involved in the representation and processing of numerical quantity.

A 2003 meta-analysis of fMRI studies put forward a model of the involvement of the parietal cortex in numerical and mathematical processing that predicts the existence of three different parietal circuits involved in different aspects of processing and representation (Dehaene, Piazza, Pinel, & Cohen, 2003). In the first circuit, bilateral regions of the IPS are thought to help in the internal representation of quantity. Consistent with early neuropsychological models and recent neuroimaging research, the model predicts that in the second circuit, areas of the left temporoparietal cortex comprising the angular and supramarginal gyri (see fig. 10.2, page 204) are involved in the verbal processing of numerical information, such as mental arithmetic.

Finally, the review suggests a third circuit in bilateral regions of the superior parietal lobes (SPL) that assist attentional processes required during number processing, such as the greater attentional resources required during multidigit compared with single-digit calculation. Furthermore, these regions are thought to assist the frequently observed linkages between spatial and numerical processing (Hubbard, Piazza, Pinel, & Dehaene, 2005). Taken together, the study of the computing brain in adults has revealed the neuronal processes involved in both enumerating and calculating and has led to the delineation of models that predict the mature brain mechanisms underlying calculation.

These neuroscientific data provide new insights into how we enumerate and calculate. They also offer evidence that the psychological processes we use to guess, for example, how many birds are on a tree, are associated with brain regions that differ from those we use to calculate exactly how much interest we should receive from our investments. However, it is important to acknowledge that for neuroscientific evidence to inform both the thinking and practice of education professionals, it is necessary to evaluate how development and learning affect the computing brain. Because development and education have dramatic effects on both the function and structure of the brain

> The brain regions activated when we do approximate calculations differ from those that are activated when we do exact calculations.

(Johnson, 2001), implications from adult neuroscientific data and models for education should be drawn with caution, and the developmental evidence should be carefully considered. Predictions for education derived from the consideration of neuroscientific data alone could lead to fundamental errors, because the brains of children and adults differ both in function and structure. In view of this, this literature review now turns to an overview of studies that have investigated how the brain mechanisms underlying enumeration and calculation change over developmental time.

The Development of the Computing Brain

Brain Mechanisms Underlying the Development of Calculation Abilities

In one of the first neuroimaging studies of arithmetic development, Rivera, Reiss, Eckert, and Menon (2005) used fMRI to study the neural regions associated with addition and subtraction in children and adolescents between the ages of eight and nineteen. While their brain activity was measured using fMRI, participants viewed addition and subtraction problems (for example, 5 + 3 = 8 or 7 - 4 = 2) and had to judge whether the result displayed was correct. Participants also completed a control task in which they had to judge whether a sequence of five digits (for example, 61059 or 93263) contained a zero.

When brain activation associated with the arithmetic task was subtracted from that associated with the control task, the brain areas involved in calculation could be revealed. The authors then correlated the results of this difference with the ages of the children and adolescents to determine how the activated brain regions varied with the participants' ages. Using this analysis, Rivera and colleagues could show in which brain areas the activation either positively or negatively correlated with chronological age.

This correlational analysis uncovered brain circuits that exhibited activation during mental arithmetic, which increased with chronological age. The analysis also revealed brain regions in which the younger participants exhibited greater activation than did their older peers. Rivera and colleagues found that activation in the left inferior parietal cortex (including the anterior angular gyrus; see fig. 10.2, page 204) increased with the age of the participants. In contrast, areas of prefrontal and anterior cingulate cortex as well as other regions, such as the hippocampus (part of the brain's memory systems) and basal ganglia, exhibited decreasing activation related to the arithmetic task with increasing age. These data suggest that there are significant changes in the neural correlates of addition and subtraction as a function of age. The increasing activation of the left inferior parietal cortex suggests that the involvement of this region in adults is the outcome of a process of developmental specialization.

In addition to the positive correlation between age and brain activity in the left inferior parietal lobe, the decreasing activation of the prefrontal cortex may suggest that functions such as attention and working memory (which have been frequently associated with these frontal brain regions) are more engaged during calculation by young children than by adolescents and young adults. Finally, the decreasing activation in the hippocampus may be evidence that calculation requires less engagement of memory systems in the brain over developmental time.

The dynamic shift between engagement of the frontal cortex in younger participants toward greater engagement of the left parietal regions among adolescents clearly indicates that beginning and more mature calculators use very different brain circuitry when they solve arithmetic tasks. This suggests that the kind of instructional support must differ radically between the age groups. The greater engagement of the regions involved in working memory and attention in the younger children suggests that the processes used to solve addition and subtraction problems in these age groups are less automatized and require more effort.

> The brain networks that adults use during calculation are different from those used by children.

Implications for Education

These findings open up many educationally relevant questions, such as what factors explain the age-related shift in brain activation? How might different instructional approaches mediate this shift? In other words, how do different ways of teaching math change the brain? Studies have shown that activation of the left inferior parietal cortex increases when adults are trained in arithmetic problem-solving tasks (Delazer et al., 2003; Ischebeck, Zamarian, Egger, Schocke, & Delazer, 2007). Such training studies should also be conducted with children to examine whether similar training-related shifts can be observed and, if so, whether various approaches to arithmetic instruction have different effects on the activation of the parietal cortex. By comparing different ways of teaching math using brain imaging, the effects of various instructional approaches can be systematically compared. Another question might be, Do individual differences in the mathematical competence of children of the same age influence the degree to which the children recruit regions of the left hemisphere that are associated with more mature calculation? In other words, do children who are mathematically more competent recruit their left parietal cortex more than children in the same grade who are less mathematically competent?

Taken together, the data reported by Rivera and colleagues suggest that the development of calculation skills is associated with a dynamic pattern of changes in the brain circuitry engaged during calculation. The findings further indicate that the verbal code in the left hemisphere emerges over developmental time. The fact that brain regions known to assist with calculation in adults become increasingly involved in mental arithmetic over the course of development is important. As discussed earlier, too often empirical evidence from adults and predictions from neuropsychological models are applied to children without a thorough consideration of the developmental processes that affect the brain regions that are activated during particular tasks. The research results suggest that regions of the prefrontal cortex play a critical role during calculation in younger children. And because the prefrontal cortex is typically associated with cognitive processes that support task performance—such as cognitive control, working memory, and attention—these findings suggest that children need to draw on these supporting cognitive skills during calculation, and that they only gradually start to use those structures associated with calculation in the adult brain. From an instructional perspective,

Computation mistakes in children may not necessarily reflect a lack of computational ability, but rather a lack of working memory resources or attentional focus.

these skills illustrate that computation mistakes in children may not necessarily reflect a lack of computation ability, but rather a lack of working memory resources or attentional focus.

Brain Mechanisms Underlying the Development of Number Magnitude Processing

The findings that the brain circuits activated during arithmetic tasks change over developmental time raise the question of whether similar developmental changes can also be found when more basic tasks are tested. As discussed earlier, the numerical distance effect has been used to examine the brain regions engaged during the processing of numerical quantity. Because behavioral studies have shown that the distance effect decreases over developmental time (Holloway & Ansari, 2008; Sekuler & Mierkiewicz, 1977), it is possible that there are age-related changes in the functional neuroanatomy associated with numerical distance. To address this question, Ansari, Garcia, Lucas, Hamon, and Dhital (2005) used fMRI to measure brain activation in children (average age of ten years) and adults while they compared the relative quantities of single-digit Arabic numerals. The results revealed that, consistent with prior evidence, numerical distance activated the bilateral region of the parietal cortex. In the group of children, however, the strongest effect of numerical distance on brain activation was found in the prefrontal cortex. Thus, consistent with the study of calculation discussed earlier (Rivera et al., 2005), over developmental time, there appears to be a shift away from the engagement of the prefrontal cortex toward increasing engagement of the parietal cortex.

In a subsequent study, Ansari and Dhital (2006) examined whether similar age-related changes in the neural correlates of the numerical distance effect could be found when participants were asked to compare nonsymbolic numerical quantities. Both adults and children were asked to judge which of two arrays of squares was numerically larger, and the numerical distance between the groups of squares was systematically varied. The results, consistent with those reported by Ansari and colleagues (2005), revealed a greater effect of numerical distance on the parietal cortex in adults as compared to children.

These combined findings demonstrate age-related specialization of brain circuits for both calculation and numerical quantity processing. The available evidence suggests that the left inferior parietal cortex (comprising the supramarginal and angular gyri shown in fig. 10.2, page 204) increases in calculation-related activation as a function of chronological age. Conversely, bilateral regions of the intraparietal sulcus are more engaged during numerical quantity processing in adults than in children. Other data also support this frontoparietal shift in the activation underlying both calculation and numerical quantity processing (Cantlon et al., 2009; Kaufmann et al., 2006; Kucian, von Aster, Loenneker, Dietrich, & Martin, 2008). See figure 10.4 for an illustration of this age-related shift from reliance on frontal regions to increasing recruitment of the parietal cortex for both the processing of numerical quantity as well as calculation.

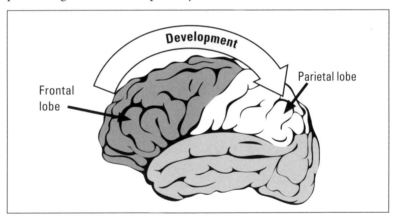

Figure 10.4: An illustration of the developmental shift from activation of the frontal lobe in young children to increasing activation of the parietal cortex with age.

Disorders of the Computing Brain

This review of literature reveals three principal insights into the computing brain:

1. The parietal cortex is associated with the processing of numerical quantity and mental arithmetic problems.

2. Within the parietal cortex, the IPS is associated with the processing and representation of numerical quantity, while

regions of the left inferior parietal cortex (comprising the angular and supramarginal gyri) are engaged when adults calculate.

3. Brain areas activated during quantitative judgments and mental arithmetic change over developmental time, with age-related decreases in the activation of the prefrontal cortex and increasing activation of areas of the parietal cortex.

These data from adults and children raise the question whether the neuronal architectures involved in quantity processing and calculation are disordered in individuals with mathematical difficulties. As mentioned at the beginning of this chapter, around 3 to 5 percent of the population is estimated to suffer from a specific inability to calculate, typically referred to as developmental dyscalculia (DD). Individuals with DD have scores on tests of verbal and nonverbal intelligence that are within the normal range but exhibit a specific impairment on tests of calculation. Furthermore, recent studies have indicated that children with DD have difficulties in processing numerical quantity (Landerl, Bevan, & Butterworth, 2004). In addition to DD, impairments of numerical and mathematical processing have also been observed in individuals with genetic developmental disorders (see De Smedt, Swillen, Verschaffel, & Ghesquiere, 2009, on 22q11.2 deletion syndrome; Mazzocco, 2009, on Turner syndrome; and O'Hearn & Luna, 2009, on Williams syndrome).

Neuroimaging Investigations Into Developmental Dyscalculia

Currently, only a handful of investigations exist that examine the neural correlates of mathematical difficulties in children with DD and those with genetic developmental disorders. Nevertheless, investigations of the brains of individuals with impairments in numerical and mathematical processing indicate that abnormalities of both the function and structure of the parietal cortex are associated with mathematical difficulties. In the first fMRI study of DD, Kucian and colleagues (2006) measured brain activity associated with both approximate and exact calculation in children with DD and their typically developing peers. The authors found that individuals with

DD showed weaker and more diffuse activation during both exact and approximate calculation as well as during a quantity comparison task (judging which of two sets of objects on a screen is numerically larger). The authors also found reduced activation among children with DD in the left IPS. These findings indicate that the neural activation patterns during numerical and arithmetic tasks differ between children with and without developmental dyscalculia.

Neural activation patterns during numerical and arithmetic tasks differ between children with and without developmental dyscalculia.

In another fMRI study, Price, Holloway, Räsänen, Vesterinen, and Ansari (2007) measured the brain activation of children with and without DD while the children compared which of two arrays of squares was numerically larger. By doing so, the authors could investigate the effect of numerical distance on the brain activation of children with and without DD. As expected, typically developing children exhibited greater activation in the right IPS when comparing squares separated by a relatively small numerical distance (for example, five versus six squares, or a distance of one) compared to a relatively large numerical distance (two versus eight squares, or a distance of six). In contrast, children with DD exhibited less activation of their right IPS for both comparisons, and they did not exhibit a distance effect on the activation of the parietal cortex.

This lower activation and absence of a distance effect in the IPS during nonsymbolic quantity comparison suggest an atypical functioning of the IPS for even the most basic numerical tasks. More recently, Mussolin and colleagues (in press) used fMRI to investigate the brain activation of children with DD and their typically developing peers when comparing symbolic numbers (Arabic numerals). Consistent with the results of Price and colleagues, the authors found reduced activation of the right IPS as well as the left superior parietal lobe.

Investigations of the neural regions involved in mathematical difficulties in individuals with genetic developmental disorders have been just as limited as investigations into the neural correlates of DD. However, Molko and colleagues (2003) used fMRI to investigate the brain activation of individuals with Turner syndrome while they performed calculation tasks. Like participants with DD, individuals with Turner syndrome exhibited atypical functioning of the IPS during calculation tasks.

In addition to the functional deficits, structural abnormalities of the parietal cortex in individuals with DD have also been observed. Specifically, Rotzer and colleagues (2007) found that individuals with DD exhibit reduced gray-matter volumes in the right IPS in a region very close to the location of the functional abnormalities just discussed. Moreover, in their study of individuals with Turner syndrome, Molko and colleagues also observed abnormalities in the structure of the parietal cortex in these individuals. Taken together, the evidence from brain imaging of individuals with mathematical difficulties points to clear atypical function and structure of the IPS. It is possible, therefore, that the developmental specialization of regions within the parietal cortex that are involved in numerical and mathematical tasks is atypical in individuals with mathematical difficulties.

Educational Implications of Research

From an educational point of view, these data are significant in several ways. First, they clearly demonstrate that mathematical difficulties are associated with a measurable brain-level impairment, in terms of both brain function and structural abnormalities. Second, these brain abnormalities can be observed during very basic numerical tasks (such as judging which of two squares is numerically larger), suggesting that calculation problems in children with mathematical difficulties may originate in the inability to process and represent numerical quantity. Such findings indicate that children with mathematical difficulties may benefit from instructional approaches that teach them about numerical quantity in both symbolic and nonsymbolic formats. This could include activities in which children have to match symbolic representations (such as Arabic numerals and number words) with nonsymbolic arrays (such as a collection of objects or dots). During such activities, educators could ask children to judge whether the collection of objects is equal to the number represented by the Arabic numeral or number word. When the symbolic and nonsymbolic representations of number are unequal, a conversation could revolve around what would be needed to make them unequal or why they are unequal.

Such activities do not always need to be focused on drawing children's attention to the relationships between symbolic and nonsymbolic representations of number, but could involve activities that highlight similarities between different representations of number, both symbolic (for example, house numbers versus thermometer level or the weight indicator on a scale) and nonsymbolic (for example, a group of different kinds of objects). Activities such as these will strengthen children's understanding of numerical magnitude and will also strengthen their understanding that number is an abstract property of sets, such that seven apples and seven bananas are the same number of objects, despite the fact that they are different kinds of fruit, with different physical appearances, weight, taste, and so on. Many board games involve simple manipulations of numerical magnitude, such as rolling a die and then moving a piece up or down on the board the corresponding number of times. It has been shown by Robert Siegler and his colleagues that playing such simple board games strengthens children's understanding of numerical magnitude (Siegler & Ramani, 2008, 2009).

Children with mathematical difficulties may benefit from instruction that teaches them about numerical quantities in both symbolic and nonsymbolic formats.

Individual Differences in the Computing Brain

Thus far we have considered evidence from groups of participants and discussed studies that average performance and brain activation patterns from several participants. From an educational point of view, however, such studies tell us little about those individual differences in children's performance that are pervasive in the classroom. Indeed, neuroscientific investigations traditionally focus on averages rather than individual data points in order to better understand patterns of data that can be generalized across participants.

Difference in Competence

There have been some attempts to use noninvasive neuroimaging methods to gain insights into how patterns of brain activation during the performance of educationally relevant tasks vary as a function of individual differences. In a 2007 study, Grabner and colleagues selected adult participants who varied in their mathematical competence from relatively low to relatively high levels as assessed by a standardized test of mathematical intelligence, and at the same time performed within the normal range (average performance) on nonmathematical tests of intelligence. The brain activity of these participants was measured using fMRI while they verified the correctness of single- and multidigit multiplication problems (for example, $4 \times 3 = 12$ or $5 \times 2 = 10$). The authors then correlated individual differences in the participants' performance on the test of mathematical intelligence with the fMRI measurements of their brain activation during calculation.

The results revealed that those individuals with higher mathematical intelligence recruit their left angular gyrus more during multiplication than those with lower mathematical competence. Note that none of these individuals could be said to have developmental dyscalculia, because participants' scores on the test of mathematical intelligence were well within the typical range. These findings indicate that the level of mathematical achievement is associated with the degree to which areas associated with calculation are activated during mental arithmetic tasks.

Differences in Strategy Use

In addition to individual differences in competence, another important individual differences variable in calculation is strategy use. It is well established that both children and adults use a variety of strategies when solving mental arithmetic problems (Siegler, 1999). In order to investigate whether brain circuits are engaged as a function of strategy use, Grabner and colleagues (2009) employed fMRI to measure the brain activation of a group of adults while they solved problems of four arithmetic operations. After the completion of the fMRI measurement, participants were asked to solve half of the problems again and to indicate after each problem what problem-solving strategy they used. Participants could choose between whether they had retrieved the answer from memory (for example, "It just popped into my head") or whether they had used a procedural strategy ("I counted in my head from the larger number" or "I divided the problem into several steps").

These self-reports were used to sort the brain images into those problems for which participants said they used a retrieval strategy versus a procedural strategy. The comparison of these brain images revealed greater activation in the left angular gyrus for retrieval. In contrast, the brain images of participants who used a procedural problem-solving strategy were associated with greater activation in frontal regions of the brain. These results illustrate that different problem-solving strategies are associated with the activation of segregated brain regions. Importantly, these findings also show that self-reported strategy use can be used to predict brain activation patterns, and thereby validate self-report methods to glean insights into the problem-solving strategies that individuals use during mental arithmetic tasks.

Interestingly, the brain regions revealed by these contrasts bear a striking resemblance to the positive and negative correlations between children's age and brain activation during calculation, reported by Rivera and colleagues (2005) and discussed earlier. Specifically, they found that while activation in the left inferior parietal lobe increases over developmental time, activity in frontal regions during mental arithmetic tasks decreases over developmental time. Because these findings associate retrieval strategies with greater activation in the left inferior parietal lobe and procedural strategies with the engagement of the frontal cortex, combining the two findings might indicate that the frontoparietal shift in activation reflects, at least partially, an age-related decrease in the use of procedural calculation strategies coupled with an increasing reliance on retrieval strategies. In other words, as children get older, they build up a storage of arithmetic facts, which they can retrieve without having to resort to effortful calculating strategies. So as we get older, we rely more on remembering and less on calculating.

These studies suggest that neuroimaging can reveal the neural correlates of individual differences in calculation. Some evidence exists that different instructional strategies lead to separable patterns of brain activation (Lee et al., 2007; Sohn et al., 2004). These studies also reveal differences in brain activation associated with different problem-solving strategies in the presence of data showing equivalent reaction times and accuracy for the different strategies. Such data demonstrate that

Functional imaging can reveal educationally meaningful differences that are not obvious by looking at behavioral data alone.

functional imaging can reveal educationally meaningful differences between conditions that are not obvious from looking at behavioral data alone.

Future Directions

This chapter has provided an overview of the brain mechanisms underlying number processing and computation in children and adults as well as individuals with mathematical difficulties. Although substantial progress has been made in our understanding of the brain regions underlying our ability to compute and how these regions develop and break down in individuals with mathematical difficulties, many open questions remain.

One of the biggest challenges facing neuroscientific studies of the computing brain is to investigate how the brain activation underlying the processing of quantity and problem solving during mental arithmetic tasks is changed by education and experience. As earlier chapters in this volume have discussed, studies of reading and the brain have shown that structured intervention can lead to a normalization of atypical patterns of brain activation among dyslexic individuals (Eden et al., 2004; Shaywitz et al., 2004; Temple et al., 2003). Such findings raise the question whether educational programs designed to improve the calculation skills of children with mathematical difficulties can lead to similar neuronal changes. The findings also suggest that mathematical difficulties are characterized by atypical activation of the parietal cortex. Therefore, researchers should investigate whether educational remediation programs can lead to a normalization of activation in individuals with mathematical difficulties or, more generally, how training programs for numeracy and arithmetic change brain activation patterns.

Although there have been some studies investigating the neural correlates of mathematical difficulties, more investigations into brain mechanisms of various levels of mathematical achievement are needed. In addition to studying children with mathematical difficulties, more exploration into the brain mechanisms associated with high levels of mathematical achievement should be undertaken. Currently a bias

Cognitive neuroscience also should study children who excel in mathematics, as their development also needs to be fostered.

exists in cognitive neuroscience toward the exploration of mathematical difficulties. However, from an educational point of view, the study of children who excel in mathematics is as important because these students' development also needs to be fostered. Neuroscience might provide some novel insights into young math prodigies, which may in turn influence instructional approaches to foster the development of such individuals. Furthermore, longitudinal research that tracks the neural activation patterns within individuals as they develop is necessary to evaluate differences in brain abnormalities between individuals who exhibit transient versus persistent difficulties in computation.

In addition to measuring the effect of mathematics instruction on brain function, future studies of the brain mechanisms underlying computation need to capture educationally meaningful variables, such as mathematics anxiety and the effect of pressure to succeed on calculation performance. It is important, too, that researchers take motivational and socioeconomic variables into account when designing neuroimaging studies and selecting research participants. Although some studies have begun investigating more complex mathematical processes, such as fractions, algebra, and calculus (Jacob & Nieder, 2009; Krueger et al., 2008; Qin et al., 2004), more investigations of these higher-level processes are needed. These investigations will make neuroscientific studies relevant to the entire spectrum of mathematics educators and will further our understanding of how the brain does mathematics.

Most neuroimaging experiments are very time consuming and costly, and in the case of fMRI, involve participants lying supine in the opening of a powerful magnet. This experimental situation is very different from a real classroom environment. Future neuroscientific studies, therefore, should investigate mathematical processing in experimental situations more similar to actual mathematics classrooms. Methods such as functional near-infrared spectroscopy (NIRS) may be suitable for use with multiple participants in a classroom setting.

It is also very important to acknowledge that neuroscientific data alone cannot lead to improvements in our understanding of the complexity involved in typical and atypical development of numerical and mathematical skills. Insights into the brain mechanisms involved in numeracy and arithmetic provide only one piece of the puzzle. It is important, therefore, for educators to draw on multiple sources, ranging from cognitive science to international comparisons of education standards to inform their practice.

Educators also have a profound role to play in the future of mind, brain, and education. Specifically, it is important that educators critically question many of the so-called brain-based educational approaches and materials that claim to be based on neuroscientific approaches. Are these advertised books and tools based on peer-reviewed empirical research (research that was reviewed by other researchers before publication)? Furthermore, educators must be critical when they hear or read "simple truths" about the brain. These often turn out to be false or represent oversimplifications of what is known about the brain, such as the notion of learning styles or the argument that there are left-brained and right-brained individuals. Many of these neuromyths are quite pervasive. Just because the advertisements for a certain product or textbook claim it is based on brain research does not automatically mean that it was informed by reliable and valid neuroscientific research.

In relationship to the research discussed in this chapter, educators can help spread understanding about developmental difficulties in numeracy and mathematics (that is, developmental dyscalculia) among fellow educators and parents. Partly because the research on both typical and atypical development of numeracy and mathematics lags so far behind the research on reading, there is less awareness that children can present with mathematical learning difficulties that are independent of their other abilities—and that these children require special attention. Educators can share their knowledge of the neuroscience research and help ensure that children receive all the support they need to succeed in mathematics.

References

Ancker, J. S., & Kaufman, D. (2007). Rethinking health numeracy: A multidisciplinary literature review. *Journal of the American Medical Informatics Association, 14*(6), 713–721.

Ansari, D. (2005). Time to use neuroscience findings in teacher training. *Nature, 437*(7055), 26.

Ansari, D., & Coch, D. (2006). Bridges over troubled waters: Education and cognitive neuroscience. *Trends in Cognitive Sciences, 10*(4), 146–151.

Ansari, D., & Dhital, B. (2006). Age-related changes in the activation of the intraparietal sulcus during nonsymbolic magnitude processing: An event-related functional magnetic resonance imaging study. *Journal of Cognitive Neuroscience, 18*(11), 1820–1828.

Ansari, D., Fugelsang, J. A., Dhital, B., & Venkatraman, V. (2006). Dissociating response conflict from numerical magnitude processing in the brain: An event-related fMRI study. *Neuroimage, 32*(2), 799–805.

Ansari, D., Garcia, N., Lucas, E., Hamon, K., & Dhital, B. (2005). Neural correlates of symbolic number processing in children and adults. *Neuroreport, 16*(16), 1769–1773.

Berch, D. B., & Mazzocco, M. M. M. (2007). *Why is math so hard for some children? The nature and origins of mathematical learning difficulties and disabilities.* Baltimore: Paul H. Brookes.

Burbaud, P., Degreze, P., Lafon, P., Franconi, J. M., Bouligand, B., Bioulac, B., et al. (1995). Lateralization of prefrontal activation during internal mental calculation: A functional magnetic resonance imaging study. *Journal of Neurophysiology, 74*(5), 2194–2200.

Bynner, J., & Parsons, S. (1997). *Does numeracy matter?* London: Basic Skills Agency.

Cantlon, J. F., Libertus, M. E., Pinel, P., Dehaene, S., Brannon, E. M., & Pelphrey, K. A. (2009). The neural development of an abstract concept of number. *Journal of Cognitive Neuroscience, 21*(11), 2217–2229.

De Smedt, B., Swillen, A., Verschaffel, L., & Ghesquiere, P. (2009). Mathematical learning disabilities in children with 22q11.2 deletion syndrome: A review. *Developmental Disabilities Research Review, 15*(1), 4–10.

Dehaene, S. (1992). Varieties of numerical abilities. *Cognition, 44*(1–2), 1–42.

Dehaene, S., Piazza, M., Pinel, P., & Cohen, L. (2003). Three parietal circuits for number processing. *Cognitive Neuropsychology, 20*(3–6), 487–506.

Dehaene, S., Spelke, E., Pinel, P., Stanescu, R., & Tsivkin, S. (1999). Sources of mathematical thinking: Behavioral and brain-imaging evidence. *Science, 284*(5416), 970–974.

Delazer, M., Domahs, F., Bartha, L., Brenneis, C., Lochy, A., Trieb, T., et al. (2003). Learning complex arithmetic—an fMRI study. *Cognitive Brain Research, 18*(1), 76–88.

Duncan, G. J., Dowsett, C. J., Claessens, A., Magnuson, K., Huston, A. C., Klebanov, P., et al. (2007). School readiness and later achievement. *Developmental Psychology, 43*(6), 1428–1446.

Eden, G. F., Jones, K. M., Cappell, K., Gareau, L., Wood, F. B., Zeffiro, T. A., et al. (2004). Neural changes following remediation in adult developmental dyslexia. *Neuron, 44*(3), 411–422.

Gerstmann, J. (1940). Syndrome of finger agnosia, disorientation for right and left, agraphia and acalculia. *Archives of Neurology and Psychiatry, 44,* 398–408.

Gerstmann, J. (1957). Some notes on the Gerstmann syndrome. *Neurology, 7*(12), 866–869.

Grabner, R. H., Ansari, D., Koschutnig, K., Reishofer, G., Ebner, F., & Neuper, C. (2009). To retrieve or to calculate? Left angular gyrus mediates the retrieval of arithmetic facts during problem solving. *Neuropsychologia, 47*(2), 604–608.

Grabner, R. H., Ansari, D., Reishofer, G., Stern, E., Ebner, F., & Neuper, C. (2007). Individual differences in mathematical competence predict parietal brain activation during mental calculation. *Neuroimage, 38*(2), 346–356.

Gruber, O., Indefrey, P., Steinmetz, H., & Kleinschmidt, A. (2001). Dissociating neural correlates of cognitive components in mental calculation. *Cerebral Cortex, 11*(4), 350–359.

Henschen, S. E. (1919). Über sprach-, musik-, und rechenmechanismen und ihre lokalisationen im grobhirn. *Zeitschrift für die gesamte Neurologie und Psychiatrie, 52,* 273–298.

Henschen, S. E. (1925). Clinical and anatomical contributions in brain pathology. *Archives of Neurological Psychiatry, 13,* 226–249.

Holloway, I. D., & Ansari, D. (2008). Domain-specific and domain-general changes in children's development of number comparison. *Developmental Science, 11*(5), 644–649.

Hubbard, E. M., Piazza, M., Pinel, P., & Dehaene, S. (2005). Interactions between number and space in parietal cortex. *Nature Reviews Neuroscience, 6*(6), 435–448.

Ischebeck, A., Zamarian, L., Egger, K., Schocke, M., & Delazer, M. (2007). Imaging early practice effects in arithmetic. *Neuroimage, 36*(3), 993–1003.

Jacob, S. N., & Nieder, A. (2009). Notation-independent representation of fractions in the human parietal cortex. *Journal of Neuroscience, 29*(14), 4652–4657.

Johnson, M. H. (2001). Functional brain development in humans. *Nature Reviews Neuroscience, 2*(7), 475–483.

Kaufmann, L., Koppelstaetter, F., Siedentopf, C., Haala, I., Haberlandt, E., Zimmerhackl, L. B., et al. (2006). Neural correlates of the number-size interference task in children. *Neuroreport, 17*(6), 587–591.

Krueger, F., Spampinato, M. V., Pardini, M., Pajevic, S., Wood, J. N., Weiss, G. H., et al. (2008). Integral calculus problem solving: An fMRI investigation. *Neuroreport, 19*(11), 1095–1099.

Kucian, K., Loenneker, T., Dietrich, T., Dosch, M., Martin, E., & von Aster, M. (2006). Impaired neural networks for approximate calculation in dyscalculic children: A functional MRI study. *Behavior and Brain Function, 2,* 31.

Kucian, K., von Aster, M., Loenneker, T., Dietrich, T., & Martin, E. (2008). Development of neural networks for exact and approximate calculation: A fMRI study. *Developmental Neuropsychology, 33*(4), 447–473.

Landerl, K., Bevan, A., & Butterworth, B. (2004). Developmental dyscalculia and basic numerical capacities: A study of 8-9-year-old students. *Cognition, 93*(2), 99–125.

Lee, K., Lim, Z. Y., Yeong, S. H., Ng, S. F., Venkatraman, V., & Chee, M. W. (2007). Strategic differences in algebraic problem solving: Neuroanatomical correlates. *Brain Research, 1155,* 163–171.

Mazzocco, M. M. (2009). Mathematical learning disability in girls with Turner syndrome: A challenge to defining MLD and its subtypes. *Developmental Disabilities Research Review, 15*(1), 35–44.

Molko, N., Cachia, A., Riviere, D., Mangin, J. F., Bruandet, M., Le Bihan, D., et al. (2003). Functional and structural alterations of the intraparietal sulcus in a developmental dyscalculia of genetic origin. *Neuron, 40*(4), 847–858.

Moyer, R. S., & Landauer, T. K. (1967). Time required for judgements of numerical inequality. *Nature, 215*(109), 1519–1520.

Mussolin, C., De Volder, A., Grandin, C., Schlogel, X., Nassogne, M. C., & Noel, M. P. (in press). Neural correlates of symbolic number comparison in developmental dyscalculia. *Journal of Cognitive Neuroscience.*

O'Hearn, K., & Luna, B. (2009). Mathematical skills in Williams syndrome: Insight into the importance of underlying representations. *Developmental Disabilities Research Review, 15*(1), 11–20.

Organisation for Economic Co-operation and Development. (2004). *Learning for tomorrow's world: First results from PISA 2003.* Paris: Author.

Pinel, P., Dehaene, S., Riviere, D., & Le Bihan, D. (2001). Modulation of parietal activation by semantic distance in a number comparison task. *Neuroimage, 14*(5), 1013–1026.

Price, G., Holloway, I., Räsänen, P., Vesterinen, M., & Ansari, D. (2007). Impaired parietal magnitude processing in developmental dyscalculia. *Current Biology, 17*(24).

Qin, Y., Carter, C. S., Silk, E. M., Stenger, V. A., Fissell, K., Goode, A., et al. (2004). The change of the brain activation patterns as children learn algebra equation solving. *Proceedings of the National Academy of Sciences, 101*(15), 5686–5691.

Rivera, S. M., Reiss, A. L., Eckert, M. A., & Menon, V. (2005). Developmental changes in mental arithmetic: Evidence for increased functional specialization in the left inferior parietal cortex. *Cerebral Cortex, 15*(11), 1779–1790.

Rotzer, S., Kucian, K., Martin, E., Aster, M. V., Klaver, P., & Loenneker, T. (2007). Optimized voxel-based morphometry in children with developmental dyscalculia. *Neuroimage, 39,* 417–422.

Rueckert, L., Lange, N., Partiot, A., Appollonio, I., Litvan, I., Le Bihan, D., et al. (1996). Visualizing cortical activation during mental calculation with functional MRI. *Neuroimage, 3*(2), 97–103.

Sekuler, R., & Mierkiewicz, D. (1977). Children's judgments of numerical inequality. *Child Development, 48,* 630–633.

Shalev, R. S., Auerbach, J., Manor, O., & Gross-Tsur, V. (2000). Developmental dyscalculia: Prevalence and prognosis. *European Child Adolescent Psychiatry, 9 Suppl 2,* II58–64.

Shaywitz, B. A., Shaywitz, S. E., Blachman, B. A., Pugh, K. R., Fulbright, R. K., Skudlarski, P., et al. (2004). Development of left occipitotemporal systems for skilled reading in children after a phonologically-based intervention. *Biological Psychiatry, 55*(9), 926–933.

Siegler, R. S. (1999). Strategic development. *Trends in Cognitive Sciences, 3*(11), 430–435.

Siegler, R. S., & Ramani, G. B. (2008). Playing linear numerical board games promotes low-income children's numerical development. *Developmental Science, 11,* 635–661.

Siegler, R. S., & Ramani, G. B. (2009). Playing linear number board games—but not circular ones —improves low-income preschoolers' numerical understanding. *Journal of Educational Psychology, 101,* 655–661.

Sohn, M. H., Goode, A., Koedinger, K. R., Stenger, V. A., Fissell, K., Carter, C. S., et al. (2004). Behavioral equivalence, but not neural equivalence—Neural evidence of alternative strategies in mathematical thinking. *Nature Neuroscience, 7*(11), 1193–1194.

Temple, E., Deutsch, G. K., Poldrack, R. A., Miller, S. L., Tallal, P., Merzenich, M. M., et al. (2003). Neural deficits in children with dyslexia ameliorated by behavioral remediation: Evidence from functional MRI. *Proceedings of the National Academy of Sciences, 100*(5), 2860–2865.

Mariale M. Hardiman

Mariale M. Hardiman, EdD, interim Dean of the Johns Hopkins University School of Education, joined the University in 2006 as Assistant Dean of Urban School Partnerships and Chair of the Department of Interdisciplinary Studies after serving in the Baltimore City Public Schools for more than thirty years. As the principal of Roland Park Elementary/Middle School, Dr. Hardiman led the school to its designation as a Blue Ribbon School of Excellence. During her tenure as principal, she devised a teaching framework, the Brain-Targeted Teaching Model, which connects research-based effective instruction with elements from the brain sciences to inform teaching and learning.

Dr. Hardiman collaborated with colleagues to develop the Johns Hopkins University School of Education's Neuro-Education Initiative, supported by the Johns Hopkins School of Medicine's Brain Science Institute. The Neuro-Education Initiative brings to educators relevant research on cognition and learning.

Dr. Hardiman has written articles and books and lectured on topics related to school leadership and the intersection of research in the neurosciences with effective teaching strategies, including meaningful integration of the arts. Dr. Hardiman earned her undergraduate and graduate degrees from Loyola University Maryland and her doctorate from Johns Hopkins University.

In this chapter, Dr. Hardiman discusses what neuroscience is telling us about the nature of creativity and how the arts can develop creativity and innovative thinking. She also explains the Brain-Targeted Teaching Model and how it can help teachers integrate the arts with different subject content at all grade levels.

Chapter 11

The Creative-Artistic Brain

Mariale M. Hardiman

*Every grand American accomplishment, every inno-
vation that has benefited and enriched our lives,
every lasting social transformation, every moment
of profound insight any American visionary ever
had into a way out of despair, loneliness, fear and
violence—everything that has from the start made
America the world capital of hope, has been the fruit
of the creative imagination, of the ability to reach
beyond received ideas and ready-made answers to
some new place, some new way of seeing or hearing
or moving through the world. Breathtaking solutions,
revolutionary inventions, the road through to freedom,
reform and change: never in the history of this country
have these emerged as pat answers given to us by our
institutions, by our government, by our leaders. We
have been obliged—to employ Dr. King's powerful
verb—to dream them up for ourselves.*

—Michael Chabon, The Obama Arts Policy
Committee, 2009

The strength of a nation, the very backbone of success in a global
economy, depends on a workforce capable of creativity and innovation. Yet as leaders lament, many students leave school lacking those

essential skills. Educating the citizens of tomorrow will require the redesign of school policies and practices so that students are not merely acquiring information but also are applying knowledge in novel ways. New research from the brain sciences is shedding light on the neural processes involved in creative thinking.

Studies show that, compared to tasks requiring conventional kinds of thinking, creative thinking appears to engage more complex neural networks. Recent studies also are demonstrating the power of the arts to enhance cognition and learning. By using the arts as a teaching methodology, educators can better prepare students to become creative thinkers and meet the demands of the 21st century. This chapter discusses research in creativity and the arts and offers a teaching framework, the Brain-Targeted Teaching Model, which demonstrates an effective way to meet the challenges of a standards-based system and at the same time foster 21st century skills.

> Studies show that, compared to tasks requiring conventional kinds of thinking, creative thinking appears to engage more complex neural networks.

The Need for Creativity in Schools

Despite a rapidly changing society, American education has changed little during the past fifty years. Americans have seen rapid growth in communications and media industries, revolutionary practices in business and technology, and blazing discoveries in medical research and treatment. Yet typical classrooms in schools across the country today look much the same as those of years gone by. From the early 20th century, American schools have been designed to reflect the factory-driven notion that education should mass-produce workers in order to prepare a workforce for an Industrial Age economy. In this view, students are considered empty vessels into which educators pour factual knowledge and then test the "product" for efficiency. Features of Industrial Age-based schools such as physical structures, same-age groupings, class schedules, and standard grading systems were geared to march students through an efficient system until they were able to join a rather predictable workforce.

While the world has experienced a seismic shift toward a knowl-edge-based, information-driven era, the policies and practices of

American schools are still like those of the factory-driven institutions of yesteryear. In an attempt to hold schools accountable for student learning, high-stakes testing has reduced the view of a sound education to the ultimate standardization—namely, performance on multiple-choice tests. Educators often lament that the so-called art of teaching in today's schools requires merely coverage of a large body of content standards taught just in time to be tested on yearly assessments. Administrators and teachers feel mounting pressure to produce ever-increasing scores on these assessments, which have come to determine not only job security for educators but also housing prices for neighborhoods.

Many teachers would agree that this focus on testing often leaves little room in the curriculum and scant time in the school day to engage learners in activities that require creativity, innovation, critical thinking, and problem solving. Yet those are the competencies identified as essential for the workforce of the future by the advocacy group, the Partnership for 21st Century Skills (www.p21.org). The rapidity of technological development is changing the nature of work at a dizzying pace. It is no wonder that the mismatch between school practices and workforce requirements has led many business leaders to feel that graduates lack sufficient skills to compete in the new global economy. It is clear that education policies and practices must reflect this demand for a new kind of workforce. Educators must heed the call by designing instruction that will develop and foster the creative mind.

What Is Creativity, and Can We Teach It?

Creativity is most often defined as the ability to produce work that is both original and useful in some way, either aesthetically or practically. It requires bringing something novel into being and transforming the existent (Andreasen, 2005).

A common myth in our culture is that creativity comes from some unusual talent or great intelligence. It is widely thought that highly creative thinking abilities are bestowed on gifted artists or great minds such as Einstein, whose major discoveries occurred before his thirtieth birthday, or Newton, who developed calculus at the age of nineteen.

Psychologist Joy Paul Guilford (1962), however, argues that intelligence and creativity are not the same; he proposes that divergent thinking is the hallmark of creativity. As opposed to convergent thinking that seeks a single solution as the "correct" answer, divergent thinking leads to multiple solutions, all recognized as appropriate. Guilford posits that creativity can be measured by observing: ideational fluency, or the number of new ideas that a subject generates; the novelty of those ideas; and flexibility of the mind, or the ability to produce multiple types of ideas.

> A common myth in our culture is that creativity comes from some unusual talent or great intelligence.

E. Paul Torrance (1965), who produced the most widely used assessments of creativity, offers the following description:

> I have tried to describe creative thinking as taking place in the process of sensing difficulties, problems, gaps in information, missing elements; making guesses or formulating hypotheses about these deficiencies; testing and retesting them; and finally in communicating the results. (p. 8)

While definitions of creativity abound, most seem to reflect Harvard Professor David Perkins' (2001) notion that creativity is breakthrough or "outside-the-box" thinking that involves patterns of thought different from ordinary problem solving. Finding an alternate route when a road is blocked, for example, is certainly problem solving, but few would consider that a creative act.

Most descriptions of creativity include the ability to produce novel ideas or products after acquiring a certain proficiency of content knowledge. According to Mihaly Csikszentmihalyi (1996), creative individuals demonstrate mastery of a domain of knowledge or skill followed by an ability to demonstrate diverse thinking and ideational fluency to move that knowledge to a new level. One of the most distinguishing characteristics of Csikszentmihalyi's definition is the capacity to experience "flow" or to feel a timeless oneness during a creative act. *Flow* describes the experience of being so engaged in an activity that one achieves a state of concentration resulting in complete absorption with the task.

This description often leads one to believe that creativity is a quality that people possess, not necessarily one they develop. As such, creativity has been traditionally viewed as an innate quality bestowed on us through the luck of the gene pool. Some scholars, including creativity expert Sir Ken Robinson (2001), agree that creativity comes naturally to certain people—yet they also propose that creativity can and should be taught. The challenge for educators is to move beyond the convergent-thinking tasks that dominate educational practice and are the hallmark of accountability measures. Instead, teachers must design instruction to engage students in divergent thinking to generate multiple and varied approaches to problem solving.

Neuroscience and Creativity

Neurologist Kenneth Heilman and his colleagues (2003) also agree that creativity includes the demonstration of divergent thinking, which involves coactivation and communication among brain regions that are not ordinarily strongly connected during noncreative activities. They believe that highly creative people have a high level of specialized knowledge and are capable of divergent thinking mediated by the brain's frontal lobe. Creativity requires abilities that are associated with frontal-lobe processing, such as working memory and sustained attention (Fink, Benedek, Grabner, Staudt, & Neubauer, 2007). But as Paul Howard-Jones (2008) notes, "There is no single part of our brain responsible for our creativity. Creative thinking is a complex thought process that calls upon many different cognitive functions and involves many different regions distributed throughout the brain" (p. 7).

As research in creativity has expanded, it is commonly accepted that activities associated with creative thinking produce differentiated patterns of activity across multiple regions of the brain (Fink et al., 2007). Using the electroencephalogram (EEG) to measure brain activity, Andreas Fink and his colleagues found that during tasks regarded as highly creative, more areas of the brain are active than during tasks that require conventional or customary thinking. Rosa Aurora Chávez-Eakle and her colleagues (2007) also found differentiation in brain activity for individuals who demonstrate high degrees of creativity. Using the Torrance Tests of Creative Thinking (TTCT) to assess fluency, originality, and flexibility of ideas, these researchers measured differences in cerebral blood flow between highly creative individuals and average control subjects. Subjects who scored in the highly creative range on the TTCT showed significantly greater activity in brain structures involved in cognition, emotion, working memory, and novelty response, thus providing additional evidence of specific neural networks associated with creative thinking.

During highly creative tasks, more areas of the brain are active than during tasks requiring conventional thinking.

A surprising addition to the study of creativity is the work of Bruce Miller of the Memory and Aging Center at the University of California, San Francisco. His lab documented sudden bursts of creativity after patients experienced frontal lobe damage. He noted that patients who lost abilities in language and social skills also lost inhibition, which triggered creative work across multiple domains (Kraft, 2007).

This link between the loss of inhibition and high levels of creativity was also found in a recent study by Johns Hopkins University researchers Charles Limb and Allen Braun (2008) of the National Institutes of Health. Using functional magnetic resonance imaging (fMRI), Limb and Braun observed brain activity of professional jazz pianists during the spontaneous playing of improvisational jazz. They compared this condition to one in which the same musicians played a jazz score they had memorized. The researchers noted significant differences in brain activity between the two conditions. During improvisation, brain scans showed a widespread deactivation of the lateral prefrontal cortex, which is typically associated with self-regulation, self-monitoring, focused attention, and inhibition. Turning off this brain area may be associated with a type of "defocused, free-floating attention that permits spontaneous unplanned associations, and sudden insights or realizations" (Limb & Braun, 2008, p. 2). The researchers also found increased activity in the medial prefrontal cortex linked with self-expression and individuality.

Studies showing the link between improvisation and creativity coincide with the work of Keith Sawyer (2006), who makes a strong case for using improvisation to promote innovation and creative problem solving. While studying both jazz and theater groups, Sawyer observed that the collaborative and improvisational nature of group work inspires the successful production of novel products.

Improvisation and collaboration are potentially powerful tools for fostering creativity in children. As Sawyer points out, one of the most effective ways to bring students together for this type of learning is through the arts. The visual and performing arts provide opportunities for students to demonstrate new patterns of thinking and learning.

The Arts as a Portal to Creativity

In the seminal publications *Critical Links* and *Third Space,* Richard Deasy (2002; Stevenson & Deasy, 2005), former director of the Arts Education Partnership, demonstrates the power of the arts in transforming student learning and fostering imagination, creativity, and innovation. Deasy identified learning capacities that the arts foster, such as:

- Persistence in sustaining concentrated attention to a task

- Symbolic understanding by using multiple modes to communicate ideas

- Resilience in overcoming frustration and failure

- Engaged learning through absorption in content

- Collaborative learning as a member of group processes for acquiring and manifesting knowledge

Researchers in the behavior, cognitive, and neurosciences have also begun to demonstrate how the arts support learning across multiple domains. Ellen Winner and Lois Hetland (2007), for example, conducted a study in Boston-area schools regarding the effects of arts programs on students' learning. Resisting the notion that the arts might improve standardized scores in reading and math, their analysis pointed to the thinking skills that the arts address but that are rarely seen in other parts of the curriculum. They identified critical mental habits that students who participated in robust arts programs developed. In addition to the technical craft that students learn through the arts, the authors believe that the arts teach vital mental processes, or "studio habits of mind," that contribute to a student's overall capacity for creative thinking. These specialized skills include:

- Persistence to work on projects over a sustained period of time

- Expression of one's personal voice

- Making relevant connections of school work to the outside world

- Envisioning mental images to perceive in novel ways

- Innovation through exploration of the surrounding world

- Reflective self-evaluation to analyze, judge, and rework projects

The authors suggest that these thinking skills translate across the curriculum and are sustainable throughout life.

Cognitive and neuroscience research has begun to make connections to how the arts affect nonartistic domains. Emily Cross and colleagues (2006), for example, have demonstrated how music and dance assist memory processes through the mediation of mirror neurons. Such neurons appear to fire similarly when a subject performs an action and when the subject watches the same action performed by someone else. In 2008, the Dana Foundation Arts and Cognition Consortium released a series of studies conducted by leading neuroscientists that found a tight correlation between exposure to the arts and improved skills in cognition and attention for learning (www.dana.org).

Creativity in the Classroom

There should be no question that all children deserve instruction in a wide range of arts programs that includes vocal and instrumental music, visual arts, theater, dance, and creative writing. No school should have to choose between hiring an arts teacher or a remedial reading specialist because of budgetary constraints or the need to prepare for accountability testing. A full range of experiences in arts and cultural activities must be considered as important to assessments of effective schools as are students' test scores (Hardiman, 2009).

The Brain-Targeted Teaching Model

My argument here, however, is that arts and cultural programs are not sufficient by themselves. Effective instruction must include integrating the arts into teaching methodologies as a powerful way to foster creative, divergent thinking. While many systems exist to help teachers design an arts-integrated curriculum, teachers who have implemented the Brain-Targeted Teaching Model (Hardiman, 2003;

> Effective instruction must include integrating the arts into teaching methodologies as a powerful way to foster creative, divergent thinking.

2006) have demonstrated its effectiveness for promoting creative application of learning objectives while infusing the arts across content areas. In a study that compared the Brain-Targeted Teaching Model to traditional teaching, children who were instructed with the model demonstrated deeper understanding of content and application of learning goals (Bertucci, 2006).

The Brain-Targeted Teaching Model is not a curriculum nor a marketed product. Rather, it is a framework for planning effective instruction informed by cognitive theory and research from the neurological and cognitive sciences. The model was designed while I was a school principal and draws from research-based best practices as well as the experiences of effective teachers who represent multiple schools, grade levels, and content areas. The model (see fig. 11.1, page 236) presents six stages, or "brain targets," of the teaching and learning process. The components of the model include Brain Target One: setting the emotional climate for learning; Brain Target Two: creating the physical learning environment; Brain Target Three: designing the learning experience; Brain Target Four: teaching for mastery of skills, content, and concepts; Brain Target Five: teaching for extension and application of knowledge; and Brain Target Six: evaluating learning.

Following are descriptions of each brain target accompanied by quotations from teachers who have implemented this model in their classrooms. These exceptional teachers are eager to share best practices and tips for implementation. Their quotations, in the "From the Experts" feature boxes, present authentic experiences and field-tested learning activities to guide colleagues who seek to implement creative and artistic teaching activities in their own classrooms.

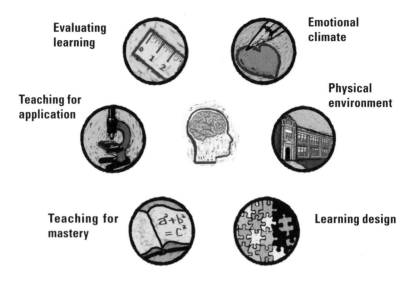

Evaluating learning

Emotional climate

Teaching for application

Physical environment

Teaching for mastery

Learning design

Figure 11.1: The six parts of the Brain-Targeted Teaching Model.

Brain Target One: Setting the Emotional Climate for Learning

Neuroscientists have established the existence of intricate interactions between the emotional and cognitive brain systems (Immordino-Yang & Damasio, 2007; Posner & Rothbart, 2007). The work of Joseph LeDoux (1996) highlighted the important role that the limbic system, the brain's emotional center, plays in influencing thinking and learning. Reducing stress and establishing a positive emotional climate in the classroom is arguably the most essential component of teaching (see chapter 4 in this volume). Therefore, the Brain-Targeted Teaching Model begins with purposeful strategies to foster a supportive climate in the classroom through routines, rituals, and positive communications. Additionally, for each new learning unit, teachers design activities that will assure that students are engaged with the content on an emotional level. The infusion of the visual and performing arts is an effective way to tap into children's emotional response systems to enhance learning.

From the Experts: Catherine Gearhart, First-Grade Teacher

Brain Target One, setting the emotional climate for learning, is like a perfume that scents all of the Brain Targets. Emotions are such a powerful component of learning that they influence all areas of a Brain-Targeted Teaching (BTT) unit. As I design the BTT unit, I keep in mind the importance of creating a safe and nurturing emotional climate so my students can operate at a comfort level where they are willing to take risks. Established routines give the students a sense of involvement and control. For instance, I have a morning meeting where students greet each other and share a positive thought, such as their favorite thing to eat for breakfast. The ritual only takes a few minutes each day, yet it creates a powerful bond among classmates and with the teacher. Maintaining these emotional connections during academic times keeps my students engaged and open to challenges.

The emotional climate is essential for promoting personal involvement, as students are encouraged to put something of themselves into their work products. It is a time when their inhibitions must be low and their "flow" high. For each unit, I choose an arts-integrated activity such as creating a poster, performing a skit, or writing a letter in character. Students will better engage in activities that require critical thinking if they feel confident and supported. Additionally, when I am assessing student learning, I believe that it is most important to continue to promote the emotional connection, letting students know that this is their opportunity to "show what they know." In my classroom, assessments are celebrations of learning. Throughout all of the Brain Targets, the emotional climate is crucial to success.

Brain Target Two: Creating the Physical Learning Environment

Establishing a positive emotional climate is also supported by Brain Target Two, which promotes use of the physical learning environment to enhance creativity and artful learning. Cognitive scientists tell us that the brain's visual attending mechanism is strongly influenced by novelty in the environment (Posner & Rothbart, 2007). Other physical elements, such as lighting, also seem to be important in student

Student achievement levels were higher in classrooms with natural and full-spectrum lighting compared to cool-white fluorescent light.

performance. For example, researchers have demonstrated up to an 18 percent increase in the achievement levels of students who were taught in classrooms with the most natural and full-spectrum lighting compared to classrooms illuminated mainly by cool-white fluorescent light (Kosik & Heschong, 2000).

In implementing the Brain-Targeted Teaching Model, the physical learning environment becomes a vehicle for making artful learning come alive. The classroom reflects order, beauty, and an ever-changing display of student-generated artworks that demonstrate learning.

From the Experts: Amanda Barnes, Third-Grade Teacher

From the very first day of school I try to put myself in my students' shoes. They spend more time in my classroom during a given week than they spend in their homes. This thought is always on my mind, especially since beginning my work with the Brain-Targeted Teaching Model. Creating the physical learning environment is crucial for my students because it influences their feelings of comfort and confidence.

With each Brain-Targeted Teaching unit that I plan, I change the setting of my classroom. Redesigning bulletin boards, changing seating arrangements, and displaying unexpected materials all engage and intrigue my students. They come to class excited to learn, and they look forward to seeing how the classroom changes from lesson to lesson.

As in many schools, my classroom has harsh fluorescent lights, so I have added lamps to soften the lighting, and I always keep my window shades up to allow as much natural light as possible. I use stimulating scents in the room, such as peppermint and vanilla, and I often play soft classical music when my students are engaged in routine activities. When they are completing higher-order thinking tasks, such as a mathematics problem, I minimize noise and distractions to allow for maximum concentration and focus. I also add terrariums, rugs, and pictures to help bring a comfortable "home-like" feel to the room. I find it important to ensure that all additions to my classroom are purposeful, and I am always careful to avoid overstimulation.

My students have come to appreciate and expect novelty and beauty in the classroom.

Brain Target Three: Designing the Learning Experience

As teachers begin to plan learning units in the Brain-Targeted Teaching Model, the third brain target encourages designing the learning experience in a way that is compatible with the cognitive processes of holistic and visual thinking. In traditional instruction, teachers write lesson plans that present information in sequential order. They typically follow a curriculum guide or textbook chapter, test the material, and then move on to the next unit. Too often, they make few connections to activities within the unit or to other content. This approach may not take advantage of the brain's natural learning system. The concept of *patterning* refers to cognitive processes of categorizing new stimuli into concepts that are either familiar or novel and then combining these concepts to create new patterns of thinking and understanding. Prior experience provides a filter through which students create this new meaning. As biologist John Medina (2008) points out, the brain processes the general idea first before focusing on details. By teaching general concepts first, Medina suggests, students will demonstrate a 40 percent improvement in understanding of content.

After determining the content standards and learning goals for a unit of study, this target encourages teachers to give students "big-picture concepts" of content through visual representations, such as graphic organizers. Teaching disconnected bits of information is like asking students to put together a jigsaw puzzle without ever having seen the overall image. Such teaching may result in students not only failing to acquire conceptual understanding, but also failing to retain the various disjointed facts and details. As Daniel Pink (2006) writes, the ability to understand "relationships between relationships" may be one of the most important skills for 21st century learning.

> The ability to understand "relationships between relationships" may be one of the most important skills for 21st century learning.

From the Experts: Susan Rome, Eighth-Grade Teacher

As I first taught the American history unit on the factors that escalated the conflict between the North and the South that led to the Civil War, I found so many resources in the form of primary source documents,

continued →

From the Experts: Susan Rome, Eighth-Grade Teacher
(continued)

music, photographs, and artifacts. While I wanted to use all of these multisensory components to engage students in deep learning experiences, I also needed to focus on addressing content standards and the objectives in the curriculum scope and sequence guide. I realized that it would be important to establish structure to scaffold the components of the unit. I designed the unit following the stages of the Brain-Targeted Teaching Model and realized that thinking of the unit as a whole and constructing a visual web would help to clarify for myself (and of course the students!) WHAT we were going to learn and HOW we were going to learn it.

This gave students the big picture concept of the unit and how the activities were interrelated to the content. It encouraged the kind of visual thinking that fosters creative ideas. We used movement, drama, song, various forms of creative writing, and even cooking to learn about that era in our history. The result was that students understood core concepts of the unit better, saw relationships clearly among the components of the unit, understood how the activities related to their learning, and knew how each activity would be assessed. This pre-planning made a huge difference in students' enjoyment of the unit and resulted in much deeper conceptual understanding of the content.

Brain Target Four: Teaching for Mastery of Skills, Content, and Concepts

After determining the unit goals and objectives and designing a big-picture map of the unit, the next component of the Brain-Targeted Teaching Model asks teachers to focus on planning activities that will promote deep learning of content and skills. The fourth brain target promotes mastery of content through multiple, arts-based activities that stimulate long-term memory.

Leading researcher in memory and Nobel Prize winner Eric Kandel (2006) explains that long-term memory requires the encoding and consolidation of new information into the brain's permanent storage networks. He explains that long-term memory requires the growth of new synaptic connections and the synthesis of new proteins. Creating long-term memory typically demands repeated, spaced repetitions of input. Larry Squire (2004) tells us that the most important factor in determining how well we remember information is the degree to which we rehearse and repeat that information.

The challenge for educators is to provide enough repetition of key learning objectives and to do so through multiple strategies that engage students' interest and attention. One way to present information in varied and enriching ways is through arts-based learning activities. Integrating the arts into content instruction has the potential to transform learning and is a natural way to cultivate creativity in children (Stevenson & Deasy, 2005).

> Integrating the arts into content instruction has the potential to transform learning and is a natural way to cultivate creativity in children.

From the Experts: Georgia Woerner, Middle/High School Science Teacher

Knowing how to integrate the arts into the curriculum is one of the most important skills for classroom teachers. The arts promote the kind of thinking about the content that is difficult to achieve in traditional teaching practices. Teaching science can be deeply creative, yet with so much content to cover, instruction often results in memorization of procedures and facts and not the kind of experimentation that science promotes. When I began teaching science, I would never have thought that the arts would compliment teaching, yet they have become powerful tools for creative learning. In a botany unit, for example, students studied the content through the botanical illustrations of naturalist artists and scientists such as Darwin, Catesby, and Audubon.

Botanical illustrations revealed the interconnectedness of science and art, as scientific knowledge is displayed through the strict rules of traditional botanical paintings. Students used dissection of plant specimens while studying life cycles and evolutionary changes of species. They then used their observational drawings of various forms of plants to create original botanical paintings and sculptures. Compared to teaching this unit through traditional methods, students were more engaged, assessments demonstrated deeper understanding, and the sense of investigation and discovery made the science classroom come alive.

Brain Target Five: Teaching for Extension and Application of Knowledge

Using the arts to achieve mastery of content is an important step in a sound program of instruction. The next target of the Brain-Targeted Teaching Model incorporates the idea that lifelong learning best occurs when students are able to apply knowledge to tasks that require them to solve problems. Thus, the fifth target encourages divergent patterns of thinking as students generate ideas, identify multiple solutions to problems, design plans of action, and apply learned content to real-world contexts. Using knowledge meaningfully requires students to extend thinking by examining concepts in deeper, more analytical ways that require the brain to use multiple and complex systems of retrieval and integration.

From the Experts: Alexander Fleming, Middle School Social Studies Teacher

In teaching the sixth-grade course in ancient civilizations, it is challenging to see how the content can connect to the students' own lives in tasks that apply the learning to real-world contexts. We use the concepts of geographical information to help students see its influence in the development of culture. After students have learned some of the major themes of the units, they then apply this knowledge by working in groups to create their own version of a primitive culture. For their "tribe," the students build shelters, determine food supply, and craft religious beliefs and relevant artifacts.

This lesson gives them a better understanding of the content than they could get merely through reading the textbook chapter. It also leads them to a deeper connection to their own cultural experiences. In the final activity that connects to real-world application, students examine how the geography of the city has shaped their neighborhoods, family traditions, and their lives.

Brain Target Six: Evaluating Learning

While Brain Target Six is the last stage of the Brain-Targeted Teaching Model, each stage of the model includes evaluation activities. The goal of evaluation is to provide relevant feedback about performance so that students can adjust learning habits and teachers can make sound instructional decisions. Cognitive science supports what teachers know by experience—notably that immediate feedback and purposeful retrieval of information strengthen the consolidation of learning and promote long-term memory (Karpicke & Roediger, 2008). The Brain-Targeted Teaching Model supports the use of multiple creative evaluation measures for unit objectives and activities.

From the Experts: Clare Grizzard, Arts Integration Specialist, Grades K–8

As an arts specialist working with classroom teachers, evaluating learning in the Brain-Targeted Teaching Model (BTT) speaks to my way of teaching: promoting divergent thinking, open-ended problem solving, and expression of a personal connection to the curriculum. The arts offer us a long tradition of alternative assessment strategies. In collaborating with teachers in the design of BTT units, we use portfolios extensively to exhibit the students' efforts and progress. The portfolio contents are chosen by the students and the teacher, and include reflective writing and self assessment relative to the content students are learning. During the unit, students are able to review their portfolios, which provide them with continual feedback, enable them to recognize growth, and allow them to reset their own goals.

While some traditional methods such as quizzes and tests are still part of our units, most of the evaluation of student learning is based on performance of real tasks, such as the creation of a product, a performance, a composition, or a design. We use rubrics that measure individual growth, and customize them for learning differences among students. In designing the rubrics, we determine the elements that comprise the task, design descriptions of expected performance, and create levels of proficiency. Students are given the rubric at the start of the task so they know the goals and outcomes for learning. The arts are a perfect vehicle for authentic assessment.

A New Paradigm

As the examples from the Brain-Targeted Teaching Model demonstrate, promoting creativity is enhanced when teachers follow a cohesive framework for planning and implementing instruction that integrates the arts. Unfortunately, merely giving teachers such a model will not substantially change how children are taught. Teachers need not only tools, but also robust training and, most importantly, sound education policies that support innovative teaching (Rotherham & Willingham, 2009).

Policymakers must examine the amount of content they expect teachers to cover within the school year and how mastery of that content can best be measured. The research community also has an important role in expanding interdisciplinary neurological and cognitive science research to study how the arts provide a platform for creative thinking. And higher education and teacher preparation programs must present coursework that supports that platform. Parents and stakeholders also have an important role in making clear to school districts their expectation that developing creativity is as important as proficiency in traditional course content.

Educating children for tomorrow will demand a paradigm shift from current practices and strong collaboration of professionals across multiple disciplines. Creativity and innovation are the promise of our children's future. As thought leaders, it is critical that educators demonstrate those very skills to re-envision and reshape education.

References

Andreasen, N. C. (2005). *The creating brain: The neuroscience of genius.* New York: Dana Press.

Bertucci, P. (2006). *A mixed-method study of a brain-compatible education program of grades K–5 in a Mid-Atlantic inner-city public elementary/middle school.* Unpublished doctoral dissertation, Johnson & Wales University.

Chávez-Eakle, R. A., Graff-Guerrero, A. G., García-Reyna, J. C., Vaugier, V., & Cruz-Fuentes, C. (2007, November). Cerebral blood flow associated with creative performance: A comparative study. *NeuroImage, 38*(3), 519–528.

Cross, E. S., Hamilton, A. F., & Grafton, S. T. (2006). Building a motor simulation de novo: Observation of dances by dancers. *NeuroImage, 31*(3), 1257–1267.

Csikszentmihalyi, M. (1996). *Creativity: Flow and the psychology of discovery and invention.* New York: HarperCollins.

Deasy, R. J. (Ed.). (2002). *Critical links: Learning in the arts and student academic and social development.* Washington, DC: Arts Education Partnership.

Fink, A., Benedek, M., Grabner, R. H., Staudt, B., & Neubauer, A. C. (2007). Creativity meets neuroscience: Experimental tasks for the neuroscientific study of creative thinking. *Methods, 42*(1), 68–76.

Guilford, J. P. (1962). Potentiality for creativity. *Gifted Child Quarterly, 6*(3), 87–90.

Hardiman, M. (2003). *Connecting brain research with effective teaching: The Brain-Targeted Teaching Model*. Landam, MD: Scarecrow Press.

Hardiman, M. (2006). Teaching model for the brain. In S. Feinstein (Ed.), *The Praeger handbook of learning and the brain* (pp. 473–481). Westport, CT: Greenwood Publishing Group.

Hardiman, M. (2009). The arts will help school accountability. *Arts Education in the News, 7*(2), 1–2.

Heilman, K. M., Nadeau, S. E., & Beversdorf, D. O. (2003, October). Creative innovation: Possible brain mechanisms. *Neurocase, 9*, 369–379.

Howard-Jones, P. (2008). *Fostering creative thinking: Co-constructed insights from neuroscience and education*. Bristol, United Kingdom: The Higher Education Academy, Education Subject Centre.

Immordino-Yang, M. H., & Damasio, A. (2007). We feel, therefore we learn: The relevance of affective and social neuroscience to education. *Mind, Brain, and Education, 1*(1), 3–10.

Kandel, E. R. (2006). *In search of memory: The emergence of a new science of mind*. New York: W. W. Norton.

Karpicke, J. D., & Roediger III, H. L. (2008). The critical importance of retrieval for learning. *Science, 319*(5865), 966–968.

Kosik, K. S., & Heschong, L. (2000). *Daylight makes a difference: Daylight in the classroom can boost standardized test scores and learning*. (ERIC Document Reproduction Service No. ED451683)

Kraft, U. (2007). Unleashing creativity. In F. E. Bloom (Ed.), *Best of the brain from* Scientific American: *Mind, matter, and tomorrow's brain* (pp. 9–19). New York: Dana Press.

LeDoux, J. (1996). *The emotional brain: The mysterious underpinnings of emotional life*. New York: Simon & Schuster.

Limb, C. J., & Braun, A. R. (2008). Neural substrates of spontaneous musical performance: An fMRI study of jazz improvisation. *Public Library of Science One, 3*(2), 1–9.

Medina, J. (2008). *Brain rules: 12 principles for surviving and thriving at work, home, and school*. Seattle: Pear Press.

Perkins, D. (2001). *The eureka effect: The art and logic of breakthrough thinking*. New York: W. W. Norton.

Pink, D. H. (2006). *A whole new mind: Why right-brainers will rule the future*. New York: Penguin Group.

Posner, M. I., & Rothbart, M. K. (2007). *Educating the human brain*. Washington, DC: American Psychological Association.

Robinson, K. (2001). *Out of our minds: Learning to be creative*. West Sussex, United Kingdom: Wiley & Sons.

Rotherham, A. J., & Willingham, D. (2009). 21st century skills: The challenges ahead. *Educational Leadership, 67*(1), 16–21.

Sawyer, R. K. (2006, April). Educating for innovation. *Thinking Skills and Creativity, 1*(1), 41–48.

Squire, L. R. (2004, November). Memory systems of the brain. A brief history and current perspective. *Neurobiology of Learning and Memory, 82*(3), 171–177.

Stevenson, L. M., & Deasy, R. J. (2005). *Third space: When learning matters.* Washington, DC: Arts Education Partnership.

Torrance, E. P. (1965). *Rewarding creative behavior: Experiments in classroom activity.* Englewood Cliffs, NJ: Prentice Hall.

Winner, E., & Hetland, L. (2007). Arts for our sake: School arts classes matter more than ever—but not for the reasons you think. *Boston Globe.* Accessed at www.boston.com/news/globe/ ideas/articles/2007/09/02/art on December 8, 2008.

Kurt W. Fischer

Kurt W. Fischer, PhD, leads an international movement to connect biology and cognitive science to education, and is founding editor of the journal *Mind, Brain, and Education*, which received the award for Best New Journal by the Association of American Publishers. As Director of the Mind, Brain, and Education Program and Charles Bigelow Professor at the Harvard Graduate School of Education, he conducts research on cognition, emotion, and learning and their relation to biological development and educational assessment. He has discovered a general scale that provides assessments of learning and development in any domain. His books include *The Educated Brain* and *Mind, Brain and Education in Reading Disorders*.

Katie Heikkinen

Katie Heikkinen, MEd, received her degree in Mind, Brain, and Education from the Harvard Graduate School of Education in 2007. She is a doctoral candidate in the Human Development program, where she focuses on the assessment of adult development. Katie attended Harvard College, where she studied visual attention in experienced meditators. She worked in Sweden in alternative education and in Boulder, Colorado at Ken Wilber's Integral Institute. She is currently on the faculty of the Integral Theory program at John F. Kennedy University, where she teaches multiple intelligences theory and cognitive science.

In this chapter, the authors suggest some new ways of thinking so that the collaboration between neuroscientists and educators can successfully improve teaching and learning now and in the foreseeable future.

Chapter 12

The Future of Educational Neuroscience

Kurt W. Fischer and Katie Heikkinen

A teacher sits alone in her classroom after the last bell of the day has rung. She has done a quick Google Scholar search on reading disabilities and is skimming through the latest research report. Although she understands the basics of the experimental paradigm, it still seems disconnected from what she experiences in the classroom on a day-to-day basis. Somehow, no one ever seems to research the questions that really concern her. Frustrated, she clicks on an ad in the sidebar: "Brain-based reading program! Guaranteed results! Only $199!" The purveyors of the flashy website at least seem to understand the problems she faces in the classroom, but can these allegedly scientific claims be trusted?

Across town, a different scene is unfolding at the local teaching hospital. Around a large meeting table, physicians, nurses, and research biologists are discussing a pressing problem. The medical professionals have encountered a series of patients who react differently from most people to a leading medication. Together with the research biologists, they plan a study to investigate the potential genetic underpinnings of the difference. Thanks to the insight provided by the doctors and nurses, the biologists have an exciting new problem to study—a problem that will both shed light on fundamental biological processes and provide potential new treatment options for doctors and patients.

Research in medicine and education, it seems, have gone down different paths (Fischer, 2009). Although there is a quantity of research linked to education, most of it perpetuates a disconnect between researchers and practitioners. Practitioners lack access to high-quality information, are rarely part of research teams, and seldom find their specific needs and questions addressed. Researchers, particularly in the so-called hard sciences, such as neuroscience or cognitive science, typically have their own agendas and give little thought to the immediate practical impact of their research, regardless of how relevant it could be to education. Researchers study questions that interest them, working in their research institution far away from education settings.

In contrast, scientists at teaching hospitals do research that often has an immediate effect on medical practice. The same is true in other research partnerships, such as in the pharmaceutical, cosmetics, and automobile industries. Research is shaped by the pragmatic needs of the consumer, and products are shaped by that research, in a mutual feedback loop. The same has not occurred in education. Unlike in other fields, there is little productive synergy between research and practice that leads to innovations in the classroom or new directions in research. In 1896, John Dewey proposed the establishment of laboratory schools as the nexus for education research, but even so-called lab schools do not typically engage in education research, despite their name (Hinton & Fischer, 2008). For the most part, education has not been the beneficiary of research-practice partnerships.

> For the most part, education has not been the beneficiary of research-practice partnerships.

What passes as research in most school systems stems from large standardized-testing initiatives—from No Child Left Behind in the United States to the Programme for International Student Assessment (PISA) in Europe and other regions. Although these initiatives do provide valuable data, they fall far short of the standards upheld in other research partnerships. Would a carmaker be satisfied in testing its products' performance twice a year on a racetrack? Surely not. How the cars perform on real roads under real driving conditions is vital information. So, too, must the effectiveness of schooling be assessed under real conditions, with researchers, teachers, and students all contributing to study design, especially in what we call "research schools," which are the education equivalent of teaching hospitals (Fischer, 2009; Hinton & Fischer, 2008).

At the same time that research and development have been neglected in education, teachers and parents in the real world have been inundated with claims about the brain and what it reveals about learning. Images of the brain "lighting up" abound in the popular press. It seems as though nearly every day a new headline exclaims how scientists have found the spot in the brain for some mental or emotional phenomenon. This brain craze has spread into education, where countless "brain-based" educational products and services are offered. How can educators separate the reasonable brain-based claims from the unreasonable claims? What does research on the brain really have to say about education?

Mind, Brain, and Education

Clearly, education research is in need of reform and improvement, and the popular fields of neuroscience and genetics must be brought into the fold. In response to these elements, a new field has emerged across the globe. In 1998, independent groups of researchers and practitioners in Paris, Tokyo, and Cambridge, Massachusetts, began major efforts to connect biology and cognitive science with education (della Chiesa, Christoph, & Hinton, 2009; Fischer, Immordino-Yang, & Waber, 2007; Koizumi, 2004). Within a few years, the groups in these three cities and elsewhere began to collaborate, and in 2004, they joined with others to found the International Mind, Brain, and Education Society. In 2007, they launched the journal *Mind, Brain, and Education.*

Mind, brain, and education, or MBE, is an interdisciplinary field that aims to bring the latest research methods to bear on education problems—and to include the wisdom of teachers and other practitioners in research paradigms (Coch, Michlovitz, Ansari, & Baird, 2009; Fischer, Daniel, et al., 2007; Fischer, 2009; Goswami, 2006;

Kuriloff, Richert, Stoudt, & Ravitch, 2009). A key element of MBE is that bidirectional relationship—researchers influencing practice and practitioners influencing research.

Educators are integral to the research process, not incidental, as in most cognitive and neuroscience research. According to the International MBE Society's website, the society's "principal goal is to foster dynamic relations between neuroscience, genetics, cognitive science, development, and education so that each field benefits from and influences work in the others, including questions asked, phenomena addressed, and methods employed" (http://imbes.org/mission.html). Thus, mind, brain, and education supports the development of an educational neuroscience that is strongly interdisciplinary, contextualized, and pragmatic.

> Educators are integral to the research process, not incidental, as in most cognitive and neuroscience research.

Obstacles to Collaboration and New Ways of Thinking

Before exploring the nature of this new kind of collaborative research and the means to support it, we must first ask about factors that might stand as obstacles. What might prevent productive relationships between researchers and practitioners? What might cause education research to be less than effective?

An important contribution of cognitive science in the last fifty years has been the analysis of the language that people use to describe their thinking. A close analysis of language can reveal a person's mental models, such as the key metaphor that underlies a person's conception of something. Research has uncovered many such mental models, or ways of thinking. Lakoff and Johnson (1980) laid out the framework for studying mental models through linguistic analysis, and Vidal (2007) discusses the mental models about the nature of the brain that developed throughout the 20th century. Mental models are unavoidable, and most serve us well. But some models get in the way of outcomes we desire. This is certainly the case in education and education research. To get beyond these less desirable mental models, we all have to "change our minds." We need to think about learning, the mind, development, and research in a new way.

From Brains in Buckets to Brains in Bodies

The current dominant model of the human mind in Western societies views the brain as the core organ that carries most of consciousness and learning. Vidal calls this model "brainhood," whereby the brain is viewed as the source of personhood and self (Vidal, 2007). When we are influenced by this mental model—and most of us in the West are—we tend to equate individuals with their brain. If we could just figure out the right life-support systems for it, Suzy's brain in a bucket would be the same as Suzy. When Suzy learns, she puts knowledge in her brain, which she can later access, much like a computer can access the data in its hard drive.

This model helps explain why images of the brain in popular media are so seductive. If we view the brain as the seat of the self—the modern soul—then access to its interior holds a deep charm. But the brain lights up, or experiences various patterns of activation, in a whole system—a body. Although it seems obvious, we often forget that our brains are part of our bodies, not the other way around. Brains are completely impacted by our physical health, nutrition, hormonal systems, and our relationships. What is more, brains depend on embodied action to develop. We learn by acting on the world, not merely thinking about it or hearing about it.

Viewing learning as an embodied process can advance education research in important ways. This perspective fully acknowledges the role of physical health in learning, inviting discussions of school-based nutrition and fitness programs. It focuses on the importance of action in learning, thus encouraging assessments that also include action. This perspective helps validate the perspective of teachers who work with bodies every day! Teachers' understanding of the whole child—body and all—is vital, and it can help researchers take a more holistic stance in their research agendas.

> Teachers' understanding of the whole child— body and all—is vital, and it can help researchers take a more holistic stance in their research agendas.

From Conduits to Construction Sites

Another potent metaphor is the conduit metaphor of learning (Lakoff & Johnson, 1980), whereby learning is treated as involving the direct transfer of knowledge from one person to another. Teachers have an idea, give it to their students, and then the students have it. Implicit to the conduit metaphor is the idea that learning is a passive process. If knowledge can simply be handed to us, then all a learner needs to do is receive it. Students who cannot display the ideas they are given are judged to be lazy or stupid, or the teacher is judged to have done a poor job at transmitting the knowledge.

Of course, learning is not so simple. Knowledge is based in activity, activity that then shapes how our brains work. The conduit model needs to be replaced with a model that focuses on the active construction of knowledge (Baldwin, 1894; Fischer & Bidell, 2006; Piaget, 1952; Singer, 1995). Information cannot be simply received; it needs to be worked with, questioned, and tested. In this way, classrooms are like construction sites, where the raw materials of instruction are transformed and tested as students build their own understandings.

In this view, learning is active, embodied, and contextualized. Good teachers know this; good assessments just need to catch up. Similarly, the most productive education research will study learning in context—in situations where people actually build knowledge. This means moving beyond standardized testing and moving toward designing studies that include realistic learning tasks or investigate learning in real time in classrooms.

From Ladders to Webs

Many teachers have sat through lectures on Piaget's four stages, in which the sensory-motor infant is compared to the preoperational child, the concrete-operational child, and the formal-operational adolescent. This simple view of linear stages encourages a ladder metaphor of development, whereby development is construed as a simple progression up a ladder from one stage to the next. Although Piaget made enormous contributions to understanding cognitive development, the science has moved on to a more nuanced view, emphasizing the construction process and the many differences between learning in distinct domains and different people (Dawson & Stein, 2008; Fischer & Bidell, 2006; Mascolo & Fischer, in press).

Psychologists have studied the active construction of knowledge for decades, and recent methodological advances have produced tools to analyze learning pathways. Learning pathways are a description of how a skill develops along a common scale, or universal ruler. This common scale denotes increasing complexity, which involves the differentiation and coordination of an increasing number of components. For example, understanding addition requires understanding the principles of the number line, and understanding multiplication builds on understanding addition. Each skill builds on a simpler skill. The levels on the universal ruler seem to involve different organizations of brain networks to support particular organizations of skills (Fischer & Bidell, 2006).

Because different types of skills pass through the same stages of this universal ruler, researchers can construct diverse learning pathways that nonetheless share a common scale. For example, one student's level of reasoning about world history might be advanced, while that same student's level of reasoning about physical science might be rudimentary, and his or her reasoning about multiplication might be somewhere in between. So at what stage does the student reason? With the huge amount of variability in expertise that every person exhibits, this question makes very little sense. Instead, researchers conceive of development as a web of independent strands or learning pathways.

The developmental web in figure 12.1 (page 256) depicts multiple skills or learning pathways. Each one passes through the same developmental levels, but largely at its own pace. A single skill might split off into two component skills, which are differentiated in development, or two skills might merge as they are integrated in development.

In the figure, the line representing each pathway truncates at its highest current level of skill. Different skills truncate at different places, showing that there is variability in expertise in any individual. In addition, learning pathways emphasize the importance of support: students can typically perform at a higher level under conditions of contextual support (optimal level) compared to a lower level when performing independently or without practice (functional level). At its simplest, support involves contextual priming of the key parts of a skill and leads to a higher level of performance. For example, when students hear a definition of multiplication, they can use that definition to produce a higher level of performance in explaining multiplication. However, they often can sustain that higher level for only a few minutes, after which the effect of the support dissipates and their performance drops.

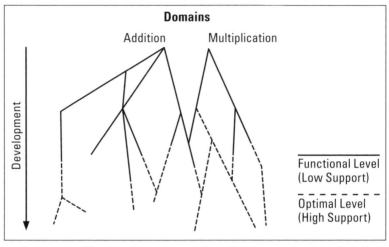

Figure 12.1: The developmental web and range for the domains of addition and multiplication.

Skill webs have several important advantages over the ladder metaphor. They emphasize variability within a single person, showing how each person has a unique pattern of skill development *across* strands as well as variation with contextual support *within* a strand. For a given strand (or content area), each of a person's skills may be at a different level of complexity, and also its complexity varies with degree of support. The web also emphasizes variability across people: one person's most poorly developed skill may be another person's most highly developed skill.

At the same time, webs capture shared patterns. Although there is a great deal of variability, the same skill at the same level shares important properties across people—not only the same complexity, but also often similar concepts and relationships among concepts. In addition, different skills at the same level share properties, most notably their complexity, the relations among components, and the ways that skills build across levels. This common ruler allows the creation of learning pathways that capture both shared patterns and learning differences.

These learning pathways can then be coordinated with curricula, task characteristics, and teaching techniques. For example, Dawson and Stein (2008) researched the development of physical science concepts and worked with a team of teachers to create an assessment for classroom use in middle school. This collaborative process is an example of the kind of process that can produce research that has implications for teaching and learning practices.

The process of collaboration begins with the establishment of a relationship between researchers and teachers (see fig. 12.2). After collaborators identify learning goals, they embed assessments in the curriculum to serve as the foundation for research into the development of specific learning pathways. In their study, Dawson and Stein (2008) investigated the concept of energy, using a short quiz, or "teaser," that asked students to explain the behavior of a bouncing ball. The researchers found that the youngest middle school students often stated the reason the ball bounces as, "It has bounciness inside!" Concepts such as potential or kinetic energy were not meaningful until much later in learning.

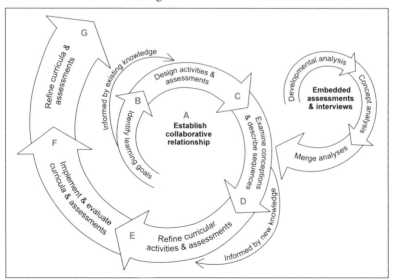

Source: Dawson & Stein, 2008. Figure created by Theo Dawson and used with permission.

Figure 12.2: The cycles of research and application in education.

After developing the learning sequence, information about how key concepts are learned can then inform curriculum. For example, the concept of conservation of energy is often listed in state curriculum frameworks as a learning goal for around the end of middle school. However, the full concept requires very high-level thinking, and children simply cannot do even a coarse approximation in seventh, eighth, or even ninth grade. This research suggests that the state frameworks need to be revised to more accurately reflect how and when concepts are most typically constructed.

Learning sequences can also inform assessment. Dawson and Stein (2008), in step E of their process (fig. 12.2, page 257), worked with teachers to create an assessment that would allow the teachers to code student performance for developmental level using a rubric. This rubric served as a useful tool to help teachers understand their students' varied needs and to tailor instruction to meet those needs. As teachers implement the assessment, further data can be collected, the assessment can be revised, and the cycle of research and application can continue.

Viewing development as a web instead of a ladder has yielded promising research methods that can give both educators and researchers important insights into how learning takes place, including differences between content areas and students. These insights, then, can lead to better tailoring of interventions to individual learning needs and better construction of curricula and teaching tools based on common learning pathways.

From Linear Growth to Dynamic Systems

The ladder metaphor is closely linked to a linear view of development, which views a child as an independent actor, all alone moving up a standard developmental sequence. A linear model of growth is also cumulative: changes add up, and any transitions are arbitrary lines in the sand of continuous change, not stage-like or abrupt (nonlinear). However, research (van Geert & van Dijk, 2002; Schwartz & Fischer, 2005; Thelen & Smith, 1994) has shown that much of development can be explained using dynamic systems theory, which uses nonlinear and dynamic mathematics to model growth, development, and learning.

Ordinarily most people think linearly and struggle with explaining nonlinear phenomena, such as the motion of liquid up a straw. We tend to think that sucking pulls liquid up, but in reality, sucking reduces air pressure within the straw, causing the liquid to be pushed upwards in a complex, dynamic system of forces. So the linear model of "sucking = pulling liquid up" must be replaced with a nonlinear model of "sucking = reducing air pressure in straw >>> relatively higher pressure on surrounding liquid >>> liquid is pushed into the area of relatively lower pressure" (Grotzer, 2004, p. 20).

The same is true in education. We struggle to explain complex developmental change because we seek simple explanations that focus on linearity, single-agent causality, and polar dichotomies. Examples include a static conception of intelligence and the nature/nurture debate. Intelligence is treated statically as a fixed attribute that explains behavior. Nature and nurture are viewed as simple opposites rather than complexly intertwined factors. A dynamic systems view of development focuses on studying the developing person in all of his or her variability, in a specific functional context. Rose and Fischer (2009) explain that this approach starts with two principles: "(1) Multiple characteristics of person and context collaborate to produce all aspects of behavior; and (2) variability in performance provides important information for understanding behavior and development" (p. 264).

What does it mean to say personal characteristics and context collaborate to produce behavior? To put it simply, no behavior can be understood solely by looking at the person alone; the context is absolutely inseparable. Understanding the context is essential for understanding the behavior. However, too often behaviors are assumed to be static, unchanging, or characteristic of the person (for example, "Billy is hyperactive."). This approach ignores the important role of context in shaping behavior ("Billy's daycare situation is not a good fit."). Context always shapes behavior—at the same time as behavior shapes the context—in a dynamic, nonlinear system. In other words, specific behaviors *emerge* from the combination of person and context.

Emergence is an important quality of dynamic systems. Emergence "refers to the coming-into-existence of new forms or properties through ongoing processes intrinsic to the system itself" (Lewis, 2000, p. 38). With emergence, change is not continuous: new forms arise as the system changes. These major nonlinear qualitative reorganizations have been seen in many contexts. For example, walking emerges from crawling as a result of increasing coordination of muscular and perceptual systems. This is a qualitative shift in locomotion, rather than a gradual change. There is no need for explicit instruction or innate programming (Thelen & Smith, 1994). Similarly, abstract thought develops from the coordination of representations (Fischer & Bidell, 2006). An abstraction such as "fairness" refers to a general, intangible characteristic of equity or equality, which is qualitatively different from the concrete representations it subsumes, such as "waiting for your turn" or "getting equal amounts of candy" or "following the same rules."

The second characteristic of a dynamic-systems approach focuses on variability as a source of information in research. With traditional linear models, attention focuses on finding the child's "true" competence, and variability is ignored or treated as error. In dynamic systems, variability is embraced as an information source, a place to find patterns to identify factors that affect behavior. For example, one important source of variability in performance is the presence or absence of support.

> One important source of variability in performance is the presence or absence of support.

Under conditions of support (priming of key components of a performance), people can act at a much higher level than without support. Viewing this variability as valuable information highlights the role of support and sheds light on different patterns of growth: students assessed under conditions of high support show clear stage-like jumps or drops in performance (a qualitative reorganization), while students assessed with low support show instead continuous growth, which often appears to be linear instead of discontinuous (fig. 12.3). Stage-like change thus comes and goes, depending on support.

Another important source of variability is the process of microdevelopment, whereby people construct small-scale changes in their skills, which cumulate in a developmental process towards large-scale changes (Schwarz & Fischer, 2005). Microdevelopmental changes occur

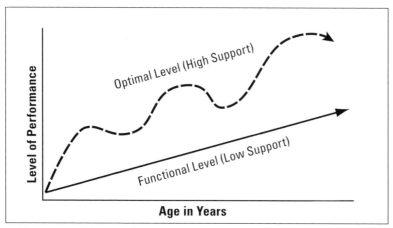

Figure 12.3: The developmental patterns for optimal and functional levels: spurts versus continuous growth.

in the short run and gradually establish relatively stable knowledge as large-scale change. For example, Granott (2002) studied people attempting to explain the behavior of a small robot. When people first began interacting with the robot, they were unfamiliar with it and did not understand it. So they used their most basic skills to analyze the robot's actions. Using these low-level skills allowed them to get to know the robot and begin coordinating more complex understandings of its behavior. The complexity of their explanations moved up and down as they learned, starting low and gradually moving up, but then falling back down again as conditions changed (for example, the robot moved in a new and unexpected way). This variability is how learning-in-the-moment occurs, with skills moving up and down, up and down. At the same time, these short-term changes in understanding add up to the long-term changes that occur over years of learning and development.

A dynamic-systems approach to development has several important advantages over a more linear approach. A dynamic-systems approach embraces both the personal characteristics and the context of the learner. It can use information about variability to explain the emergence of new properties and the microdevelopmental shifts that occur in the moment of learning. All together, this perspective provides a more real-life view of the learner, including the learner's real-world context, and moves both forward and backward in learning.

From Neuromyths to Neuroscience

As with the teacher in the opening vignette, businesses eagerly exploit neuroscience to sell commercial products to parents and teachers interested in the brain. Unfortunately, most of these brain-based products exploit "neuromyths," attractive-sounding beliefs about the brain that are largely false. John Bruer (1997) noted that neurobiological findings related to synaptogenesis, critical periods, and enriched environments have been leveraged to make inappropriate educational recommendations. Since then, neuromyths have become even more commonplace. The explosion of neuroscience research has made brain images pervasive—and persuasive—in popular media (McCabe & Castel, 2008; Weisberg, Keil, Goodstein, Rawson, & Gray, 2008), and most educators have been exposed to initiatives linking the brain to education (Pickering & Howard-Jones, 2007). In its 2007 report on brain-based learning science, the Organisation for Economic Co-operation and Development described eight prevalent neuromyths, all of them wrong:

- Ages zero to three years are more important than any other ages for learning.

- There are critical periods for learning important skills such as language.

- We only use 10 percent of our brains.

- Some people are left-brained, and some are right-brained.

- Men's brains and women's brains are very different.

- Young children can learn only one language at a time.

- Memory as a general capacity can be improved.

- People can learn as they sleep.

The neuromyths that are prevalent today seem to stem, in part, from the "brain in a bucket" mental model. But even with a more embodied, contextualized, and dynamic view of the learner, the exact role of neuroscience in education remains unclear. The prevalence of neuromyths gives teachers false hope, as they seek a truth believed to be "out there," ready to be discovered and delivered to them. In the quest to understand the brain, people often seek quick fixes and magic bullets. Some scholars, in the face of these myths and their peddlers, have pushed the discourse regarding neuroscience and education in the opposite direction. These "neuro-deniers" know that they cannot believe the hype around brain-based education and instead seek to break the connection between neuroscience and education. Bruer (1997) famously claimed that the link between neuroscience and education is "a bridge too far" and that neuroscience will not make valuable contributions to education. Egan (2002) goes so far as to doubt the role of both neuroscience and cognitive science in education research.

Both neuro-hypers and neuro-deniers have it wrong. Neuroscience can make real contributions to education, but it is a slow, gradual process that requires an important set of preconditions for doing research that relates to education practice and policy. Katzir and Paré-Blagoev (2006) note that rigorous educational neuroscience research requires falsifiable theory linking "specific skills to specific educational goals or tasks," and then linking those skills "to specific brain functions and structures" (p. 57). These theories must then be tested using appropriate experimental methodology, in a way that can distinguish between competing theories or rival hypotheses. Finally, the educationally relevant interpretations that stem from these empirically supported theories must be implemented and assessed. In this way, data from neuroscience can serve as one of many converging lines of evidence to support educational change.

Findings in Dyslexia

Dyslexia research provides a good example of an appropriate use of neuroscience findings in education (Fischer, Goswami, Geake, & Task Force on the Future of Educational Neuroscience, 2010). Katzir and Paré-Blagoev (2006) note that dyslexia research features strong hypotheses about the role of specific skills in reading performance, and these skills are linked to brain function and structure. As an example, they cite the role of phonological processing in dyslexia. Because dyslexia is commonly imagined as a visual deficit—and some research supports this view (for example, Schneps, Rose, & Fischer, 2007)—the role of listening seems less clear.

> Dyslexia research provides a good example of an appropriate use of neuroscience findings in education.

Yet evidence suggests that for alphabetic languages such as English, most "children with dyslexia have difficulty developing an awareness that words, both written and spoken, can be broken down into smaller units of sounds, such as phonemes, onsets, rhymes, and syllables," which is called phonological processing (Katzir & Paré-Blagoev, 2006, p. 59). Such research thus makes a clear connection between a specific skill (phonological processing) and an educationally relevant skill (reading). This specific skill can then be connected to specific patterns of brain activation in dyslexics and nondyslexics. Because activation patterns differ in the two groups in ways that implicate phonological processing, there is additional evidence that the phonological process-ing model of dyslexia is correct, at least as one component of dyslexia. We also have information that is potentially valuable for educational practice (Fischer, Goswami, Geake, & & Task Force on the Future of Educational Neuroscience, 2010). Because phonological processing plays a large role in learning to read in alphabetical languages, most children should benefit from an increased focus on oral language in classrooms.

Sesame Street provides another kind of example of ways that research in general can help to improve educational practice. From its founding, *Sesame Street* was based on practical research to deter-mine what was effective at motivating children watching the show on television and helping them to learn. Gerald Lesser (1974), one of the founders of *Sesame Street,* established a general research program to test practices and assess their effectiveness. For example, the initial plan was that all characters on the show would be human beings, because the creators believed that children would respond better emotionally to people. However, when the Muppets became an option, Lesser and others tested them with children, finding that, contrary to their beliefs, children strongly engaged with the Muppets and learned effectively from them. Research on learning environments can test many kinds of practical questions like this one and thus help improve educational effectiveness.

Making It Happen

The five new ways of thinking that we have outlined are essential for the future of educational neuroscience. Neuroscience, cognitive science, and developmental science have contributed valuable insights to the field of education in the past and are well poised for further contributions in researcher-practitioner partnerships. But certain changes are needed to pave the way for this kind of interdisciplinary collaboration. In addition to new ways of thinking, educational neuroscience needs to develop the pragmatic infrastructure required to support new kinds of research (Fischer, 2009). To reach the potential of grounding education effectively in research requires improving infrastructure by establishing communication about research between scientists and educators, creating research schools, sharing databases on learning and development, and establishing a new profession of educational engineers.

From One-Way to Two-Way Relationships

The current model of education research too often positions educators as passive recipients of research findings. Yet many other fields benefit from productive research partnerships that produce usable knowledge. We must build on the integration of research and practice that occurs in these fields by creating a strong infrastructure that joins scientists with educators to study effective learning and teaching in education settings. Science and practice both provide many potentially powerful tools to improve education, but a true educational neuroscience will require collaboration. Practitioners and researchers must establish two-way, reciprocal relationships, working together to formulate research questions and methods that will move both science and teaching forward. This two-way collaboration is the only way that education can benefit from the kind of usable knowledge regularly created in fields such as medicine, cosmetics, and agriculture.

> Practitioners and researchers must establish two-way, reciprocal relationships, to formulate research questions that will move science and teaching forward.

From Schools to Research Schools

Research schools are similar to teaching hospitals, where researchers and practitioners work together to refine medical techniques and build medical knowledge related to practice and research (Hinton & Fischer, 2008). Research schools should be real-life schools closely affiliated with universities, where educators and researchers work together to create research that illuminates education practice and policy and to train future researchers and practitioners.

From Data Poor to Data Rich

Research schools can take the lead in establishing databases that track data on student learning. These databases should eventually be shared at the national and international levels. Steps in this direction have been made, as for example, the state databases for No Child Left Behind, the National Daycare Study (NICHD, 2006), and the PISA international assessments created by the OECD (2007). But we must move beyond simple standardized testing and include information about how learning occurs in real-life settings for learning, incorporating rich data on individual differences and learning pathways.

From Educators to Educational Engineers

Finally, a new class of education professional is needed, the educational engineer, who will act as a translator between research and practice. An educational engineer can help apply findings from cognitive science and neuroscience to learning in classrooms and can engineer educational materials and activities that are grounded in research and that promote learning.

Conclusion

Teachers who are interested in the biological, cognitive, and developmental aspects of learning should not have to sit in their classrooms alone with Google Scholar as their only resource. Moreover, they should not have to view themselves as passive recipients of the conduit of knowledge from scientists on high down to education. Instead, they should be active participants in the research process. Their knowledge provides vital insights that can move science forward, just as insights from practicing doctors inform basic medical research. Researchers interested in topics relevant to education should embrace this knowledge and allow their research programs to be shaped by practical needs. Together, researchers and practitioners can lay the groundwork for a true science of education.

References

Baldwin, J. M. (1894). *Mental development in the child and the race: Methods and processes with seventeen figures and ten tables.* New York: Macmillan.

Bruer, J. T. (1997). Education and the brain: A bridge too far. *Educational Researcher, 26*(8), 4–16.

Coch, D., Michlovitz, S. A., Ansari, D., & Baird, A. (2009). Building mind, brain, and education connections: The view from the Upper Valley. *Mind, Brain, and Education, 3*(1), 26–32.

Dawson, T. L., & Stein, Z. (2008). Cycles of research and application in education: Learning pathways for energy concepts. *Mind, Brain, and Education, 2*(2), 90–103.

della Chiesa, B., Christoph, V., & Hinton, C. (2009). How many brains does it take to build a new light? Knowledge management challenges of a transdisciplinary project. *Mind, Brain, and Education, 3*(1), 16–25.

Egan, K. (2002). *Getting it wrong from the beginning: Our Progressivist inheritance from Herbert Spencer, John Dewey, and Jean Piaget.* New Haven, CT and London: Yale University Press.

Fischer, K. W. (2009). Building a scientific groundwork for learning and teaching. *Mind, Brain, and Education, 3*(1), 2–15.

Fischer, K. W., & Bidell, T. R. (2006). Dynamic development of action and thought. In W. Damon & R. M. Lerner (Eds.), *Theoretical models of human development: Handbook of child psychology* (6th ed., Vol. 1, pp. 313–399). New York: Wiley.

Fischer, K. W., Daniel, D. B, Immordino-Yang, M. H., Stern, E., Battro, A., & Koizumi, H. (2007). Why mind, brain, and education? Why now? *Mind, Brain, and Education, 1*(1), 1–2.

Fischer, K. W., Goswami, U., Geake, J., & Task Force on the Future of Educational Neuroscience. (2010). The future of educational neuroscience. *Mind, Brain, and Education, 4*(2), 68–80.

Fischer, K. W., Immordino-Yang, M. H., & Waber, D. P. (2007). Toward a grounded synthesis of mind, brain, and education for reading disorders: An introduction to the field and this book. In K. W. Fischer, J. H. Bernstein, & M. H. Immordino-Yang (Eds.), *Mind, brain, and education in reading disorders* (pp. 3–15). Cambridge, United Kingdom: Cambridge University Press.

Goswami, U. (2006). Neuroscience and education: From research to practice? *Nature Reviews Neuroscience, 7*(5), 406–413.

Granott, N. (2002). How microdevelopment creates macro-development: Reiterated sequences, backward transitions, and the Zone of Current Development. In N. Granott and J. Parziale (Eds.), *Microdevelopment: Transition processes in development and learning* (pp. 213–242). Cambridge, United Kingdom: Cambridge University Press.

Grotzer, T.A. (2004, October). Putting science within reach: Addressing patterns of thinking that limit science learning. *Principal Leadership, 5,* 16–21.

Hinton, C. , & Fischer, K. W. (2008). Research schools: Grounding research in educational practice. *Mind, Brain, and Education, 2*(4), 157–160.

Katzir, T., & Paré-Blagoev, E. J. (2006). Applying cognitive neuroscience research to education: The case of literacy. *Educational Psychologist, 41*(1), 53–74.

Koizumi, H. (2004). The concept of "developing the brain": A new natural science for learning and education. *Brain & Development, 26*(7), 434–441.

Kuriloff, P., Richert, M., Stoudt, B., & Ravitch, S. (2009). Building research collaboratives among schools and universities: Lessons from the field. *Mind, Brain, and Education, 3*(1), 33–43.

Lakoff, G., & Johnson, M. (1980). *Metaphors we live by.* Chicago: University of Chicago Press.

Lesser, G. S. (1974). *Children and television: Lessons from* Sesame Street. New York: Random House.

Lewis, M. D. (2000). The promise of dynamic systems approaches for an integrated account of human development. *Child Development, 71*(1), 36–43.

Mascolo, M. F., & Fischer, K. W. (in press). The dynamic development of thinking, feeling, and acting over the lifespan. In R. M. Lerner & W. F. Overton (Eds.), *Handbook of life-span development: Biology, cognition, and methods across the lifespan* (Vol. 1). Hoboken, NJ: Wiley.

McCabe, D. P., & Castel, A. D. (2008). Seeing is believing: The effect of brain images on judgments of scientific reasoning. *Cognition, 107,* 343–352.

National Institute of Child Health and Development, Early Child Care Research Network. (2006). Child-care effect sizes for the NICHD study of early child care and youth development. *American Psychologist, 61,* 99–116.

Organisation of Economic Co-operation and Development. (2007). *Understanding the brain: The birth of a learning science.* Paris: Organisation of Economic Co-operation and Development, Centre for Educational Research and Innovation.

Piaget, J. (1952). *The origins of intelligence in children.* New York: International Universities Press.

Pickering, S. J., & Howard-Jones, P. (2007). Educators' views on the role of neuroscience in education: Findings from a study of UK and international perspectives. *Mind, Brain, and Education, 1*(3), 109–113.

Rose, L. T., & Fischer, K. W. (2009). Dynamic systems theory. In R. A. Shweder (Ed.), *The child: An encyclopedic companion* (pp. 264–265). Chicago: University of Chicago Press.

Schneps, M. H., Rose, L. T., & Fischer, K. W. (2007). Visual learning and the brain: Implications for dyslexia. *Mind, Brain, and Education, 1*(3), 128–139.

Schwartz, M. S., & Fischer, K. W. (2005). Building general knowledge and skill: Cognition and microdevelopment in science learning. In A. Demetriou & A. Raftapoulos (Eds.), *Cognitive developmental change: Theories, models and measurements* (pp. 157–185). Cambridge, United Kingdom: Cambridge University Press.

Singer, W. (1995). Development and plasticity of cortical processing architectures. *Science, 270*(5237), 758–764.

Thelen, E., & Smith, L. B. (1994). *A dynamic systems approach to the development of cognition and action.* Cambridge, MA: MIT Press.

van Geert, P., & van Dijk, M. (2002). Focus on variability: New tools to study intra-individual variability in developmental data. *Infant Behavior & Development, 25*(4), 340–374.

Vidal, F. (2007). Historical considerations on the brain and self. In A. Battro, K. W. Fischer, and P. Lena (Eds.), *The educationed brain: Essays on neuroeducation* (pp. 20–42). Cambridge, United Kingdom: Cambridge University Press.

Weisberg, D. S., Keil, F. C., Goodstein, J., Rawson, E., & Gray, J. R. (2008). The seductive allure of neuroscience explanations. *Journal of Cognitive Neuroscience, 20*(3), 470–477.

Glossary

alexia. The inability of a reader to read words by sight.

alphabetic principle. The understanding that spoken words can be broken down into phonemes, and that written letters represent the phonemes of spoken language.

amygdala. The almond-shaped structure in the brain's limbic system that encodes emotional messages to long-term memory.

axon. The neuron's long and unbranched fiber that carries impulses from the cell to a neighboring neuron.

Broca's area. A region of the brain located behind the left temple that is associated with speech production.

cerebrum. The largest of the major parts of the brain, controlling sensory interpretation, thinking, and memory.

computerized tomography (CT, formerly CAT). An instrument that uses X-rays and computer processing to produce a detailed cross-section of the brain and other body structures.

cortex. The thin but tough layer of cells covering the cerebrum that contains all the neurons for cognitive and motor processing.

dendrite. The branched extension from the cell body of a neuron that receives impulses from nearby neurons through synaptic contacts.

dopamine. A neurotransmitter associated with movement, attention, learning, and the brain's pleasure and reward system.

dyscalculia. A persistent developmental problem in learning to process numbers.

dysgraphia. A persistent developmental problem in learning to write.

dyslexia. A persistent developmental problem in learning to read.

electroencephalograph (EEG). An instrument that charts fluctuations in the brain's electrical activity via electrode attached to the scalp.

event-related potential (ERP). An electrical signal emitted by the brain in response to a stimulus such as a picture or a word. The signals are detected by electrodes attached to the scalp.

frontal lobe. The front part of the brain that monitors higher-order thinking, directs problem solving, and regulates the excesses of the emotional system.

functional magnetic resonance imaging (fMRI). An instrument that measures blood flow to the brain to record areas of high and low neuronal activity.

grapheme. The smallest part of written language that represents a single phoneme in the spelling of a word.

hippocampus. A brain structure that encodes information from working memory into long-term memory.

magnetic resonance imaging (MRI). An instrument that uses radio waves to disturb the alignment of the body's atoms in a magnetic field to produce computer-processed, high-contrast images of internal structures.

magnetoencephalograph (MEG). An instrument that measures fluctuations in the brain's magnetic fields via electrodes attached to the scalp.

neurogenesis. The growth of new neurons.

neuromyth. An assumption about the brain that has little or no scientific evidence to support it.

neuron. The basic cell making up the brain and nervous system, consisting of a cell body, a long fiber (axon) that transmits impulses, and many short fibers (dendrites) that receive them.

neuroplasticity. The brain's lifelong ability to reorganize neural networks as a result of new experiences.

neurotransmitter. One of several dozen chemicals stored in the axon sacs that transmit impulses from neuron to neuron across the synaptic gap.

nonconscious. A mental state of behaving or responding without conscious awareness of doing so.

number sense. In its limited form, this refers to the ability to recognize that an object has been added or removed from a collection.

numeracy. The ability to reason with numbers and other mathematical concepts.

occipital lobe. The rear part of the brain responsible mainly for visual processing.

orthography. The written system that describes a spoken language. Spelling and punctuation represent the orthographic features of written English.

parietal lobe. The region of the brain responsible for sensory perception as well as reading, writing, language, and calculation.

phoneme. The smallest units of sound that make up a spoken language.

phonological awareness. The ability to recognize and manipulate phonemes as well as the recognition that sentences are comprised of words and that words are comprised of syllables that can be broken down into phonemes.

phonology. The component of grammar that studies the sound patterns of a language, including how phonemes are combined to form words as well as patterns of timing, stress, and intonation.

positron emission tomography (PET). An instrument that traces the metabolism of radioactively tagged sugar in brain tissue producing a color image of brain activity.

prefrontal cortex (PFC). The brain region located just behind the forehead believed responsible for cognitive processing, including decision making, higher-order thinking, and controlling emotional responses.

prosody. The rhythm, cadence, accent patterns, and pitch of a language.

reticular activating system (RAS). The dense formation of neurons in the brain stem that controls major body functions and maintains the brain's alertness.

semantics. The study of how meaning is derived from words and other text forms.

synapse. The microscopic gap between the axon of one neuron and the dendrite of another.

syntax. The rules and conventions that govern the order of words in phrases, clauses, and sentences.

temporal lobe. The region on each side of the brain responsible for memory and auditory processing.

transcortical magnetic stimulation (TMS). The use of brief magnetic pulses applied to the scalp to disrupt parts of a neural network in order to observe its influences on the performance of specific tasks.

unconscious. A physical state of being unresponsive to people and other environmental stimuli.

visual word form area. A region of the human brain that responds specifically to words and letters.

Wernicke's area. The region of the brain, usually located in the left hemisphere, thought to be responsible for sense and meaning in one's native language(s).

working memory. The temporary memory wherein information is consciously processed.

Index

A

abstraction
  computing brain overview, 216
  emergence of abstract thought, 260
  mathematical brain overview, 173–176
academic achievement. *See* student
  achievement
academic intuition. *See* intuition
acalculia, calculating brain overview,
  185
accountability measures, creativity and,
  231, 234
activations of brain areas. *See* brain-area
  activations
addition (operation). *See also* arithmetic; mathematics
  calculating brain overview, 180,
    182–184, 189, 192, 193
  computing brain overview, 205,
    208–209
  learning pathways and, 255–256
  mathematical brain overview, 165,
    167, 171, 172
addresses, remembering, 170–171
adolescents. *See also* age differences
  brain research in 1990s, 15–16, 18
  calculating brain overview, 182
  computing brain overview, 208–209
  reading brain construction, 142
  reading brain overview, 125
  speech and language processing,
    87–88, 101
adults. *See also* age differences
  brain research in 1990s, 16, 17
  calculating brain overview, 182–184,
    189–191, 195

  computing brain overview, 202–213,
    216–219
  mathematical brain overview, 169, 171
  reading brain construction, 139,
    141–143, 147, 150, 152
  reading brain overview, 114–122, 124,
    126–127
  speech and language processing, 89,
    97, 98, 101, 102
affective and social neuroscience. *See*
  social and affective neuroscience
affective filter, Krashen's, 49, 53
age differences. *See also specific age*
  groups, e.g., adolescents
  brain research in 1990s, 15–17
  calculating brain overview, 180–183,
    191
  computing brain overview, 208–213,
    217–218
  creative-artistic brain overview, 228,
    231–233
  mathematical brain overview, 171
  neuroimaging technology overview, 39
  reading brain construction, 144–148,
    151
  reading brain overview, 122–125
  speech and language processing, 89,
    96–103
aggression, brain research in 1990s, 15–16
agraphia, calculation deficits and, 203
alexia, reading brain overview, 114–115,
  117
algebra
  computing brain overview, 220
  mathematical brain overview, 173–175
algorithms
  calculating brain overview, 188–190

On Excellence in Teaching
Edited by Robert Marzano
The world's best education researchers, theorists, and staff developers deliver a wide range of theories and strategies focused on effective instruction.
BKF278

21st Century Skills: Rethinking How Students Learn
Edited by James Bellanca and Ron Brandt
Education luminaries reveal why 21st century skills are necessary, which skills are most important, and how to help schools include them in curriculum and instruction.
BKF389

Ahead of the Curve: The Power of Assessment to Transform Teaching and Learning
Edited by Douglas Reeves
Leaders in education contribute their perspectives of effective assessment design and implementation, sending out a call for redirecting assessment to improve student achievement and inform instruction.
BKF232

On Common Ground: The Power of Professional Learning Communities
Edited by Richard DuFour, Robert Eaker, and Rebecca DuFour
Examine a colorful cross-section of educators' experiences with PLCs. This collection of insights from practitioners throughout North America highlights the benefits of a PLC.
BKF180